A BROAD & BALANCED CURRICULUM IN PRIMARY SCHOOLS

Sara Miller McCune founded SAGE Publishing in 1965 to support the dissemination of usable knowledge and educate a global community. SAGE publishes more than 1000 journals and over 800 new books each year, spanning a wide range of subject areas. Our growing selection of library products includes archives, data, case studies and video. SAGE remains majority owned by our founder and after her lifetime will become owned by a charitable trust that secures the company's continued independence.

Los Angeles | London | New Delhi | Singapore | Washington DC | Melbourne

A BROAD & BALANCED CURRICULUM IN PRIMARY SCHOOLS

EDUCATING THE WHOLE CHILD

SUSAN OGIER

SAGE | Learning Matters

Learning Matters
An imprint of SAGE Publications Ltd
1 Oliver's Yard
55 City Road
London EC1Y 1SP

SAGE Publications Inc.
2455 Teller Road
Thousand Oaks, California 91320

SAGE Publications India Pvt Ltd
B 1/I 1 Mohan Cooperative Industrial Area
Mathura Road
New Delhi 110 044

SAGE Publications Asia-Pacific Pte Ltd
3 Church Street
#10-04 Samsung Hub
Singapore 049483

Editor: Amy Thornton
Senior project editor: Chris Marke
Project management: Deer Park Productions
Marketing manager: Lorna Patkai
Cover design: Wendy Scott
Typeset by: C&M Digitals (P) Ltd, Chennai, India
Printed in the UK

First published in 2019

Library of Congress Control Number: 2019940722

British Library Cataloguing in Publication Data

A catalogue record for this book is available from the British Library

ISBN 978-1-5264-6943-4
ISBN 978-1-5264-6942-7 (pbk)

CONTENTS

ABOUT THE EDITORS AND CONTRIBUTORS

The editors

Susan Ogier is Senior Lecturer in Art and Design on a range of courses at the University of Roehampton. Susan has many years of experience in teaching in early years and primary schools, specialising in art and design. She actively promotes visual art in education through innovative research projects and international collaborations. Susan has published a number of books, curriculum materials, book chapters and peer-reviewed journal articles, and frequently presents at conferences in both the UK and Europe. Her most recent publication, *Teaching Primary Art and Design* (2017) is a core text for student and trainee teachers in the UK and abroad.

Tony Eaude is an independent research consultant. Tony was a class teacher in primary schools for 13 years before becoming the head teacher of a multicultural primary school for nine years. He then studied for a doctorate looking at how teachers of young children understand spiritual development. Since 2003 he has been an independent researcher and author. He has published extensively on themes related to spiritual, moral, social and cultural development, the education of the whole child and the expertise of primary classroom teachers and how this can be developed. More details of his work can be seen on **www.edperspectives.org.uk**.

The contributors

Genea Alexander has worked in education as both a primary teacher and Senior Lecturer for many years. Currently a Senior Lecturer in Primary Education at the University of Worcester, Genea teaches on undergraduate and postgraduate education courses, having led the Primary PGCE course. Genea's research and teaching interests include pedagogy and professional practice, the arts and primary languages education and she is co-author of several publications, including the invaluable teacher and trainee teacher text: *The Teachers' Standards: Understanding and Evidencing Effective Practice* (2016), which is currently being revised and updated for second edition publication. Genea is a Fellow of the Higher Education Academy and a committee member of the National Primary Teacher Education Council.

Nick Corston is a CEO and founding member of STEAM.Co., a non-profit project that advocates, inspires and actions creativity. Nick has a Master's degree in Engineering. Before a career change to set up STEAM Co., Nick worked in marketing.

Teresa Cremin, an ex-teacher and teacher educator, is now Professor of Education (Literacy) at the Open University. Her research, often involving teachers as researchers, mainly explores teachers' literate identities and practices and children as readers and writers. A Fellow of the Academy of Social Sciences, the Royal Society of Arts and the English Association, Teresa is a Trustee of UKLA and co-editor of the journal *Thinking Skills and Creativity*. She has written/edited nearly 30 books, with *Experiencing Reading for Pleasure in the Digital Age* (Sage, 2019) forthcoming. Teresa is passionate about developing readers for life and leads a professional user-community website based on her research into reading for pleasure: **https://researchrichpedagogies.org/research/reading-for-pleasure**.

Richard Dunne is head teacher of Ashley C of E Primary School in Walton on Thames. The school is an Ofsted-graded Outstanding School and has developed a curriculum of learning built around the principles of Harmony in the natural world. This combines core academic skills with a purposeful enquiry-based approach to learning. The school has won awards for energy conservation, food growing and provision, and for its New Leaders in Sustainability expeditions to Chamonix in the Alps.

Pinky Jain is Principal Lecturer in Primary Education School International, School Quality and Primary Mathematics Lead. Pinky is passionate about education, especially the professional development of trainee teachers and the teaching of maths in schools. She taught in a range of schools and HEIs before joining the University of Worcester in 2011. Pinky teaches on the BA QTS and PGCE (Primary Mathematics Modules, Professional Studies and Independent Research Modules), is Subject Leader for Primary Mathematics and is Programme Leader for the PGCE Mathematics Specialist Pathway. Pinky completed her PhD in Primary Mathematics Education from the University of Nottingham where she developed a model to support the understanding of children's prior knowledge in the primary maths classroom. Pinky's research interests are in the fields of primary maths teaching and professional development.

Emilie Martin is a freelance writer and teacher. She has taught in primary schools across London, most recently at Ashley C of E Primary School, alongside Richard Dunne. She is a contributor in the Harmony Project, which promotes the application of Harmony principles in education, food and farming, and has researched and documented the development of a curriculum based on principles of Harmony at Ashley School.

Rachel Mason is Emeritus Professor of Art Education at the University of Roehampton London. She has taught art and art education in England, Australia and the USA and is well known for her research and publications on multicultural, cross-cultural and international art education. She is a former President and Vice President of the National Society for Education in Art and Design and founded and edited the *International Journal of Education through Art*. Her books include *Art Education and Multiculturalism* (1996), *International Dialogues in Visual Culture, Education and Art* (with Teresa Eca, 2010), *Beyond Multicultural Art Education: International Perspectives* (with Doug Boughton 1999 and published in 2002). From 2008 to 2011 she directed the Images and Identity Curriculum and Development Project, funded by the European Commission, in which teams of researchers in six European countries investigated the potential contribution of art education to citizenship learning.

Aimee Quickfall is Head of Programmes for Primary and Early Years Foundation Stage at Bishop Grosseteste University in Lincoln. Previously she was a primary and early years teacher for 13 years, teaching every year group from Nursery to Year 6. In a previous life she gained a philosophy degree at the University of Nottingham and has been working philosophical enquiry into her life (and teaching) ever since.

Michael Rosen is Professor of Children's Literature at Goldsmiths, University of London where he co-devised and co-teaches the MA in Children's Literature. He has published in the region of 200 books for children and adults and is a former Children's Laureate. He is the presenter of a programme about language, *Word of Mouth*, on BBC Radio 4 that has been running since 1998. He has written a book for children and teachers on writing poetry *What is Poetry?* (Walker Books) and a further three booklets for teachers on writing and reading. Michael writes a monthly open 'letter' to the Secretary of State for Education in the *Guardian* where he critiques government policy on schools from the standpoint of a parent.

Julie Sutton has many years of teaching experience in both primary schools and higher education. She is currently a Senior Lecturer in Primary Education at the University of Worcester where she is the Cohort Leader for the Post Graduate Primary School Direct course and leads on both Foundation Subjects and Primary Music. Julie's research interests include music education, pedagogy and professional practice and the creative curriculum. She has presented at conferences and is the co-author of several book chapters. As chair of the Worcestershire Music Education Hub, Julie has successfully led a music research project on the quality of music education in schools which is to be disseminated to a wider audience at regional and national level. She is a fellow of the Higher Education Academy and a committee member of the National Primary Teacher Education Council.

Kate Thorpe is Lecturer in Primary Education at the IoE, University College London. She has worked as a lecturer in Education in France at the Oratoire Teacher Training College. Her specialist areas are Art and Design, Learning and Teaching and MFL. Kate has also worked extensively as an educational consultant in China, France, Jordan and the UK. Her research interests are: creative teaching and learning both within and outside of the classroom; creative interdisciplinary curriculum; metacognition; AfL; and considering the place of a holistic approach to education.

Maria Vinney is Senior Lecturer in Teacher Education, University of Winchester. Maria is a Senior Lecturer in Teacher Education, specialising in Primary Art and Design and Expressive Arts at the University of Winchester. Maria has extensive experience as a primary teacher and head teacher, championing children and the arts in education. Maria offers CPD for teachers and support staff as an Educational Arts Consultant in schools and early years settings.

Robert Watts is Senior Lecturer in Art and Design Education at Roehampton University, London. In 2016 he completed a PhD entitled *Children's Perceptions of Beauty: Exploring Aesthetic Experience through Photography*. The research investigated how children reflect upon and articulate their perceptions of beauty and examined how these perceptions relate to philosophical thinking about aesthetic experience. Robert trained as a painter and taught in London schools before joining Roehampton in 2000. He led the MA Art, Craft and Design Education programme from 2005 to 2015 and is currently Course Leader for PGCE Secondary Art and Design. He is the co-editor of *Teaching Art and Design 3–11* and *Readings in Primary Art Education*, and has written several articles for international journals. Robert has published over 200 creative projects for teachers, a selection of which are available on his website at: **www.artandeducation.co.uk**.

Tessa Willy is Associate Professor, School Director of Teacher Education at Kingston University. She started her career teaching in primary and secondary settings across the UK and in Malawi. Since moving into higher education, she has been Programme Leader for the PGCE Primary course at the University of Roehampton, later joining the UCL Institute of Education. Her areas of interest are the ethics of geography, notably climate change and social justice. Tessa is a participating member of the Editorial Board of the Geographical Association's journal *Primary Geography*.

Carrie Winstanley has taught in schools and higher education for more than twenty years and is currently Professor of Pedagogy at Roehampton University, London, with a particular responsibility for learning and teaching. She works on undergraduate and postgraduate (taught and research) programmes and with university staff. She is the author of various books, papers, edited collections and study guides, has served on the Executive Council of the Philosophy of Education Society of Great Britain for many years and has a background in educational psychology. She is particularly interested in pedagogy and the concept and practice of creating challenge for learners, particularly able learners with learning difficulties, disabilities and disadvantage. Carrie is particularly committed to encouraging children and adult learners to embrace museum and gallery visits as an essential aspect of their learning.

FOREWORD

This is a timely and important book. It can help to answer some of the questions which are increasingly being asked about primary school curricula in the UK.

The formal requirements of national curricula typically reflect the perspectives of those with most power to influence them. In the UK, some bold experiments are being reviewed. The time is right for approaches which seek to more carefully balance subject knowledge and learner motivation through more engaging curricula and the expertise of teachers.

For example, in the opinion of many, the 2014 curriculum for England is narrow, subject focused and constrained by high-stakes assessment. Politicians in the formative period of its development declined to take much of the advice they were offered by professional teachers and researchers. Whilst some children can respond to very high expectations, others are less able to do so. Concern about pupil well-being, mental health, demotivation and stress are being heard far too often. In short, there is accumulating evidence that the 2014 curriculum requires significant change to respond to the actual needs of young learners.

And how best will our children thrive? How can their daily educational experiences be enriched? What do they really need to know and understand for the future?

There is almost always a tension between 'what is' and 'what might be' in educational provision. This book constructively enters that debate by imagining, advocating and demonstrating a broader, more balanced and more enriching curriculum for young children.

In particular, the authors recognise that the creative arts and humanities have been dramatically squeezed in recent years, and they demonstrate their potential to all-round education and the enrichment of school experience. This book is based on optimism and commitment.

The editors and contributors deserve congratulations and thanks.

Andrew Pollard

Professor of Policy and Practice, UCL Institute of Education

INTRODUCTION

UNDERSTANDING THE CONTEXT OF CHILDREN'S LIVES: SUPPORTING HOLISTIC EDUCATION

SUSAN OGIER AND TONY EAUDE

THE WORLD WILL NEVER STARVE FOR WANT OF WONDERS; BUT ONLY FOR WANT OF WONDER.

(G.K. CHESTERTON, TREMENDOUS TRIFLES (1901)

This book will help you think about the role of the primary teacher in educating 'the whole child', and in particular how to ensure that you provide a broad and balanced curriculum. In this Introduction we shall, explore briefly what we mean by 'the whole child', discuss why a broad and balanced curriculum is so important yet sometimes so difficult to implement within the current climate, and introduce some key themes to be considered throughout the whole book.

Let's start with the legal position. The Education Act 2002 states that:

> The curriculum for a maintained school or maintained nursery school satisfies the requirements of this section if it is a balanced and broadly based curriculum which – (a) promotes the spiritual, moral, cultural, mental and physical development of pupils at the school and of society, and (b) prepares pupils at the school for the opportunities, responsibilities and experiences of later life.

> (Education Act 2002, Part 6.78)

THE CURRICULUM FOR A MAINTAINED
SCHOOL OR MAINTAINED NURSERY SCHOOL
SATISFIES THE REQUIREMENTS OF THIS
SECTION IF IT IS A BALANCED AND BROADLY
BASED CURRICULUM WHICH
(A) PROMOTES THE SPIRITUAL, MORAL,
CULTURAL, MENTAL AND PHYSICAL
DEVELOPMENT OF PUPILS AT THE SCHOOL
AND OF SOCIETY, AND
(B) PREPARES PUPILS AT THE SCHOOL FOR
THE OPPORTUNITIES, RESPONSIBILITIES
AND EXPERIENCES OF LATER LIFE.

- EDUCATION ACT 2002, PART 6.78

Although the 2002 Education Act remains law in England, the curriculum in English primary schools has increasingly become narrowly focused towards certain aspects of two 'core' subjects (for example, the Phonics Test, the Spelling, Punctuation and Grammar (SPAG) Test and, recently, times tables). The 2014 version of the National Curriculum, and worries about data when inspection takes place, have meant that almost every other curriculum area has been marginalised in the frantic rush to ensure that children score highly in tests in these areas. Children's spiritual, moral, social and cultural development, which is examined in more detail in Chapter 3, is rarely at the top of any school's agenda, and activities related to the humanities and the arts are often left out, or done in a cursory way, in many schools.

So, what has happened to make many primary schools ignore this law and concentrate mainly on numeracy and literacy? Accountability and data seem to be the new drivers for education, rather than the children's needs, as understood by teachers. Under a political agenda that forces schools to battle in a 'survival of the fittest' educational jungle, competition and accountability are top priorities for leadership teams. League tables exist to try and show how well teachers and schools are doing, and children themselves are often faced with a curriculum that is distant from their own human needs. Pressures are high and primary education has become a place where children are constantly being 'made ready' for the next stage of education – and pass the next test.

For example, Early Years is now often seen mainly as preparation for Year 1 so that children are 'school-ready' while much of Key Stage 2 has focused on trying to ensure that children are 'secondary-ready'. We must not forget that Year 1 children are only five and six years old. In many countries children of this age are not even in formal education for another one or two years – and there are good reasons for this, as in these systems, children are valued for *being a child*, and not just a little adult who can't yet do things quite well enough. David Almond's poem, *The Tester* (see page 5), demonstrates how deeply the current desire for testing has become embedded – and dreaded – by children and teachers alike.

Learning and socialising through play is being wiped off of the educational landscape to the detriment of many children, especially those from disadvantaged backgrounds. According to psychologist Peter Gray, *play* functions as the major means by which children:

1. develop intrinsic interests and competencies;

2. learn how to make decisions, solve problems, exert self-control, and follow rules;

3. learn to regulate their emotions;

4. make friends and learn to get along with others as equals;

5. experience joy.

(2011: 443)

In other words, play is an essential part of how young children learn how to live and become happy, confident and responsible people.

All children need opportunities to explore, to be creative and to find out about themselves and the world they live in through activities associated with science, the arts, the humanities and much more. The importance of these is explored throughout the book. We are hoping to persuade you that having a broad and enriching range of experiences is an essential part of every child's education and explore what this means in greater depth.

What has happened to childhood?

Research by Whitebread *et al.* (2012) shows that there has been a sharp decline in children's free play within the recent past, and that this is a common decline across the Western world. Many factors affect the reasons for this decline, such as family pressures, which mean parents do not have time to play with their children; parents' anxiety over safety, which means children are not allowed to play outside; and an increase in screen use at young ages, which can result in physical and social isolation. Some of the responsibility, however, must lie within schools, where children spend at least six hours a day, 195 days of the year – and this figure itself is increasing. If children attend breakfast and homework clubs, they can be in institutional care for 11 or 12 hours a day. Whitebread notes that prescriptive educational policies imposed on schools have limited even early years practitioners from planning for, and allowing children to, play. Over-supervision and restrictive practices that curb children's natural physical, emotional, spiritual and creative development means that their inability to develop good learning behaviours, which should enable them to socialise effectively and serve them well for life ahead, is a time-bomb waiting to explode.

The issue is compounded by the fact that many newly qualified teachers have had very limited training to teach a wide and varied curriculum (Spielman, 2018), and therefore have little understanding of how or what to teach when faced with subjects other than formulaic versions of English and maths. The crisis in teacher recruitment and retention has led to fast and furious methods of teacher training being trialled. These sometimes preclude new teachers, who have come through such routes, from understanding the wider context for learning, or knowing how to engage and motivate children with age-appropriate learning experiences.

In some academy chains and very large schools, many teachers are expected to use bought-in schemes over which they have no control. The thinking is that the schemes ensure consistency across multiple year group classes. But one Year 2 teacher, who worked in such a school, noted that she was so overwhelmed with having to plough through prescribed lesson plans that she barely had time to smile at the children. So it is no wonder the broad and balanced curriculum is in danger of becoming extinct in some areas, and especially in some age groups (SATs years, for example). It is, as we have seen, statutory for primary schools to teach across the curriculum but in such circumstances 'topic' work often becomes a fairly superficial nod towards a 'creative' or broad curriculum.

What does 'educating the whole child' mean?

We argue for a holistic education, the 'education of the whole child'. As Eaude (2018) indicates, any person has many different elements to their identity as a person: physical, mental, spiritual, moral, social and cultural, cognitive, emotional, aesthetic and many others. While we may try to isolate these in order to examine them, these all affect each other, just as physical and mental health are

THE TESTER ISOLATES US.
HE PUTS US ON OUR OWN WITH A TEST PAPER.
HE ISOLATES US FROM OUR OWN
TRUE UNDERSTANDING.
HE ISOLATES US FROM OUR
COMPANIONS.

HE TURNS WHAT SHOULD BE FLUENT AND JOYOUS INTO A
PROBLEM AND A TASK.

IT IS NOW SOMETHING WE MUST BE
ACCOUNTABLE FOR.

SO WE FALL OUT OF LOVE WITH IT,
OUT OF LOVE WITH LANGUAGE,

OUT OF LOVE WITH
OURSELVES.

DAVID
ALMOND

CHRIS RIDDELL

interlinked. So, we should see each child as a whole person – and try to understand how to assess and to teach him or her as such.

Young children grow up in an increasingly globalised world. UNESCO (2014) emphasises that global citizenship and education for sustainable development are closely linked and require:

- *cognitive skills* – where learners acquire knowledge, understanding and critical thinking about global issues and the interconnectedness/interdependency of countries and different populations;

- *socio-emotional skills* – by which learners have a sense of belonging to a common humanity, sharing values and responsibilities and holding rights and showing empathy, solidarity and respect for differences and diversity;

- *behavioural skills* – as a result of which learners act effectively and responsibly in local, national and global contexts for a more peaceful and sustainable world.

(Bourn *et al.*, 2016: 12–13)

However, a holistic education is not just about learning skills. The challenges of growing up in a world of diversity and constant change requires qualities such as respect, resilience and empathy, and the disposition and motivation to manifest these qualities in different situations. The chapters in this book reflect this and are designed to help you to focus on strengthening these in the children in your class.

REFLECTION

What do you remember most from your own primary school experiences?

Perhaps it was the trip to the park to look for minibeasts, or being read to at story time while sitting outside on a warm day? Maybe you remember being enthralled by the theatre group that came to visit, or the joy of singing your heart out in the school choir? For many children, a residential visit was incredibly important. The likelihood is that the things you remember as key learning and formative experiences will be the immersive ones, where you were engaged intellectually, physically and emotionally, and because your teachers planned a wide and varied curriculum to inspire you and to make you feel excited about learning and the future. *You* are now the teacher and it is your job – and your privilege – to inspire your pupils and encourage them to feel hopeful and excited about the future. This book is designed to help you to do that.

The structure of this book

This book brings together expert voices from the world of primary education to suggest what best practice looks like in different areas of children's learning. This will help you to reflect on, and understand more, what children need in order to develop and flourish as well-rounded human beings, so that you can consider how to embed these factors in your own curriculum design.

You can expect to:

- develop a greater understanding of the need for children to have access to a broad and balanced, creative and motivating curriculum that is relevant to them and will prepare them for their future lives;

- engage in practical and intellectual discussion, based on research and underpinned by theoretical perspectives, with case studies from schools and the world beyond school, which will challenge your thinking and enable you to critically reflect on what is needed to adopt a holistic approach;

- feel inspired, confident and reassured that you can provide a full curriculum of high quality experiences for children while ensuring high standards are maintained in all areas.

The book is divided into three sections based on key concepts as outlined below although each chapter is written so as to be accessible as a stand-alone topic. Each chapter makes reference to aspects of the Teachers' Standards that the content addresses and echoes the philosophies that underpin the research and theories discussed. These are collected together in three main sections: 1. The child; 2. The curriculum; 3. The teacher.

PART 1: *Understanding the Context of Children's Lives: Supporting Holistic Education*

Helps us focus on the child as an individual – as the person in front of you, in your classroom – in ways that help them discover their place in the world. It discusses children's emotional, spiritual, moral, social and cultural development and self-identity (Chapters 2 and 3). Chapter 1 considers the role of creativity and Chapter 4 that of the arts, especially in relation to emotional and mental health. In Chapter 5 we discover how 'learning to think', especially through philosophical methods of enquiry, can be encouraged across the whole curriculum and in Chapter 6 we show how a broad and balanced curriculum promotes an environment where all children are included.

PART 2: *Making Learning Meaningful: Teaching and Assessing a Broad and Balanced Curriculum*

Is about how different subjects contribute to the education of the whole child and how the curriculum can be designed to enable this. It offers models of excellence as case studies to help you contextualise theories introduced by the authors. Chapter 7 sets the tone by inviting us to gain a deeper understanding of the humanities as areas of learning where an enquiry approach is central to developing different types of knowledge. Chapter 8 demonstrates the reality and relevance of arts integration by discussing the importance of understanding visual culture and the role of images in twenty-first-century education. Chapter 9 develops this concept by exploring how the spoken word is essential in enabling children to learn how to write, and that this can, itself, be framed as an art form. Chapter 10 looks at how, and what, young children learn through an interaction with nature, and provides food for thought on the impact of children's dis-association with the natural world. In Chapter 11, ways in which mathematics can contribute to a holistic curriculum are explored, emphasising that a blend of discrete subject teaching together with cross-curricular links is essential, so that children understand the application of maths in real-life situations. In a similar vein, Chapter 12 argues that an emphasis on science, technology and maths need not exclude the arts, but that there is a natural symbiosis between them. Chapter 13 considers the implications for the assessment of the whole child, giving innovative examples and pointing out how this must inform planning and teaching rather than being seen as a separate enterprise.

PART 3: *The Reflective Teacher: Developing as a Professional in the Primary Classroom*

Encourages you to critically reflect, and decide, on what kind of teacher you want to be and where your priorities lie for the children in your class. It will, we hope, help you to remember what drove you to become a teacher in the first place: to make a positive difference to children's lives. Chapter 14 returns to the idea of holistic learning and examines the link with creativity across the curriculum. Chapter 15 highlights the importance of personal beliefs and passions and building bridges from children's own interests in creating a culturally responsive, child-centred curriculum. Chapter 16 considers different models of professionalism to argue for one based on 'extended professionality'. In Chapter 17, the importance of creative teaching through gaining agency in planning and teaching the curriculum, and so empowering and motivating children, is emphasised, while Chapter 18 offers a light-hearted view (with serious undertones) on some of the commonly taken-for-granted myths in relation to classroom organisation, behaviour management and inclusion.

The final chapter reflects on some of the key points to highlight why the education of the whole child and a broad and balanced curriculum is so important, recognising that in the current climate doing so presents many challenges, but ones that the best schools – and teachers – manage to overcome. It reminds us that for young children the world is still a place of wonder, exploration and enjoyment, and that a crucial part of the teacher's role is to encourage children to wonder, to be curious, to explore and to discover their world and their own place within it.

References

Bourn, D., Hunt, F., Blum, N. and Lawson, H. (2016) *Primary Education for Global Learning and Sustainability – A Report for the Cambridge Primary Review Trust.* Cambridge: CPRT.

Eaude, T. (2018) Addressing the needs of the whole child: implications for young children and adults who care for them. *International Handbook of Holistic Education.* Abingdon: Routledge, pp. 61–9.

Education Act (2002) Part 6.78. Available at: **https://www.legislation.cov.uk/ukpga/2002/32/contents** (accessed 19 February 2018).

Gray, P. (2011) The decline of play and the rise of psychopathology in children and adolescents. *American Journal of Play, 3* (4): 443–63.

Spielman, **A.** (2017) *Enriching the Fabric of Education*. Festival of Education, speech transcript, available at: **https://www.gov.uk/government/speeches/amanda-spielmans-speech-at-the-festival-of-education**

Tough, **P.** (2013) *How Children Succeed*. London: Random House.

UNESCO (2014) *Global Citizenship Education. Preparing Learners for the Challenges of the 21st Century*. Paris: UNESCO.

Whitebread, **D.**, **Basilio**, **M.**, **Kuvalja**, **M. and Verma**, **M.** (2012) *The Importance of Play*. Belgium: TIE.

HOW TO USE, AND READ, THIS BOOK

YOU MAY, OF COURSE, WISH TO READ THE BOOK STRAIGHT THROUGH, OR PICK OUT CHAPTERS OF PARTICULAR INTEREST TO YOU IN YOUR STUDIES, OR IN RELATION TO SCHOOL EXPERIENCE.

WE HOPE THAT, ULTIMATELY, YOU WILL HAVE READ THE WHOLE BOOK.

WE HAVE INCLUDED REFLECTIVE QUESTIONS AND CASE STUDIES IN EACH CHAPTER TO ENCOURAGE YOU, INDIVIDUALLY OR IN A GROUP WITH YOUR PEERS, TO REFLECT ON THE IDEAS PRESENTED AND TO CONSIDER AND FIND POSSIBLE SOLUTIONS TO SOME OF THE CHALLENGES YOU WILL FACE AS A TEACHER.

WE SUGGEST THAT YOU READ EACH CHAPTER QUITE SLOWLY AND THINK ABOUT HOW IT REFLECTS YOUR OWN PHILOSOPHY AND THE DILEMMAS AND CHALLENGES YOU FACE IN BECOMING THE SORT OF TEACHER WHO WILL INSPIRE CHILDREN.

WE HOPE THAT THIS WILL ENCOURAGE YOU TO EXPERIMENT WITH AND DISCUSS THE RESEARCH, THEORIES, IDEAS AND CONCEPTS PRESENTED HERE WITH PEERS, MENTORS AND TUTORS, AND TO FIND WAYS FOR CHILDREN TO BE ENGAGED AND MOTIVATED BY DEVELOPING LIFE-LONG LEARNING STRATEGIES SO THAT THEIR INDIVIDUAL CREATIVITIES AND TALENTS CAN FLOURISH.

WHO IS THIS BOOK FOR?

Trainee teachers and those new to teaching

Any teacher who wants a better understanding of teaching 'the whole child'

All those who want to take a fresh look at the curriculum offer in primary schools

School leadership staff responsible for changing curriculum practices across the school

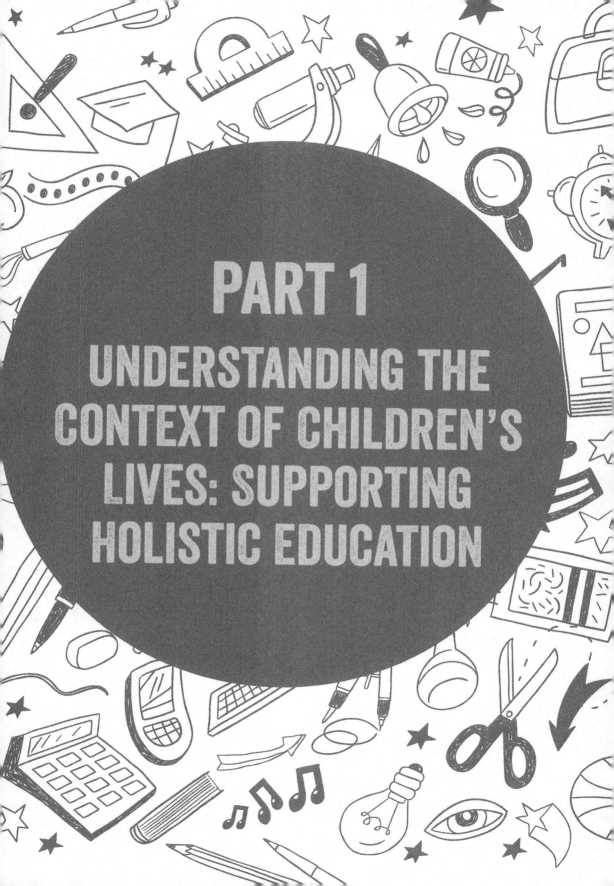

PART 1

UNDERSTANDING THE CONTEXT OF CHILDREN'S LIVES: SUPPORTING HOLISTIC EDUCATION

1

RESOURCING THE SPIRIT OF THE CHILD: CREATIVITY IN THE CONTEMPORARY CLASSROOM

KATE THORPE

CREATIVITY CAN BE SEEN AS REFLECTING THE EVERYDAY POTENTIAL AND IS NOT JUST THE PRESERVE OF THE GIFTED FEW.

(CRAFT AND JEFFREY, 2008)

KEYWORDS: CREATIVE TEACHING AND LEARNING; CREATIVITY; CURIOSITY; INCLUSIVITY; WELCOME; ETHNOGEOGRAPHY; MUTUALLY RESPECTFUL; PERFORMATIVITY CULTURE; CRITICAL THINKING; WELL-BEING; AGENCY.

CHAPTER OBJECTIVES

This chapter:

- highlights the significance of creativity for both child and teacher
- explores definitions that are practicable for the primary practitioner in developing the notion of *resourcing the spirit of the child*
- considers how creative thinking creates a supportive and inclusive learning environment
- considers pedagogical approaches to elicit critical thinking and therefore creativity, both within and beyond the bounds of the classroom

LINKS TO THE TEACHERS' STANDARDS

Working through this chapter will enable you to meet all of the Teachers' Standards, in particular:

TS 1:   Promote good progress and outcomes by pupils

TS 2:   Set high expectations which inspire, motivate and challenge pupils

TS 7:   Manage behaviour effectively to ensure a good and safe learning environment

Part 2:   Personal and Professional Conduct

Introduction

This chapter will explore how creativity in the contemporary classroom might look and feel, and, significantly, how this will depend upon the individual teacher and their unique class. Through examining case studies and good practice, I shall illustrate how this is not an add-on or once a week instance but that instilling creativity in the classroom is essential to an inclusive, friendly and metacognitive classroom where children are happy and fulfilled. Teaching for creativity motivates both teacher and pupil, encouraging aptitudes such as problem-solving and innovative thinking (Craft, 2003). These in turn motivate deeper learning (Black and Wiliam 1998; Alexander, 2010; Fisher, 2006; Rogers and Wyse, 2015).

REFLECTION

You might consider that *'teaching for creativity is learner focused* while *creative teaching is more teacher focused'* (Craft and Jeffrey, 2004).

Reflect upon instances of your practice when you were *teaching creatively*. How did you successfully elicit creative responses from the children?

We shall reflect and find out more about this throughout the chapter and highlight that such an approach demands to be embedded into everyday practice. Creative teaching and learning is, by its nature, multi-disciplinary (Barnes, 2015), and often involves the synchronisation of two or more subjects being taught together: we shall look at this as a way to exemplify 'joined-up' learning, although we must acknowledge that the current system prefers to separate subjects in children's learning experience. The chapter summary will highlight how and why *resourcing the spirit of the child* is essential to consider as part of a teacher's repertoire of pedagogical approaches in order to ensure that the education of the whole child is paramount in our minds.

Setting the scene: considering the significance of creativity for both child and teacher

Primary schooling represents a wonderful opportunity for both teacher and child. As a teacher we have our class for one full academic year, and during this time we have the opportunity to get to know the children and to provide a holistic education, one which encourages the child to be a child: to be curious, explore, communicate, share, collaborate, reflect, imagine and learn to empathise (Early Education, 2012; Craft *et al.*, 2014; Alexander, 2010). All these are essential skills to facilitate a child to blossom, to resource their spirit.

So, what does curiosity look like? Perhaps it is about providing opportunities for the child to explore and manipulate materials and mediums in new and innovative ways. It is also about stimulating reasoning; making connections; discovering how and why things work, are designed; awakening an understanding of the reciprocal nature of the world and the child's place in it; and to find new and better ways to make our world a more sustainable place to live. As teachers we can scaffold and facilitate critical thinking, hypothesising and reflection, through providing an environment with resources and questions that invite the child to be creative and curious.

Resourcing the spirit of the child is, I suggest, the remit of each primary teacher. As we progress through this chapter we shall look at how practitioners can and do meet this aim (Craft and Jeffrey 2008). Ethereal as the concept of *resourcing the spirit of the child* may at first seem, as you will see, it is one very much founded in providing a holistic education, that considers the 'how' we teach (Craft and Jeffrey, 2004) rather than merely the 'what', or conforming to a reductive curriculum that glorifies the 3 Rs. The practitioner who knows their class, who has created a firm, mutually respectful rapport, can address their needs, educational and pastoral (Carr, 2005; Stein, 1953; Maslow, 1970), in creative ways, and can take their class on a journey in which they are all engaged.

Kite flying

Imagine a kite, apparently flitting in the sky. There are a variety of elements at play that enable the kite to fly, have direction and purpose. The guiding thread of this chapter will be for us to consider how to integrate a child-centred education into the primary school: one that complements the National Curriculum (NC). The operators of that kite are the teacher's knowledge and experience base, their ethos, their fluency and competence with employing a variety of pedagogies, their perspective on how and why resourcing the spirit of the child are of importance. The kite, as with the child, will fly if the conditions are right, and recognising the reciprocal relationship of the teacher and the child, valuing and celebrating their knowledge and experience, their virtual bags of knowledge, is essential. The tug on the kite string represents the child's curiosity. Thus the way we teach a subject, the hook or stimuli, may respond to this metaphorical tug and draw upon their curiosity to develop their knowledge and understanding.

The many-fold iterations of the National Curriculum places more or less emphasis on creativity at different times, but it is always there somewhere! A reading of the NC supports and promotes the skills required for creativity. For example,

A high-quality music education should engage and inspire pupils to develop a love of music [and their talent as musicians] and so increase their self-confidence, creativity and sense of achievement.

(NC Music, KS 1 and 2 Purpose of Study, 2013)

We can replace the word *music* for any subject. This statement is relevant for creative teaching and learning in all subjects, and promotes not only the learning and practising of the skills referred to as integral to curiosity, but also the significance and the need for us to provide learning opportunities that will foster a transposing of these skills.

If we look at the NC Programmes of Study (PoS) and Aims for Mathematics, we recognise the same skills being drawn upon:

A high-quality mathematics education therefore provides a foundation for understanding the world, the ability to reason mathematically, an appreciation of the beauty and power of mathematics, and a sense of enjoyment and curiosity about the subject.

(NC Mathematics, 2013)

Let's consider the definitions of the National Advisory Committee on Creative and Cultural Education (NACCCE, 1999) 'teaching creatively' (using imaginative approaches to make learning more interesting and effective) and 'teaching for creativity' (forms of teaching that are intended to develop children's own creative thinking or behaviour). We can begin to see how the metaphor of the kite can help us to imagine creative practices that will resource the spirit of the child.

THEORY FOCUS

Anna Craft and Bob Jeffrey in their article 'Learner inclusiveness for creative learning' (2004) make the distinction between creative teaching, which is more teacher orientated, and teaching for creativity, which is more learner orientated. Creative teaching involves intent from the teacher to teach using a creative pedagogy and may well aim to elicit creative responses from the child, but not necessarily – this is neither a prerequisite nor a definite part of this approach. Teaching for creativity aims to foster creative responses, be they through critical thinking or creating a physical product. The article analyses creative teaching and learning in detail, and with some great case studies to illustrate, might well inspire you to plan similar experiences.

REFLECTION

Reflect on lessons you've taught or seen:

- When do you think the teacher was teaching creatively?
- What was present in this pedagogy, compared with other instances of teaching?

For us in schools, at this moment in time, we could replace the word 'culture' with the term 'performativity culture' (Craft and Jeffrey, 2008) or the phrase 'accountability and high stakes school agenda' (NASUWT, 2017). This performativity culture is the result of the last decade of governmental policies specifically relating to the arts and culture, the marketisation of education, and the emphasis upon creativity now having a *value in itself, it's emphasis shifting from 'create' as a verb to 'creativity' as a noun* (Craft and Jeffrey, 2008). And, of course, in such a high-stakes society, this needs to be measured, to be accountable. As teachers, we need to balance the education and needs of our class with the requirements of Statutory Assessment Tests (SATs), so that we look beyond merely providing correct answers to a test question. We need to consider children's learning and their acquisition of skills and knowledge in a holistic, purposeful way.

What do we mean by creativity?

As a practitioner we must know our children well and relate their own knowledge and experience to our teaching. This will motivate children to try new ways of thinking, to take risks and thus to think creatively. Consider Stein's seminal work on creativity (Stein, 1953), upon which many contemporary pedagogues have built their own interpretations. Stein's explanation of the creative process can be of great use to the practitioner.

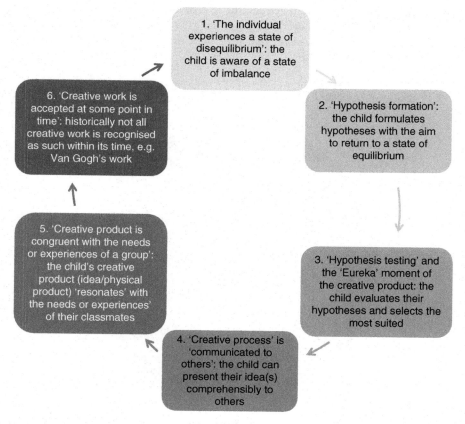

Figure 1.1   The creative process (created from Stein, 1953)

Figure 1.1 shows a summary of Stein's key elements of creativity to formulate a creative process that I hope you will find useful. Stein introduces the significance of the contextual background of the creative product, within both the historical moment and the culture in which the product is presented, and the resulting acceptance of both the initial creative process and the final product. Relating this to the classroom we can extrapolate that the child, in taking a risk to think creatively with innovation, will seek acceptance and a valuing of their attempts. Indeed, for both the child and the teacher this moment is incredibly significant. Our reception of what, to that child, is a creative and original thought or product is key: the way we respond as a teacher and role-model, will influence each child in that class.

If we recognise the individual's creative process and struggle with respect and positivity, then so will the whole group. We'll encourage them to take risks, to hypothesise, to evaluate, to be creative, to reciprocally create an environment in which the creative process is valued, ideas may be trialled, mistakes made and the spirit of the child be resourced.

Is this a classroom that stimulates curiosity? That values the child? It is a pedagogy that invites creativity, that is learner focused, and such an approach would also resource you as the teacher.

Anna Craft's analysis of creativity, from multiple perspectives (Craft, 2001) – from psychoanalysis to humanist fields – builds upon Stein's work and is most useful for us in the classroom. For our purposes, we shall consider what Craft termed 'little c creativity' (Craft, 2000), that is creativity that is reflected in the individual's 'everyday potential' (Craft and Jeffrey, 2008). It is *imaginative activity fashioned so as to yield an outcome that is of value as well as original* (NACCCE, 1999) for that child.

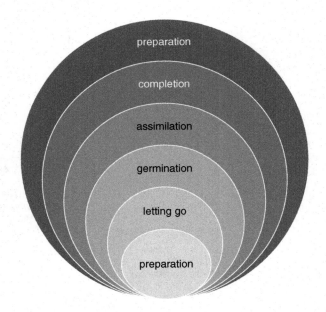

Figure 1.2 **'Spiral' model of the creative process (adapted from Craft, 2000)**

If, as Craft and Jeffrey propose, that creativity is a potentiality available to all, then little 'c' creativity makes a lot of sense. Despite the fact that a performativity culture has inevitably created tensions between education, accountability and the governmental desire to raise standards, then it also stands to reason that on balance, education may also provide a platform for creativity. Seltzer and Bentley (1999) state that *creativity can be learned* and education has a significant role to play *to reflect forms of learning which develop creative ability.*

Craft and Jeffrey (2008) found that *practitioners and creative partners from the creative and cultural sector are inspired by the changing landscape to emphasise the fostering of creativity in children they teach* and that this results in them striking a balance between this supposed *impossible tension* and moving beyond this to work with it.

As practitioners we can create learning opportunities for creative responses from children, to balance the aforementioned 'impossible tension' between a performativity culture and an education that enriches the experience, skills and knowledge of the child.

REFLECTION

Recall an instance from your own primary education when you were being creative. What did it look and feel like? These experiences of creativity are ingrained upon our consciousness as moments of deep engagement, resulting in an experience which we can vividly recall however much time has passed.

As a primary teacher, evoking such creative experiences for children is and should be a part of our pedagogical repertoire, to enrich their educational experience, to replenish the spirit of the child. We can create an inclusive environment in which children's engagement is unavoidable if we inspire and motivate them to be curious, to think and to pose questions.

For us as primary teachers, to foster an environment in which the child can engage in the creative process, we must encourage children to want to question, hypothesise, explore one another's viewpoints from a mutually respectful and critical stance, to evaluate – as we have seen in Figure 1.1. Where the child may be *imaginative, going beyond the obvious, being aware of one's own unconventionality, being original in some way. It is not necessarily linked with a product-outcome* (Craft, 2000). If we hold this overarching ethos in mind when planning we can provide opportunities for children to engage with such creative learning experiences, be they on an individual or collaborative level.

Child and teacher rapport: resourcing and valuing the individual, their differences and similarities

Part of the repertoire of a teacher is to find ways to connect meaningfully with their class. Getting to know them swiftly at the beginning of the school year creates a bond that both child and teacher can continue to nurture. Finding out about your pupils gives you insights, which may otherwise not be apparent, helps prevent a teacher making assumptions and gives the child the opportunity to be seen in a new light. Each child has their individual differences and similarities, and we as teachers want to build on both of these in order to nurture a caring, inclusive, friendly and supportive environment that values their individuality.

CASE STUDY

Nurturing a rapport

I was recently working in a school in Greater London with groups of children from Y3-Y5 identified to receive Pupil Premium funding. Part of the challenge was to gain their trust and respect swiftly to motivate them to want to work with a teacher they didn't know. Although I had a limited period of time in which to work with them the school expected results: in both academic and behavioural improvement and achievement. Having just met the children, with the emphasis put upon results, how does a practitioner balance this with what children need?

For each group, I devised a simple fun verbal activity, in which I was an equal participant rather than facilitator. Our activity is shown in Figure 1.3.

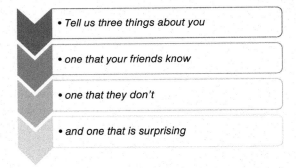

- *Tell us three things about you*
- *one that your friends know*
- *one that they don't*
- *and one that is surprising*

Figure 1.3   Verbal activity

Me going first seemed to break the ice. Also, this gave them longer to think about their responses, and they were invited to think silently (you could suggest they draw or make notes, as appropriate for your class) for a few minutes before responding. Suddenly, there were some smiles around the table. They were evidently enjoying sharing. Talking about themselves. Listening to one another. Talking about something not necessarily related to school.

This verbal, impromptu (or so it seemed to the children) activity was invaluable. It gave me insights into their interests, relationships, school and home rapports, to name but a few. They were surprised by the *something surprising* each of us told, enjoying our complicity. I told them I would take notes while they were talking to help me remember. It was a reasonably quick activity and scaffolded my future planning with regard to how to motivate and work with each child. The time was well spent, as it meant that I had begun to nurture a relationship with the children. I could relate planning to their experience and interests. Each of us knew something about the other as the exchange was reciprocal: a shared sense of agency was thus created.

Such an activity can readily be tailored to a particular class, or even a particular theme you wish to scaffold. The children's engagement and enjoyment was evidence of the value of taking time to nurture a positive and inclusive rapport between yourself and the children as well as between children themselves.

Creating a resourcing environment

Now we have identified the importance of a positive and inclusive rapport between child and teacher, we must consider the environment and how this can be resourceful in itself. We shall explore key areas within which both child and teacher interact and have varying degrees of agency through Craft's notion of 'possibility thinking'.

A key element for us as practitioners is to consider how to make the school environment inclusive and meaningful. If we aim for the child to be engaged through their imagination, exploration of thought and action, thus to be resourcing their spirit to be creative, then we must involve them in decisions about creating those environments (Craft and Jeffrey, 2004; Valentine, 2006). The teacher plays a significant role, either directly as a role-model or indirectly through facilitating an environment in which creativity is valued. The child may also become the role-model, for an 'apprenticeship approach to developing creativity' (Craft, 2001). Similarly to the socio-constructivist view of education, such a mentor (a more knowledgeable other) may be a child or adult from within or without the school.

Parallel to this, we should consistently bear in mind the invisible messages we give children. How do we welcome children into the class? What expectations do we transmit through facial responses and body gestures? Clarity of expectation and providing feedback are pivotal in providing the child with cues which they can understand, which promote pupil agency and in turn contribute to a safe and welcoming environment (Csikszentmihalyi, 2008; Crichton and McNaid, 2015). As teachers our role is to promote a child's self-esteem and self-belief, equip them with skills and knowledge to achieve and to provide them with challenges. All these elements contribute to resourcing the child, providing a holistic education and creative learning experiences.

Our role as teachers is to recognise how to motivate, value and provide for creative learning. Inclusive of balancing the decision of when to stand back, let the child explore and discover at their pace (the incubation stage), and when to intervene. Consider Craft's description of the stages of creativity: preparation, incubation, inspiration or illumination and verification, and the reciprocal relationship between teacher and pupil. We might reflect on how these relate to those identified by Stein, and whether your lessons provide opportunities for the class to engage with these stages. Perhaps the creative cycle in Figure 1.4 could aid your pedagogical approach and lesson planning;

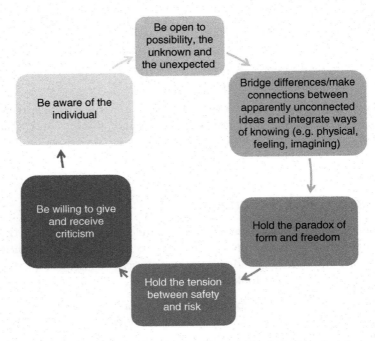

Figure 1.4   Adapted from Kessler and Craft's combined 'Creative Cycle' approach (Craft, 2001)

The *physical environment* of the classroom

REFLECTION

Imagine coming into the classroom as a child, on the first day of term, or the child that joins midway through. What could inspire, excite and engage you? How might colour or differing tones and lighting play a part in creating the atmosphere? How could the environment create a sense of welcome and inclusivity?

These key elements are ones that practitioners can control and that can have a significant impact on the child's emotional responses. Consider the organisation of the furniture, the physical use of space, the maximising of natural light, the location of displays, the accessibility of resources, reading areas, cosy corners – these should all be inclusive of autonomous-child access.

An imaginative teacher will plan for these elements, through providing books, displays, tasks etc. that give children access to their ethnogeography. In so doing the teacher enhances and values inclusive thinking by all children.

Elements such as the furniture, plants and activities can serve to *create a natural link between the inside and outside environments of the school. Fostering a link with the outside environment is important because a school as a place of learning and discovery cannot be seen to be an island* (Valentine, 2006).

Creating and maintaining your class ethos

In some ways this aspect is unique to each teacher and each class, and may or may not reflect personal interests or areas of expertise. Throughout the primary age phase, we have a wonderful opportunity to scaffold and provide a considered physical environment for the children, which celebrates and values their interests and ethnogeography and which provides attractive physical spaces as well as opportunities for collaboration or private reflection (such as a book corner, displays or an expressive table). These can be incorporated into lessons, the children's play and critical thinking tasks.

As you engage with the below case study, consider how this relates to the creative cycle (Figure 1.4) and how the teacher has created a supportive, resourcing environment to enhance learning.

CASE STUDY

Year 6

A Year 6 class were working in mixed groups, their aim being to experiment with a variety of materials to find the best material to float. They worked collaboratively, according to the lesson aims, giving them freedom to explore, thereby opening possibilities. They were to record their thinking and hypothesising at each stage, and to discuss reasons as a group. The teacher facilitated a brief period of exploration time, and then through deciding when and which groups needed guidance, posed questions that promoted reasoning and challenge to their assumptions, to 'bridge differences', test hypotheses and formulate incubation time, thus promoting focus and facilitating them to try imaginative and novel ideas.

The children had a clear understanding of their remit and were able to work collaboratively, to bridge differences in thinking and hypothesising, to make connections, take risks and evaluate. The time given to explore the materials and incubate their ideas meant that they could use prior knowledge and understanding to test their thinking. Taking risks and making mistakes was proven to be valuable. Through recording their thinking at each stage, they could evidence how their thinking had been influenced by the results and see the progression in their thinking and understanding. The teacher was sensitive to the needs of each group and child, posed a mixture of open and closed questions, and did not provide the children with an answer but motivated deeper thinking from the children. This could be called *possibility thinking* (Cremin *et al.*, 2006).

The rapport between the child and teacher was supportive and trusting, which was evident through the risk-taking, the sharing of positive criticism and the self-esteem demonstrated. For example, a number of children who often lacked focus and concentration when working on purely academic tasks were fully engaged with this work. As we have seen, the teacher created an environment in which risk-taking is encouraged, where children were respectful of one another's contributions and respectfully challenged one another's thinking, and where the learning was highly motivated, cognitive and of high quality. If creative responses from the children are regarded as valuable – and these may be take many forms, and may not represent a *neat, finished product* (Craft, 2001b) – both teacher and child recognise the significance of the learning process.

REFLECTION

As you engage with the following ideas (Figures 1.5-1.7), in light of creating your class ethos, consider the following:

- How can you implement these ideas in your classroom?
- When would you do this? At the beginning of each term? Half-termly?
- Would it enrich practice to share with other classes?
- When could the children evaluate their environment and produce their own next steps?

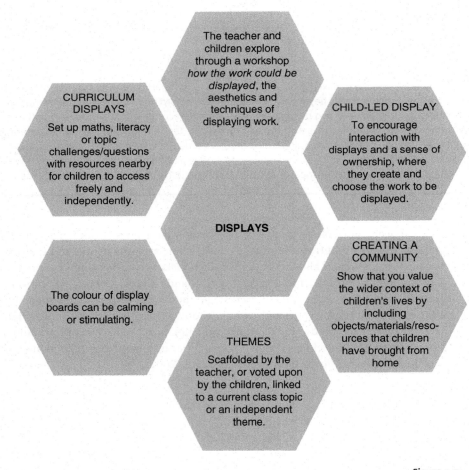

Figure 1.5   Displays

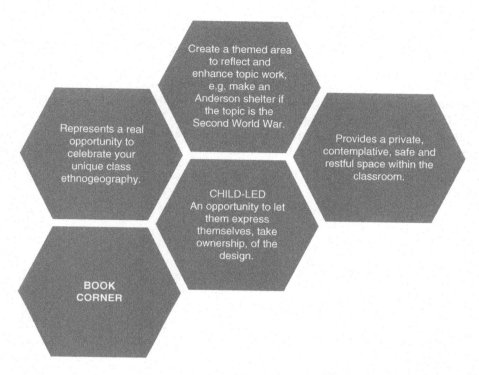

Figure 1.6   Book Corner

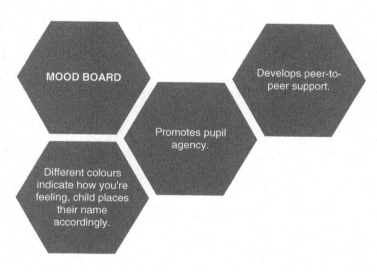

Figure 1.7   Mood Board

How do we create immersive learning environments?

A fantastic strategy and a readily available resource for all teachers to create an immersive learning environment inclusive of stimulating possibility thinking is through the posing of and responding to questions. An immersive learning environment is one where children are active learners within a multisensory, interactive environment, such as role-play, enquiry-based learning and exploratory play (Tickell, 2011). These are fundamental characteristics for effective learning and teaching (Tickell, 2011). As we have just seen in the Y6 case study, an essential part of the planning and the role of the teacher was not direct teaching, but the posing of questions and motivating a deeper level of cognition leading to deeper understanding.

REFLECTION

When do we as practitioners do this?

Are we narrowing opportunities for engagement with critical and possibility thinking, though perceiving immersive learning as only being possible for discrete subjects or topics?

How can we create opportunities for us, in our lesson planning, through to medium- and long-term planning, to foster possibility thinking?

The type of questioning is pivotal, as is to whom the questions are posed. The teacher can motivate possibility thinking through questioning, such that the initial or lead question has intent, while subsequent posing of and responding to questions could be child to child or child to teacher and from a 'what if' or 'what might be' as opposed to a 'what is' basis (Chappell *et al.*, 2008). The child could be working individually upon a problem, or working collaboratively, thus questions and responses (verbal and non-verbal) will be both generated and shared by the group. The teacher shifts their focus from directing the learning to fostering an atmosphere where the child has time to explore ideas, physical space and resources with which to experiment, explore and evaluate in imaginative and novel ways. The teacher motivates the child's sense of 'self-determining' through providing an inclusive, immersive environment, being responsive to the child through a delicate balance of when to let the flow of the child's thinking follow its natural course, thus 'standing back' and knowing when to pose open questions and provide a 'responsive intervention' (Chappell *et al.*, 2008). This will maintain focus on the problem, through motivating the child to possibility think, to imagine new alternatives. The teacher, in standing back, promotes the child's intrinsic curiosity, exploration and imaginative or creative thinking that will bridge differences, or if you prefer it assimilates those instances of cognitive dissonance. This maintains the child's sense of agency or 'self-determining' and therefore their concentration and motivation.

If we take the stance that immersive learning and creativity formulate 'the core of the curriculum' and that we as teachers should provide immersive opportunities be they verbal, physical or pictorial in process and outcome, then we are stimulating *research, reasoning and recording [which] are seen to be essential complements to the traditional '3 Rs'* (Cremin et al., 2006) and are therefore fostering creative learning.

The teacher who understands that their role is to provide opportunities for children to have owner-ship of their learning, through celebrating and valuing their funds of knowledge (Alcorn, 2016), is contributing to resourcing the spirit of the child. They are motivating children to be autonomous learners, who have some control over where, when and how their learning takes place;, where they are *the* protagonists *of their learning and are encouraged by teachers to develop projects and solve problems among themselves, using the* teacher *as a tool who can 'lend' help, information and experience when necessary* (Valentine, 2006: 11).

REFLECTION

How do you respond to the quotation above?

Can you assume the role of the 'teacher as a tool who can 'lend' help, information and experience when necessary'?

CHAPTER SUMMARY

In this opening chapter we have contextualised creativity in relation to the NC inclusive of current tensions from external forces. We have explored different avenues related to creativity in educa-tion and highlighted how such an education is holistic, should be embedded in learning in order to resource the spirit of the child, and enable that child to fulfil their potential as a well-rounded human being and member of society.

We have looked at theory and practice to guide our evolving critical thinking and adaptation of pedagogical approaches to enrich the curriculum. We have defined creativity in terms of Craft's notion of 'little c', and possibility thinking in regard to this being available to all children, fostered through a pedagogy that invites exploration, hypothesising, taking risks and making mistakes that is inclusive.

We have recognised the significance of creating a firm rapport with the child through taking the time to get to know them, their interests and skills. The research and literature we've explored, alongside examples from practice, indicate a wide range of potential gains from the promotion of pupils' creativity. In combining all these elements, then surely our kite will fly and we will be resourcing the spirit of the child.

```
┌──────────────── KEY POINTS TO CONSIDER ────────────────┐
```

- Personal development is key to good learning: helping pupils establish a framework for their own learning and increasing motivation can be achieved through engaging with creative pedagogy.
- Social, emotional and intellectual development (resourcefulness) can be promoted through collaborative practices and teamwork based on good relationships between teacher and child, as well as between children themselves.
- The learning environment itself is key to enabling children to engage with the learning process, promoting a culture of autonomy through possibility thinking.
- The concept of *resourcing the spirit of the child* is at the heart of what we do as primary teachers.

References

Alcorn, **F.D.H.** (2016) *The Omnipotent Presence and Power of Teacher-Student Transactional Communication Relationships in the Classroom: The So-Called 'Post-Race Era'*. Rotterdam: Sense Publishers.

Alexander, **R.** (2010) Conclusions and recommendations. *Children, Their World, Their Education: Final Report and Recommendations of the Cambridge Primary Review*. Abingdon: Routledge.

Barnes, **J.** (2015) An introduction to cross-curricular learning. In P. Driscoll, A. Lambirth and J. Roden (eds) *The Primary Curriculum: A Creative Approach*, 2nd edition. London: Sage, pp. 260–83.

Black, **P. and Wiliam**, **D.** (1998) Inside the black box: raising standards through classroom assessment. *Phi Delta Kappan, 80* (2): 139–48.

Carr, **D.** (2005) Personal and interpersonal relationships in education and teaching: a virtue ethical perspective. *British Journal of Educational Studies, 53* (3): 255–71.

Chappell, **K.**, **Craft**, **A.**, **Burnard**, **P. and Cremin**, **T.** (2008) Question-posing and question-responding: the heart of 'possibility thinking' in the early years. *Early Years: An International Journal of Research and Development, 28* (3): 267–86.

Craft, **A.** (2000) *Creativity Across the Primary Curriculum*. London: Routledge.

Craft, **A.** (2001) Little c creativity. In A. Craft, B. Jeffrey and Leibling (eds) *Creativity in Education*. London: Continuum, pp. 45–61.

Craft, **A.** (2003) The limits to creativity in education: dilemmas for the educator. *British Journal of Educational Studies, 51* (2): 113–27.

Craft, **A. and Jeffrey**, **B.** (2004) Learner inclusiveness for creative learning. *Education 3–13: International Journal of Primary, Elementary and Early Years Education, 32* (2): 39–43.

Craft, **A and Jeffrey**, **B.** (2008) Creativity and performativity in teaching and learning: tensions, dilemmas, constraints, accommodations and synthesis. *British Educational Research Journal, 34* (5): 577–84.

Craft, A., Cremin, T., Hay, P. and Clack J. (2014) Creative primary schools: developing and maintain pedagogy for creativity: ethnography and education, *9* (1): 16–34.

Cremin, T., Burnard, P. and Craft, A. (2006) Pedagogy and possibility thinking in the early years. *Thinking Skills and Creativity, 1* (2): 108–19.

Crichton, H. and McNaid, A. (2015) Learning Intentions and success criteria: learners' and teachers' views, *Curriculum Journal, 27* (2): 190–203.

Csikszentmihalyi, M. (2008) *Flow: The Psychology of Optimal Experience.* New York: Harper Perennial Modern Classics.

Early Education (2012) *Development Matters in the Early Years Foundation Stage (EYFS).* London: Early Education. Available at: **https://www.early-education.org.uk/development-matters**

Fisher, R. (2006) *Thinking to Learn: Helping Pupils Take Greater Responsibility for Their Own Learning.* Report. Inverness: Highland Council. Available at: **https://www.steveslearning.com/ Teacher%20Training%20resources/Fisher,%20R.%20Tools%20for%20Thinking.pdf**

Maslow, A.H. (1970) *Motivation and Personality,* 2nd edition. New York: Harper & Row.

NACCCE (1999) *All Our Futures: Creativity, Culture and Education* (Chaired by K. Robinson). Report, National Advisory Committee on Creative and Cultural Education (NACCCE). Sudbury: DfEE.

NASUWT (2017) *Creativity and the Arts in the Curriculum: A Report of Policies and Practices in England, Northern Ireland, Scotland and Wales.* Report, NASUWT, The Teachers' Union. Available online at: **https://www.nasuwt.org.uk/uploads/assets/uploaded/3535be2c-801c-46cb-b44108 10472b52a3.pdf**

Department for Education (2013) *The National Curriculum in England: Key Stages 1 and 2 Framework Document.* Available at: **https://www.gov.uk/government/publications/national-curriculum-in-england-primary-curriculum**

Pollard, A. (2014) *Reflective Teaching in Schools.* London: Bloomsbury Academic.

Rogers, S. and Wyse, D. (2015) Agency, pedagogy and the curriculum. In D. Wyse, R. Davis, P. Jones and S. Rogers (eds) *Exploring Education and Childhood: From Current Certainties to New Visions.* London: Routledge.

Seltzer, K. and Bentley, T. (1999) *The Creative Age: Knowledge and Skills for the New Economy.* Report. London: Demos.

Stein, M.I. (1953) Creativity and culture. *Journal of Psychology, 36* (2): 311–22.

Tickell, C. (2011), *The Early Years: Foundations for Life, Health and Learning: An Independent Report on the Early Years Foundation Stage to Her Majesty's Government.* DfE. Available online at: **http://www.educationengland.org.uk/documents/pdfs/2011-tickell-report-eyfs.pdf**

Valentine, M. (2006) *The Reggio Emilia Approach to Early Years Education,* 2nd edition. Report. Glasgow: Learning and Teaching Scotland.

2

CREATING SPACE TO EXPLORE SELF-IDENTITY

RACHEL MASON

YOU HAVE THE RIGHT TO AN IDENTITY – AN OFFICIAL RECORD OF WHO YOU ARE. NO ONE SHOULD TAKE THIS AWAY FROM YOU.

(ARTICLE 8: UN CONVENTION ON THE RIGHTS OF THE CHILD, UNICEF)

KEYWORDS: IDENTITY, CHILDREN, CURRICULUM, CITIZENSHIP, CONTEMPORARY ART, VISUAL IMAGES, MULTIPLE IDENTITIES.

CHAPTER OBJECTIVES

This chapter:

- summarises the current state of knowledge about personal identity and how it is formed
- explains why (i) it is important to encourage children to explore and communicate their personal and group identities and (ii) how and why art can be a useful pedagogical tool to help them do that
- argues the case for extending and developing young children's civic identifications
- describes and analyse interdisciplinary schemes of work that can be used to inspire work on exploring identity in primary classrooms

LINKS TO THE TEACHERS' STANDARDS

Working through this chapter will enable you to meet all of the Teachers' Standards, in particular:

TS 2:   Promote good progress and outcomes by pupils

TS 5:   Adapt teaching to respond to the strengths and needs of all pupils

TS 8:   Fulfil wider professional responsibilities

Part 2: Personal and professional conduct

Introduction

Why do we need to consider the role of personal identity in our work with primary aged children? This question is one that I shall attempt to answer in this chapter. I shall begin by examining existing ideas about the nature of identity and how the concept of *self* is formed. I shall also make a case for engaging with the notion of multiple identities, and discuss the key role that visual images play in children's actions and their perceptions of self. In this chapter we shall focus on curriculum, and consider the opportunities that art and citizenship education offer for exploring and expanding young children's personal, social and, especially, civic identifications. We shall end the chapter by looking at schemes of work emanating from an international research project, in which contemporary artworks were the stimulus for interdisciplinary classroom experiments that set out to enable children to explore their personal and group identities, and which will help you to value each child in your class for the unique being that they are.

What is identity and how it is formed?

Identity in the legal sense is established at birth. UNICEF's Convention on the Rights of the Child (1989) states that *parties shall undertake to respect the right of the child to preserve his or her identity, including nationality, name and family relations as recognized by law without lawful interference.* Thus we all have the right to the aspects of identity mentioned above.

This legal definition, notwithstanding the nature of identity, is contested and is theorised in different ways:

- *Psychologists* generally use the word to describe those things that distinguish individuals from each other. This is often understood as *personal identity*.

- *Sociologists*, on the other hand, tend to use it to describe *social identity* as an individual's self-concept derived from personal membership of a social group.

REFLECTION

What is your perception of the notion of personal identity?

Have you considered the relevance of exploring notions of the 'self' with pupils?

---- **THEORY FOCUS** ----

Social theory posits that the formation of *self* occurs through identification with significant others during one's biographical experience. *Family* is an especially important socialising agent that transmits skills, values and attitudes about self and others. But individuals have multiple social identifications and experience diverse levels of being or self. For example, *ethnic identity* refers to a sense of belonging to a particular ethnic group (the group that individuals feel they belong to tends to be one in which they claim heritage); *national identity* commonly refers to the sense of belonging to a particular nation or nation state. The discussion of curriculum in this chapter focuses on *citizen identity*. While this is typically defined and explored in national terms, it is linked to personal identity and influenced by a range of factors such as relations between personal and social identifications, including those of the state (Mason *et al.*, 2011).

How does our sense of self-identity impact on our lives?

Socialisation is a process by which individuals learn the norms and roles that society creates. Beginning at birth, for example, most parents treat children differently according to gender, as determined by the appearance of their genitals. But young people may question this and may have a strong sense of being the opposite gender. Questions about gender, ethnicity, nationhood and identity are currently at the forefront of political agendas and, in the theoretical discourse about them, they are either viewed as in a state of fragmentation or strengthening.

Material and symbolic resources also play an important role in shaping the way our identity evolves. Images in the visual culture that surrounds us every day may be consciously or unconsciously embedded in our imagination as icons of different aspects of our identities. TV and the Internet offer many versions of identity influenced by images circulated by global mass media and sharply focused marketing (Cote, 1996; Mayo and Nairn, 2009).

---- **REFLECTION** ----

Think about key icons or images from your own childhood. How do these affect who you have become? How do they help you to connect you with your feelings about your past, yourself and other people?

Some theorists understand *culture* and *mass media* as the most important factors in shaping an individuals' opportunities, obligations and actions. Given that visual culture and consumption impact significantly on children's actions and perceptions of self, it is my opinion that competence in analysing visual images is (or should be) a fundamental educational goal.

Cultural complexities

Changing cultural and social contexts and new relationships allow individuals to develop new or modified identities. The number of children growing up in a culture that is different from that of their parents has increased as never before in history, which Pollack and Van Reken describe as *third culture kids* (2017). We know that context plays a significant role in self-conception (Brooker, 2008: 10). Young children in today's classrooms may be experiencing and communicating *pluralist* national identities, and their self-identifications are likely to be complex and multiple. This makes your job as a primary teacher complex on multiple levels too.

While identity in a legal sense is established from birth, personal, social and cultural identity grows and changes (Woodhead, 2008). Identity is expressed through children's subjective feelings about themselves and about others. Much of their identity depends on opportunities they have, both in and out of school, for reflecting on their social relationships and making social comparisons. Human groups, such as gender, ethnic and religious groups, are fundamental categories of these kinds of anchors, and constitute an important part of our social world. We know that children's early childhood experiences have profound effects upon their schooling outcomes as a whole (Siraj-Blatchford, 2009). Research has shown that children start to construe others in categorical terms such as gender and race at a very early age (Bennet, 2011: 356–7).

Educating positive identities

Warin (2010) argues that developing a sense of self is crucial to a person's overall psychological well-being, as it enables us to take control of our lives and helps us to manage our experiences. Educating for positive identities is important. It touches on some fundamental questions facing every young child: 'Who am I?' 'Is it OK to be who I am?' and 'What is my place in the world?'

It is important also because social identifications have consequences. Research shows that children aged 5 typically show unconditional preferences for their own social and cultural in-groups (Aina and Cameron, 2011; Society for Neuroscience, 2009). They often hold very stereotyped national identifications and interpretations of people living in different countries including their own.

REFLECTION

Does this statistic surprise you? What experiences do you think might lead such young children to hold already formed stereotypical views?

Facilitating civic identifications: children are citizens too

Children are increasingly kept apart from public life. We need to embrace the political challenge of their inclusion and participation in the lives of their communities. An excellent model of this is the truly democratic paradigm of the pre-schools of Reggio Emilia in Northern Italy, where children are assumed to have the same citizens' rights as anyone else – and the same status too. Read more about the Reggio Approach and the importance that is placed upon identity formation:

https://www.reggiochildren.it/identita/reggio-emilia-approach/?lang=en

Citizenship education is concerned with *citizen identity* and understood as the legal and political status of individuals within democratic societies and their civic rights and responsibilities. Although it involves a focus on developing awareness of political procedures and institutions, the focus now is on an active curriculum element. This is on the grounds that citizens are not merely passive holders of rights, but engaged citizens who demonstrate the kinds of civic skills that will strengthen democratic culture. Some scholars argue that it is more appropriately concerned with developing attitudes, values and dispositions (Kymlicka and Opalski, 2001: 293; Waldron, 2004: 212), which has to be where our role as primary teachers lies. The aim is to endow children with the abilities to take effective action and to cherish members of society. It also provides opportunities for children to engage with critical enquiry, to question controversial issues and to learn about democracy, citizenship and government.

Identity, as an understanding of the self, therefore, becomes a recurring theme that can be revisited many times over the period of years that children spend in school: it follows a natural development curve as the child progresses through the years. Citizenship education, whether with a national or regional focus, sets a context for a child's sense of personal identity within a democratic society. The problematic nature of multiple citizenship identities, however, is not so well recognised and this is where we can look to using contemporary art to help facilitate discussion and dialogue and to provide a platform for children to explore their thoughts and ideas.

Image analysis

Given that visual culture impacts significantly on children's actions and perceptions of self-competence, analysing visual images is (or should be) a fundamental educational goal. A defining characteristic of a well-formed citizen is the capacity to make informed choices. We can use tried and tested strategies for engaging children in image analysis and deconstruction by asking questions about the images that surround us in everyday life. This is crucial for facilitating them to engage in critique and action.

Making images

Art education is concerned with self-expression and exploring personal identification. Art teachers routinely encourage their students to value art-making as a psychological manifestation of their social, cultural and individual identities, and to use visual images as a means to exchange and communicate their feelings and ideas.

THEORY FOCUS

Hoffman-Davis (2007) argues that some of the main features of art education experience that distinguish it from other subjects are the engagement with a tangible product which involves the application of imagination and agency on the part of the learner. A focus on emotion allows learners to express personal emotions and develops a capacity for empathy with others. Ease with ambiguity allows for greater variations in interpretations, and a respect for the integrity and diversity of differing viewpoints and opinions. Art lessons involving *making* are orientated toward process and experience, with the learning embodied in the process of enquiry and reflection on the process. The learner develops a contextual, tacit understanding of those processes through the direct connection with art making in which they can find a moment of personal engagement and ultimately take responsibility for their own progress.

Read *Why Our Schools Need the Arts*, by Jessica Hoffman-Davis here:

http://edpuniversity.info/ebooks-pdf/080774834X.pdf

REFLECTION

There is much debate and concern about the decline of arts in our primary schools (Cooper, 2018; NSEAD, 2016). With a deeper understanding of the benefits that arts can bring to developing the whole child, what can you do in your class to reverse that trend?

What can this look like in the classroom?

Self-portraits have long been a popular topic for art lessons, but there is a need to move beyond the common fixation on observational drawing and literal representation of physical appearance. Devising schemes of work that challenge children's sense of themselves is much more important. We can help children to explore the impact of social influences on personal identity, and set tasks that enable them to distinguish how the wider community can affect their identity. The following examples demonstrate how children's sense of personal identity was developed through the vehicle of art and citizenship education in the Images and Identity research project.

Who am I?

This topic was addressed through practical activities in which students were encouraged to explore their personal identities using collage and mixed media. One German teacher encouraged primary school children to explore and express their identity by designing an identity treasure chest, in which they could place objects, either ready-made or created by themselves, to symbolise different aspects of their identity. In an Irish school, pupils created handprints and selected words to represent their identity, then combined these together resulting in creative artworks.

Seeing Me

Under the title 'Seeing Me', pupils in a multi-racial primary school in London collaborated on creating photographic self-portraits to send to children in another country. The curriculum focused on acquiring photography skills, learning to talk about visual images and communicating about their own culture and sense of self, both visually and orally, to children in a country other than their own. The classroom had a supply of Digital-Blue cameras, offering features that enable young children to experience taking photos of each other, a computer with software for downloading the images directly from the cameras, and an interactive whiteboard for showing images to the whole class. This meant they were able to shoot, look at and discuss their photographic portraits straight away.

After a first attempt at producing a photograph that explained 'who I am', the children were given many practice sessions, to familiarise themselves with the technology.

To support children with English as an additional language much of this developmental work was completed in small groups and pairs, for example writing down things they wanted to communicate about themselves, sharing ideas and photographing each other. At one point the children were invited to bring favourite objects from home to include in their portraits. In the last lesson each child chose the image of themselves they liked best and wrote a few sentences on the computer to send to their partner school.

Family and self

Portuguese teachers selected the theme of 'Family' with the aim of advancing learner awareness of the changing nature of family as an agent of socialisation and how this influences civic identity. *Patrimony and family values are deeply embedded in societal structure in Northern Portugal, where this action research took place, and initial discussions suggested their pupils held ethnocentric and stereotypical perceptions of identity* (Moura and Sá, 2013: 183). They used contemporary art to springboard into a scheme of work that challenged their stereotypical notions of childhood and family relations.

Michael De Brito is a contemporary realist painter whose parents migrated from Portugal to New York. His large-scale oil paintings are influenced by European 'Old Masters' like Rembrandt, Manet and Velázquez. The subjects he paints are moments of everyday life, especially kitchen scenes, in which his ex-patriot family and guests sit around a table sharing conversation, food and drink. See Michael De Brito's paintings at: **https://www.artistsnetwork.com/art-mediums/oil-painting/ michael-de-brito/**

The teachers asked children (aged 10–11) to compare what they saw in the paintings with their own family backgrounds and identify aspects of family life they did/did not associate with. The ensuing discussion challenged their internalised conceptions of 'normal' family life. Consideration of a broader concept of family was enhanced through the practical activity of making papier-mâché puppets representing family members. In the process of creating these, the students were encouraged to reflect on their changing perceptions of family and challenge stereotypical views of how it is experienced. In the final activity they photographed the puppets and created picture postcards using digital media (see Figures 2.1 and 2.2).

Figure 2.1   Children's puppets in response to Michael de Brito's 2008 painting Family.

Figure 2.2   Child's postcard to a grandfather exploring notions of family

In their evaluation of this curriculum experiment the teachers concluded that engaging with De Brito's paintings had greatly facilitated discussion of their preconceptions. His images of his Portuguese family stimulated enquiry-based conversations in which the pupils exchanged stories of their own family lives, customs and traditions. Sharing these experiences and ideas, alongside exploring the artworks, had enabled them to come to terms with the idea that family is not the same for everyone and significantly developed their critical thinking skills (Moura and Sá, 2013).

Self and difference

Exploring the notion of *difference* is key for developing tolerance in our societies. Children can be taught to understand the impact of social influences on personal identity by setting tasks that enable them to distinguish how the wider community can affect their personal identity, and how this is sometimes the same and sometimes different from other people's. Teachers in the Images and Identity project developed activities designed to explore similarities and differences in the way we see ourselves and how others see us. They used questions and visual images to stimulate discussion of conflicts pupils might experience while exploring different aspects of their identity. Some questions they posed included *Who am I? How do others see me? How well do I think I know others? What does it mean to be different? Where am I from? What does it mean to be British, French etc. and a citizen of the world of social media?*

REFLECTION

What can you find out about the children that you did not already know? What do the children find out about each other to help them understand their similarities and differences?

Figure 2.3   Children dressing up/wearing masks. Photograph by Susan Ogier

Physical appearance and identity

In one British school a teacher encouraged young children to alter their defining images of themselves by getting them to use make-up and costume to change how they looked. This enabled the children to consider how appearance affects how we are perceived by others, and how by wearing different clothing for different situations we express certain aspects of our identity (see Figure 2.3). For example, a school uniform creates an identity that links children with a particular school and location; the same child wearing a football kit on a Saturday morning portrays another aspect of his identity; attire connected with religious groups denotes yet another aspect of that child's identity. Children were encouraged to photograph one another by posing in their costumes, which they then used to make personal reflections on what they had chosen to wear and why, and how the clothing had affected them emotionally.

Culture, heritage and crafts

Material culture in the form of costumes, musical instruments, monuments, patterns and motifs on textiles, etc. frequently transmits specific community and/or ethnic identities from one generation to the next. Thus analysing and comparing cultural artefacts has the potential to increase pupils' awareness of diverse heritages and lifestyles. Teachers in Portugal were especially keen to promote awareness of folk arts in a way that counteracted stereotyping and prejudice. They applied an anthropological model of art criticism (see Cuthbertson, 1982, below) to the study of artefacts from different countries, and engaged their students in discussion of different cultural traditions and lifestyles. To show how cultural identities are transmitted over generations and transformed over time they invited a contemporary textile artist who uses traditional materials and techniques to come into school. She explained her work and showed the children examples, together with the traditional artefacts that inspired the work.

Eight ways of analysing an artefact:

- Studying how it was made

- Determining how it was used

- Discussing the environment or context of the artefact

- Considering its development through time

- Comparing artefacts of similar use across cultures

- Studying the design and decoration

- Interpreting its meaning, significance and cultural value

- Considering why it is in a museum (if appropriate).

(Cuthbertson, 1982)

Identity and place

National identity commonly refers to the sense of belonging to a particular nation or nation state. As Holt-Jensen (1999: 216–27) and Knox and Marston (2004: 505) point out, dominant images of landscape frequently function as icons of national identity, and sometimes quite specific vistas turn into typifications of national landscape that help to construct ideas of distinctive national pasts, for both natives and foreigners. Tourist postcards often depict idyllic impressions of real places that represent what tourists should rather than actually do see. Tourist postcards featured centrally in a scheme developed in Ireland that engaged pupils with ways in which space and place are intrinsic to our being in the world. *How are we viewed?* After the pupils were introduced to Irish artist Sean Hillen, they were encouraged to produce paper collages from fragments of postcards and other found materials, depicting seemingly impossible landscapes that challenged stereotypical Irish representations of place.

Identity cards

In one scheme of work developed in an English school, children explored the role and function of identity cards. They explored identity in relation to photographic 'passport' portraits. They considered what they were comfortable with revealing about their identity and what they wanted to remain private. They studied examples of official ID cards from different countries and learned about their function. They studied the rules for producing passport photographs, then photographed each other using the rules. They made personal ID cards and combined portraits of themselves with photographs of objects and text that they found meaningful. Through this experience, they were able to consider their personal and collective identities, and how this is used by authorities in different ways.

Using contemporary artworks

REFLECTION

How do you feel about introducing children to citizenship themes, such as personal and group identities, through contemporary art?

Contemporary artists often question/challenge media stereotypes. A defining feature of the Images and Identity project was the use of contemporary artworks (especially photography) to prompt discussion, exploration and self-reflection about identity. Photographic portraits of young people by Wendy Ewald and Rene Djkstra and Michael De Brito's paintings of his family were especially helpful. Photographic self-portraits by Cindy Sherman and Gillian Wearing were used to stimulate discussion of physical appearance and identity since they invited questions about 'Who are we behind the mask?' Norbert Attard's installation *Where Are You From*? stimulated discussion and self-reflection about national identification and diversity in Malta.

How do I see myself and how do others see me?

Gillian Wearing is a contemporary British artist whose photographic portraits are a powerful stimulus for self-reflection on identity formation. She uses masks ranging from disguises to voice dubbing to conceal the identities of her subjects. In a series of self-portraits, she applied silicone prosthetics to herself and carefully reconstructed family photographs so as to transform herself into her mother, father and sister as young adults. Some of Gillian Wearing's photographic projects are public collaborations. In another series of portraits, she explored the relationship between public image and private identity. For the series called *Signs that say what you want them to say and not Signs that say what someone else wants you to say*, (1992–3) she photographed over 500 strangers whom she stopped in the streets of London and persuaded to write down private feelings about themselves. Then she photographed them holding up these messages. This is easy to replicate in the classroom. See Gillian Wearing's artwork at: **https://www.tate.org.uk/art/artists/gillian-wearing-cbe-2648**.

Examples of teacher questions: *Do you think the sitters are posing as themselves? What do you think their comments mean? What is the photographer trying to say? Do you think that your whole identity is visible to others? Are there some parts of your identity that you try to hide?* Both the Wearing examples challenge the assumption that identity and physical appearance go hand in hand.

Identity and human rights

Wendy Ewald is an American artist-teacher who works with young people around the world encouraging them to become photographers and acting as a translator of their images. The photograph in Figure 2.4 was taken during a one-year project in Margate, Kent, she called *Towards a Promised Land* (2003–6). It involved 22 young people recently arrived on the Isle of Thanet from places affected by war, poverty and/or political unrest, or simply as a consequence of changes in their domestic circumstances.

The full text on this photograph reads: *My name is Uryi. I came from Grodno in Belarus. It happened that we had to leave our lovely city. Now we are living in a beautiful English city, Margate, which is by the sea. I love this place, but I am always thinking about my grandmother and my friends back home* (see **http://wendyewald.com/portfolio/margate-towards-a-promised-land**).

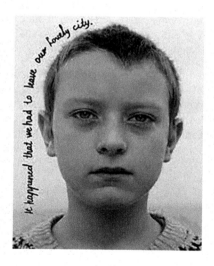

Figure 2.4   Wendy Ewald: Towards a Promised Land (2006)

Examples of teacher questions:

- Who is the boy photographed?

- Where do you think he is from?

- What do you think the photograph says about him?

- How would you feel if you had to change your identity: your name/your nationality/your school/your language?

During class discussion, the teachers concerned explained that the children in this series of images had come to the UK from other parts of the world and that they were living in a holiday seaside town, Margate, but were not on holiday. Children were directed to look more closely at them with questions like *What does the text on the pictures say? What might that mean?* Then they were informed that Wendy Ewald, felt that these children were 'invisible' and that their identities had been changed by their experiences; they were not in their own homes, with their families, in a place that they knew. The boy, Uryi, told her he had changed his name to George so that he would seem more British. Then the teachers posed the question: *Would you change your name? Why? Why not?*

Find out more about Wendy Ewald's work here: **http://wendyewald.com/**

CHAPTER SUMMARY

In this chapter I have argued for attention to move towards encouraging children to reflect on and explore relations between personal and social identities, in order to develop their sense of self. To achieve this end, I have suggested they analyse contemporary artworks, reflect on identity-related social issues or themes, and experiment with ways of developing and realising 'I' position statements in visual form. Through exploring, experimenting with and communicating personal feelings and ideas in this way I anticipate they may learn something about citizenship and personal identity and that their personal identity is not static but is something that evolves and changes as they grow.

In this approach, I have outlined contemporary artworks that project the identity of their subjects as compound personalities. These can be used as prompts to stimulate pupil interest and discussion. Providing a structured approach to image analysis is crucial in this to facilitating conversations in which critical reflection on identity-related concepts and themes takes place. In the classroom you can draw on citizenship curriculum materials to facilitate group discussion of issues and concepts associated with, for example, sharing similarities, acknowledging differences across diverse cultures, and challenging any stereotypical perceptions children may have that influence how they view people or places.

I hope that the practical examples will encourage you to provide opportunities for children to create artistic responses to identity-related issues or themes. This can play a crucial role in facilitating personal exploration, during which children construct their identities and extend individual notions of self.

```
╭──────────── KEY POINTS TO CONSIDER ────────────╮
```

- Identity is a recurring topic in both art and citizenship education. There are advantages in combining them.

- Understanding one's self and personal identity helps children to find their place in the world and to develop empathy and tolerance towards others.

- Children should have opportunities to create personal and group artistic responses to identity issues, concepts and themes.

- Children can develop the ability to analyse, interpret and critically evaluate the visual world around them. Exploring visual images both orally and in writing is (or should be) a fundamental educational goal.

- Contemporary art often documents the multi-faceted personal and collective identities of their subjects challenging social and geopolitical realities (Vella, 2013: 78).

- Another reason for using images by contemporary artists it is that they are largely neglected in school, but should be part of every child's artistic and cultural education.

Further reading

Bennett, M. (2011) Children's' social Identities. *Infant and Child Development*, 20: 353–63.

Cooper, B. (2018) *Primary Colours: The Decline of Arts Education in Primary Schools and How It Can Be Reversed*. London: Fabian Society. Available at **https://fabians.org.uk/wp-content/uploads/2019/01/FS-Primary-Colours-Report-WEB-FINAL.pdf**

Cuthbertson, S. (1982) Dialogue with objects: asking questions. *Museum Quarterly*, 84, British Columbia Museum Association.

Carter Ching, C. and Foley, B. (eds) (2012), *Constructing the Self in a Digital World*. Cambridge: Cambridge University Press.

UNCRC (n.d.) *UN Convention on the Rights of the Child in Child Friendly Language*. UNCRC/Unicef, **https://www.unicef.org/rightsite/files/uncrcchilldfriendlylanguage.pdf**

References

Aina O.E. and Cameron, P.A. (2011) *Why Does Gender Matter: Counteracting Stereotypes with Young Children*, **https://www.southernearlychildhood.org/upload/pdf**

Bennet, M. (2011) Children's social identities. *Infant and Child Development*, *20*: 353–63.

Brooker, L. and Woodhead, M. (eds) (2008) *Developing Positive Identities: Diversity and Young Children*. Early Childhood in Focus (3). Milton Keynes: Open University.

Cooper, B. (2018) *Primary Colours: The Decline of Arts Education in Primary Schools and How It Can Be Reversed*. London Fabian Society: DG3. Available at https://fabians.org.uk/wp-content/uploads/2019/01/FS-Primary-Colours-Report-WEB-FINAL.pdf

Cote, J. (1996) Sociological perspectives on identity formation: the culture identity link and identity capital. *Journal of Adolescence, 19*: 417–28.

Hoffman-Davis, J. (2007) *Why Our Schools Need the Arts.* New York: Teachers College Press.

Holt-Jensen, A. (1999) *Geography, History and Concepts.* London: Sage, pp. 216–27.

Knox, P. and Marston, S. (2004) *Places and Regions in Global Context: Human Geography*, 3rd edition. Toronto: Pearson, p. 505.

Kymlicka, W. and Opalski, M. (eds) (2001) *Can Western Liberal Pluralism Be Exported? Western Political Theory and Ethnic Relations in Europe.* Oxford: Oxford University Press, p. 293.

Mason, R. (2011) Teacher guidelines: art. *Images and Identity Training Materials*, **www.image-identity.eu/images_and_identity_folder**

Mason, R., Richardson, M. and Collins, F. (2011) School children's visualisations of Europe. *European Educational Research Journal, 11* (1): 153–74.

Mayo, E. and Nairn, A. (2009) *Consumer Kids: How Big Business Is Grooming Our Children for Profit.* London: Constable & Robinson.

Miell, D. (1990) The self and the social world. In I. Roth (ed.) *Introduction to Psychology*, Volume 1. London: Erlbaum.

Moura, A. and Sá, C. (2013) Family and citizenship. In R. Mason and C.-P. Buschkühle (eds) *Images and Identity: Educating Citizenship through Visual Arts.* Bristol: Intellect, pp. 175–98.

NSEAD (2016) *The National Society for Education in Art and Design Survey Report 2015–16.* Available at: **www.nsead.org/downloads/survey.pdf** (accessed online 6 April 2018).

Pollack, D. and Van Reken, R. (revised 2017) *Third Culture Kids: Growing Up Among Worlds.* London: Nicholas Brealey.

Schaffer, H.R. (2006) *Key Concepts in Developmental Psychology.* London: Sage.

Simeunović Bajić, N. (2009) *The Role of Media in European Identity Formation: Understanding the Complexity of Today's European Media Landscape.* Budapest: Central European University.

Siraj-Blatchford, I. (2009) Conceptualising progression in the pedagogy of play as sustained shared thinking in early childhood education: a Vygotskian perspective. *Educational and Child Psychology, 26* (2): 77–89.

Society for Neuroscience (2009) Less empathy toward outsiders: brain differences reinforce preferences for those in same social group. *Science Daily*, 1 July. Available at: **www.sciencedaily.com/releases/2009/06/090630173815.htm**

Society for Research in Child Development (2009) Awareness of racism affects how children do socially and academically. *Science Daily*, 14 November, **www.sciencedaily.com/releases/2009/11/091113083301.htm**

Vella, R. (2013) Errant identities in contemporary art education. In R. Mason and C.-P. Buschkühle (eds) *Images and Identity: Improving Citizenship through Visual Art.* Bristol: Intellect, pp. 63–80.

Waldron, F. (2004) Making the Irish: identity and citizenship in the primary curriculum. In C. Sugrue (ed.) *Curriculum and Ideology: Irish Experiences, International Perspectives.* Dublin: Liffey Press.

Warin, J. (2010) *Stories of Self: Tracking Children's Identity.* Stoke on Trent: Trentham Books.

Woodhead, M. (2008) Legal identity is conferred by birth registration. In L. Brooker and M. Woodhead (eds) *Early Childhood in Focus 3.* Milton Keynes: Open University Press.

3

SPIRITUAL, MORAL, SOCIAL AND CULTURAL DEVELOPMENT

TONY EAUDE

[SMSC DEVELOPMENT INVOLVES] . . . THE TRAINING OF GOOD HUMAN BEINGS, PURPOSEFUL AND WISE, THEMSELVES WITH A VISION OF WHAT IT IS TO BE HUMAN AND THE KIND OF SOCIETY THAT MAKES THAT POSSIBLE.

(HOUSE OF LORDS, 2006)

KEYWORDS: SPIRITUAL; MORAL; SOCIAL AND CULTURAL DEVELOPMENT (SMSC); CHARACTER; THE WHOLE CHILD; RELATIONSHIPS; ENVIRONMENTS; REFLECTION; FUNDAMENTAL BRITISH VALUES.

CHAPTER OBJECTIVES

This chapter helps you to:

- consider the place of spiritual, moral, social and cultural (SMSC) development in legislation and the Ofsted Inspection Framework;
- explore what SMSC development means and why it matters in relation to the education of the whole child and children's well-being;
- consider the challenges in making provision for children's SMSC development and ways that teachers can overcome these;
- explore how SMSC development can 'fit into' a subject-based curriculum;
- discuss the implications for primary schoolteachers, especially in terms of relationships, classroom ethos and environment

```
┌──────────────── LINKS TO THE TEACHERS' STANDARDS ────────────────┐
```

Working through this chapter will enable you to meet all of the Teachers' Standards, in particular:

TS 1: Set high expectations which inspire, motivate and challenge pupils

TS 5: Adapt teaching to respond to the strengths and needs of all pupils

TS 7: Manage behaviour effectively to ensure a good and safe learning environment

Introduction

The 2002 Education Act requires schools to provide a balanced and broadly-based curriculum which:

- promotes the spiritual, moral, cultural, mental and physical development of pupils at the school and of society; and

- prepares pupils at the school for the opportunities, responsibilities and experiences of later life.

The first of these is now usually known as spiritual, moral, social and cultural (SMSC) development. The Ofsted Inspection Framework (2018) highlights that before making their final judgement on a school's overall effectiveness, inspectors must evaluate the effectiveness and impact of the provision for pupils' spiritual, moral, social and cultural development. The Ofsted Framework sets out what inspectors are likely to be looking for, including how schools are promoting fundamental British values, which has been placed within SMSC development and is discussed towards the end of this chapter.

Both the law and the inspection framework emphasise that schools must make provision for SMSC development, but this chapter argues that there are other, more fundamental reasons and considers the implications for primary teachers. I hope to challenge some of your assumptions and prompt you to see the role of the teacher in new, thought-provoking but exciting ways.

What is spiritual, moral, social and cultural development?

As the quotation above indicates, SMSC development is about the sorts of people that children are and become, and the type of society which enables them to become purposeful and wise. However, there is no agreed definition of SMSC and many teachers are unsure what it entails. You may wish to look at how Ofsted (2018) describes what they are looking for, but wait until you have answered the following question!

REFLECTION ─────────────────

Consider what SMSC development entails. Think about each of the four elements below:

- spiritual;
- moral;
- social;
- cultural.

I expect that you will probably come up with answers which are different from other people in the group. You may find that it is hard to decide exactly what falls within each element and that they overlap.

However, my guess is that you may have made associations between

spiritual	and	religion, awe and wonder, beautiful experiences
moral		right and wrong, behaving well, values
social		getting on with each other, being kind
cultural		different backgrounds and beliefs, the arts

Spiritual is probably the one you found hardest to define. Many people immediately associate spirituality with religion, but most of the research suggests that children's spirituality should be understood more broadly. My own research (see Eaude, 2008) emphasises children searching for the answers to universal questions, set out below, which can be explored within, or outside, a religious framework.

Hay with Nye (1998) emphasise relationships and what they call value-sensing, mystery-sensing and awareness-sensing as three dimensions of children's spirituality. Their emphasis on relationships highlights that spiritual development is not just about looking inwards but is to do with interactions with other people, the world and (for some people) God or a transcendent being. In Hull's words (1998: 66), *spirituality exists not inside people, but between them.*

One phrase that captures for many teachers what spiritual development is about is 'awe and wonder'. Spirituality is often associated with beautiful and life-enhancing experiences, such as seeing an egg hatch, being moved by a lovely sunset or hearing a wonderful piece of music. However, spiritual development also involves addressing difficult and potentially painful questions.

Most people think of moral development as learning to make choices about what is right and wrong, and behaving well, a tradition called *duty ethics*. The problem, in my view, is that this approach can overlook the importance of context and most moral and ethical choices in practice are not about whether to be honest or generous, for example, but how honest or generous to be. Another tradition of moral development is *virtue ethics*, which emphasises the sort of person one is and the qualities and dispositions which enable one to make appropriate decisions. Qualities such as courage, generosity, resilience, kindness and empathy all go to make up one's character, but in a more rounded and holistic way than a view of character which emphasises grit, a stiff upper lip and the denial of emotion.

Values are the foundation of how children are motivated to behave well, based on intrinsic motivation, as discussed below. But which values one emphasises and promotes may vary depending on the culture and expectations at home. For instance, modesty matters a great deal for most children from South Asian backgrounds and patriotism is often underplayed in England compared to its significance in other societies.

Social development seems the easiest of the four components of SMSC to understand and is to do with children getting on with other people and being kind and cooperative. Social is closely associated with emotional development. Many children find cooperating and regulating their emotions difficult, especially very young children and those who are anxious. Boys, in particular, often have a limited emotional repertoire and externalise their emotions, for instance manifesting their anger through aggressive behaviour. Social and emotional development is the basis of most aspects of children's learning.

Figure 3.1   Cultural and creative learning occurs across all subject areas

Cultural development refers to various overlapping meanings related to identity and belonging, since most children will live in a world of cultural diversity, but this also refers to developing an understanding of our lives in the context of the artistic expression and traditions. The excellent report of the National Advisory Committee on Creative and Cultural Education (NACCCE, 1999), *All Our Futures*, emphasises the link between culture and creativity, with a strong focus on how the arts enhance creativity, though arguing that creativity should underpin learning in every subject area (see Figure 3.1).

How do the four elements of SMSC development relate to each other?

In Eaude (2008), I argued that the four elements of SMSC development overlap but all involve searching for answers to universal questions to do with meaning, identity and purpose. The expectations of children and teachers may be somewhat different in faith-based schools and others, with more emphasis on the religious aspect in the former, though these questions, as summarised in the following diagram, are universal:

Spiritual Who am I? Where do I fit in? Why am I here?	**Moral** How should I act? What sort of person do I want to become?
Social How should I interact with other people?	**Cultural** Where do I belong? What is my identity?

Young children ask such existential questions, though they may not do so using the same words as adults, or even words at all. For instance, they often do so in their play or through their drawings. Such questions raise some painful and puzzling issues for both adults and children and have no easy answers while children need a sense of agency and time and space to explore them.

SMSC development is more about how children learn to become people – and the sorts of people they become – than filling them with information. Although it is convenient to discuss the four elements separately, they are interlinked and overlap, and while SMSC may seem separate from cognitive development, cognition and emotion are interdependent in that one cannot learn well in the cognitive domain at times of intense emotion. Therefore children's needs have to be met holistically in ways to be discussed shortly.

Many teachers are not sure what SMSC development entails or see it as mainly about life-enhancing experiences and fairly safe, uncontroversial ideas. However, the theologian, John Hull (1998), relates spirituality to the dominant values of modern, consumerist Western societies based on money and consumption, with brands and external features presented as more important than intrinsic qualities and sees the role of education as enabling young people to be critical of inauthentic and transient values. Therefore provision for children's SMSC development may imply challenging and helping children to question many of the messages which they encounter in advertising and the media, and which are often reinforced at home, such as money, possessions and looks being the basis of success and happiness.

How should teachers promote and plan for children's SMSC development?

Some teachers argue that SMSC development happens throughout the life of a school and that one cannot really plan for it. While much happens tacitly, children require guidance and support and provision has to be planned for. The report *Schools with Soul: A New Approach to Spiritual, Moral, Social and Cultural Education* (RSA, 2014) highlights a danger that too many schools take a 'scattergun approach' that risks provision being 'everywhere and nowhere'. This raises two questions as follows.

REFLECTION

What sorts of provision should primary teachers make to promote children's spiritual, moral, social and cultural development?

Where does SMSC development 'fit into' the primary curriculum?

The obvious, though not necessarily the best, place to start answering these questions may be to think in terms of subjects. There are many opportunities in every subject area (see Figure 3.2). For instance:

Figure 3.2   Children learn SMSC concepts by exploring the world around them

- In science, the beauty of nature and the puzzling nature of the universe prompt questions about where we fit in and how we should act.

- In maths, patterns are often a source of wonder and creativity and many cultures made vital contributions to mathematics.

- In English, by hearing and reading stories, children can be encouraged to explore ethical issues and understand how other people from other times and cultures feel and respond.

- History, geography and RE are areas where children can enquire, explore and come to understand themselves and people from other cultures and societies, especially in terms of time, space and belief.

- The arts provide many opportunities for children to use their imagination and exercise creativity.

Children's SMSC development does not just happen in RE or PSHE lessons or circle time (though these may provide good opportunities). Rather, it should run like a thread through all aspects of school life, like the words in a stick of seaside rock, or be part of the school's DNA.

With the current focus on literacy and numeracy skills, many schools pay little explicit attention to SMSC development as such. However, often early years and primary schools make good provision for SMSC development through the hidden curriculum and outside the classroom. Rather than curriculum subjects, it may be more useful in planning provision for SMSC development to think of the types of:

- experiences

- environments

- relationships

which you offer, as well as opportunities within subject areas.

Primary teachers are well placed to ensure that all children have a wide range of experiences and to create and sustain the sort of environment, ethos and relationships which enhances children's SMSC development. Their expectations in terms of high standards need to relate to social and emotional development and behaviour, not just what can be easily measured in literacy and numeracy.

Young children benefit from a broad range of experiences which encourage them to exercise agency – a sense of being in control – and creativity. In a targets and outcomes-driven curriculum, adults often expect young children not to act as children, but more like little adults. Much of what helps to enhance SMSC development, such as play, stories and the arts, are enjoyable – and children must be allowed to enjoy them. But this does not mean that children should just have fun and do as they want. Children enjoy challenges as long as they are manageable and meaningful to them.

The relationship between the children and the teacher is vital in helping establish and sustain the nurturing environment which enhances SMSC development. To explore the questions outlined above, children need time and space to enquire and reflect, not just in sessions set aside for reflection, but across the whole curriculum. If children are to be able to explore, take risks and question and have a sense of belonging, environments must feel safe and inclusive and provide a range of challenges without being too competitive. But creating inclusive environments sometimes means that adults need to ensure that children do not act however they want to. So, in encouraging children to be kind and thoughtful, behaviour which excludes other children has to be challenged by the teacher and ideally by other children. And children must learn to work together, in groups, not just with their friends, if they are to become used to cooperating with those who are different.

As the playwright James Baldwin wrote, children never have been very good at listening to their elders but have never failed to imitate them. This highlights that all adults must model how to act and interact. For instance, children are expected to show respect or creativity, while adults must demonstrate respect for children and encourage divergence in their own actions. Setting a good example matters especially in relation to embedding the values which help children to be intrinsically motivated so that they act appropriately, even when unobserved and without the promise of reward and fear of punishment.

Teaching in this way is difficult if teachers are expected to cover a very full curriculum at great pace. But it is worth remembering that good provision for SMSC development is more about *how* you teach than *what* you teach and the sort of person you are as a teacher is no less important, and maybe more so, than what you know.

Can children's SMSC development be assessed?

Much of what enhances children's SMSC development is not tangible or easily measurable, which raises the following questions.

REFLECTION

How can teachers be confident that they are having an impact?

How can they track this impact?

Aspects such as relationships and ethos are vital, but they are not easily assessed and certainly cannot be measured with any validity. However, external assessment should be of the provision that schools and teachers make, rather than of individual children. One can try to make the best provision possible but never guarantee its impact.

However, primary teachers usually know their children well and build up a strong relationship over time, enabling them to assess children's progress, mostly based on 'feel' and intuition. This does not mean that teachers should ignore data, which may give some clues about children's SMSC development, for instance if they are attending more regularly or getting into fights less often. But it does imply that teachers should rely more on holistic assessment, by including many adults who know the child, where possible, and exercising professional judgement rather than relying on test scores (see Chapter 13 on assessment in this book).

What are fundamental British values and how do they relate to SMSC development?

We have seen that exploring and developing values is an important component of SMSC development. In recent years, the idea of fundamental British values, which is associated with the Prevent Strategy to combat radicalisation, has been included in SMSC development. This idea is more controversial than it may seem.

REFLECTION

Fundamental British values are defined as democracy, the rule of law, individual liberty and mutual respect and tolerance of those with different faiths and beliefs.

Do you agree that these are fundamental to being British? What would you change or include?

You may think that these values are all essential. However, values, including fundamental British values, are more debatable than they appear on the surface. The following quotation gives some idea why.

THEORY FOCUS

In a plural society like ours people agree in valuing virtues like justice and honesty but do not share the same interpretation of these terms ... The more detailed interpretation such words are given, the more difficult it is to achieve a broad consensus.

(Katayama, 2004: 70)

As Katayama suggests, there may be broad agreement on shared values, but not on what these mean or entail. This is certainly the case with fundamental British values.

Three main arguments have been made against these four values as fundamental or distinctively British. Some people such as Michael Rosen (2014) suggest that these are universal human values. Others point out that Scotland, Wales and Northern Ireland emphasise different values and that these are English rather than British. Others argue that the way fundamental British values are often presented is a nostalgic view which is not reflective of the diversity of modern Britain.

A more practical and worrying concern is that the policy focus on fundamental British values and its association with the Prevent Strategy is seen to be targeting some communities and minorities, especially presenting a stereotype of Muslims being potential terrorists, when most Muslims, as with other groups, are thoughtful and law-abiding citizens.

What do we mean by the fundamental British values chosen?

REFLECTION

What do you understand by:

- democracy
- the rule of law
- individual liberty
- mutual respect and tolerance of those with different faiths and beliefs?

Let's explore these ideas briefly, bearing in mind Katayama's words above. Most people probably regard democracy as desirable, but there are many different types of democracy and many would argue that Britain has not always been very democratic in practice.

Similarly, the rule of law is usually seen as a necessary part of a civilised society and most classrooms operate on the basis of rules, both explicit and implicit, such as how children are expected to act and interact (see Chapter 18, this volume). However, a question which children, especially in Key Stage 2, find fascinating is 'should one ever break the law? and if so when?' For instance, many of the most important social changes such as the civil rights movement in the US involved breaking the law and there is a long tradition in England of dissent.

Most people are broadly in favour of individual liberty. However, as with the rule of law, what this entails in practice is not always obvious. For instance, few people would argue that one should be free to act as one wishes when this severely constrains someone else's liberty, and children must learn that they have responsibilities as well as rights.

Although Britain often claims to be a tolerant country, the government's actions – especially towards minorities – have often not reflected this. While most teachers would wish to encourage respect and tolerance, you may think, as I do, that respect is more positive than tolerance, which seems rather grudging, and one should not tolerate some things such as racist, sexist and homophobic behaviour and attitudes.

What are the implications for teachers?

REFLECTION

Do you agree with what I have written? *(It is fine if you don't.)*

Whatever your view, what are the personal and professional implications for you as a primary teacher in promoting fundamental British values?

I hope that you will recognise that the idea of fundamental British values is more contested than it appears at first sight. However, 'not undermining fundamental British values' is included in the section 'Personal and professional conduct' of the Teachers' Standards which sets the minimum requirements for teachers' practice and conduct; and are therefore associated what it means to act, and be treated as, a professional, as discussed in Chapter 17. Teachers must therefore think carefully about how they can promote, and not undermine, fundamental British values in their own personal lives and professional practice.

Promoting fundamental British values needs to run right through how teachers teach and interact with children, as with the rest of SMSC. For instance, children learn how democracy works by participation in democratic processes rather than just learning about how Parliament operates. And teachers should, but do not always, show respect for children and their families, especially those whose beliefs and actions are different from their own. Given the importance of role-modelling in how young children especially learn, how you act and interact with other people is a vital aspect of how you help them embed the values which will help them become thoughtful and responsible citizens.

Why does SMSC development matter?

This chapter has argued that children's SMSC development is important, though too often not seen as such. Often this is associated with teachers not knowing quite what it involves or with lack of time in a busy, results-driven climate. However, the following quotation suggests a more profound reason.

> *The key reason for the marginalisation of pupils' SMSC development is time – not so much time for provision, as time for reflection about purpose.*

(RSA, 2014: 16)

Much of this chapter calls for a rather different approach to how primary teachers are currently encouraged to think about the curriculum and how to teach. The emphasis on skills in literacy and numeracy and success being measured largely in terms of test scores leaves little room, or incentive, for teachers to think deeply about the aims and purposes of education and remember what brought them into teaching. Yet if we do not think about what we are trying to achieve and focus only on a narrow range of skills, we run the risk of leaving young children unprepared for a world of complexity and change. And of teachers missing out on what is one of the wonderful but demanding aspects of teaching young children – the chance to contribute to, and see, the development of the whole child.

CHAPTER SUMMARY

This chapter has suggested that SMSC development is an essential part of the development of the whole child and a broad and balanced curriculum. It involves children having time and space to explore difficult, sometimes puzzling, questions and using their imagination and creativity. It does not mean that teachers should not challenge children or expect high standards but entails different types of challenge and views of standards. It may involve encouraging children to question many of the messages about materialism and consumerism. Doing this is very hard for teachers in the current climate, but is what many primary teachers went into teaching for.

KEY POINTS TO CONSIDER

Spiritual, Moral, Social and Cultural Development:

- has a prominent place in legislation and the Ofsted Inspection Framework and is essential to the development of the 'whole child';
- involves searching in terms of questions about identity, meaning and purpose and how people should interact with each other, which can be explored within or outside a religious framework and is not just about easy, life-affirming experiences;
- does not occur just within one subject, such as RE or PSHE, but crosses subject boundaries;
- occurs through experiences, environments and relationships, especially by example, rather than by direct instruction;
- relates to contested and controversial ideas such as 'fundamental British values';
- is not easy but an aspect which most primary teachers find very fulfilling.

Further reading

Eaude, T. (2008) *Children's Spiritual, Moral, Social and Cultural Development – Primary and Early Years*, 2nd edition. Exeter: Learning Matters.

This accessible book for students explores many issues discussed here in more depth.

Ofsted (2018) *School Inspection Handbook* (updated April 2018). Available at **https://www.gov.uk/government/publications/school-inspection-handbook-from-september-2015**

Paragraphs 142–145 outline how Ofsted defines the different elements of Spiritual, Moral, Social and Cultural Development and what inspectors will be looking for.

Royal Society of Arts (RSA) (2014) *Schools with Soul: A New Approach to Spiritual, Moral, Social and Cultural Education.* Available at **https://www.thersa.org/discover/publications-and-articles/reports/ schools-with-soul-a-new-approach-to-spiritual-moral-social-and-cultural-education**
This is a short and clearly written pamphlet about SMSC and how to make provision for it, though it is not specific to primary schools.

References

Hay, **D. with Nye**, **R.** (1998) *The Spirit of the Child.* London: Fount.

House of Lords (2006) *Hansard* (quoted in RSA, 2014: 6).

Hull, J. (1998) *Utopian Whispers: Moral, Religious and Spiritual Values in Schools.* Norwich: Religious and Moral Education Press.

Katayama, **K.** (2004) The virtue approach to moral education. In J. Dunne and P. Hogan (eds) *Education and Practice: Upholding the Integrity of Teaching and Learning.* Oxford: Blackwell, pp. 61–73.

National Advisory Committee on Creative and Cultural Education (NACCCE) (1999) *All Our Futures: Creativity, Culture and Education.* Sudbury: DfEE.

Rosen, **M.** (2014) *Dear Mr Gove: What's so 'British' About Your 'British' Values?* Available at **https:// www.theguardian.com/education/2014/jul/01/gove-what-is-so-british-your-british-values**

4

CHILD MENTAL HEALTH AND THE ROLE OF THE ARTS

SUSAN OGIER

SCHOOLS SHOULD NOT BE BOOT CAMPS FOR LEARNING HOW TO MAKE A LIVING: THEY SHOULD BE PLACES FOR LEARNING HOW TO LIVE.

(ELLIOT EISNER, 2006)

KEYWORDS: ARTS; MENTAL HEALTH; EMOTION; RESILIENCE; INCLUSION; COMMUNICATION.

CHAPTER OBJECTIVES

This chapter:

- explores reasons why children's mental health has recently become a critical issue for teachers
- examines the impact of the statutory curriculum
- questions how we recognise children with poor mental health
- examines current research and theory to support the well-being benefits of arts engagement
- considers the importance of allowing children space and time to grow emotionally as well as intellectually through arts education

---

LINKS TO THE TEACHERS' STANDARDS

Working through this chapter will enable you to meet all of the Teachers' Standards, in particular:

TS 5:   Adapt teaching to respond to the strengths and needs of all pupils

TS 7:   Manage behaviour effectively to ensure a good and safe learning environment

TS 8:   Fulfil wider professional responsibilities

Part 2:   Personal and professional conduct

Introduction

The place of the arts within state education in England is suffering an enormous decline in status (Atkinson, 2016). This situation is now the basis for a more serious debate on the creativity of the nation, as children do not have sufficient access to a full and broad curriculum that allows them to discover their artistic talents. Nor will they be able to develop those talents and interests into something that might gain them useful employment in the industries of the future (Hutchings, 2015). If young people are denied an acknowledgement of their potential as creative individuals and as useful contributors to society, we must also debate how this situation affects their mental health and well-being. In this chapter, we shall explore some of the factors impacting on the ability of schools in England to provide a broad and balanced education that includes arts subjects. We shall discuss the implications for the well-being and mental health of future generations, as overemphasis and high value continues to be placed on narrow subject content and factual learning. Furthermore, we shall consider how we might redress the imbalance and develop an inclusive and emotionally supportive way of working with children in and through the arts in our schools.

A curriculum fit for purpose?

In a foreword to the 2016 EEF review report by See and Kokotsaki on 'The impact of arts education on cognitive and non-cognitive outcomes of school aged children', Kevan Collins notes that arts education has now become a political issue.

REFLECTION

Why do you think that arts education has become a political issue? What is political about the arts?

This, Collins says, is made plain by the fact that the artist Bob and Roberta Smith stood against Michael Gove the 2015 general election and declared that 'all schools should be art schools'. It was an attempt to bring a serious issue, that so many children are not receiving their full entitlement of arts education, to the forefront of public debate.

We all know that there has been a gradual erosion of arts subjects from the curriculum in state sector schools in England, but it has never been in such steep decline as the one we have seen since the 2014 National Curriculum reforms. The pure focus on English and Maths, and the pressure to teach to the test, has had an enormous impact on how primary school teachers actually do their job. Far from being the 'generalist' that was the very nature of teaching in primary schools, the prescriptive curriculum means that there is very little time for anything else in the school day.

Despite evidence from international studies such as Winner *et al.*'s (2013) Art for Art's Sake report, which highlights wide-ranging benefits that studying arts subjects brings, the phenomenon of accountability through narrow means seems to be affecting education systems in the Western world. While countries such as China and Singapore are implementing curricula that inject creativity and innovation into the offer for children's education (West-Knights, 2017), we have turned the opposite way.

THEORY FOCUS

The National Union of Teachers' 2015 Report, *Exam Factories: The Impact of Accountability Measures in Children and Young People*, recognises that *the accountability agenda in England has changed the nature of education in wide ranging and harmful ways* (Hutchings, 2015: 1), and that these measures are undermining creative teaching and learning, which in turn limits children's potential and affects their self-esteem, confidence and mental health. The relentless pressure placed upon children to achieve in core subjects has far-reaching negative effects on children's well-being. Hutchings states that:

Children and young people are suffering from increasingly high levels of school-related anxiety and stress, disaffection and mental health problems. This is caused by increased pressure from tests/exams; greater awareness at younger ages of their own 'failure', and the increased rigour and academic demands of the curriculum.

(2015: 5)

It is also noted that due to the high-stakes testing, there has been an increase in diagnoses of ADHD, as very young children are made to sit still in a school environment that does not support the need for children's natural physical development. It is becoming clear that the 'accountability agenda' comes at the expense of teachers being able to have concern for children as individuals, making it difficult for them to achieve well by situating learning within, and for the benefit of, their own lives. This has resulted in schools becoming the 'exam factories' described by Hutchings, where children are placed on a conveyor belt at the age of four (sometimes even younger than this) and spat out at the other end – either as a 'success' or to be cast onto the second's pile.

Read the research reports here:

- **https://www.teachers.org.uk/files/exam-factories.pdf**
- **https://read.oecd-ilibrary.org/education/art-for-art-s-sake_9789264180789-en#page266**

There is no question that learning in Maths and English are absolutely key to leading a successful future life and career, but there are other equally important factors that come into play in order for children to engage and achieve, and to fulfil their personal potential. For this end, we must start with the basics – and these are social and emotional health and well-being, which can be fostered through encouraging creative play, and learning in and through the arts throughout childhood experiences. The current system has forgotten this aspect, and the following case study exemplifies the impact of a curriculum that forces children to fit in with it rather than the other way around.

CASE STUDY

A long-term outlook . . .

A five-year-old boy, Sean, is placed on the 'Oblong' table in his Reception Class at a school where ability grouping is employed as a strategy for differentiation. The 'Oblongs' are children who find it difficult to engage in a formal school curriculum and are seated together, so that 'brighter' children can get on with their work. As Sean progresses through the school, his understanding of what it means to be on the Oblong table increases, and as he develops more understanding, he is increasingly demotivated and disengaged. His self-esteem plummets, and by the time he reaches secondary school he has all but given up, feeling that school and learning are not for him.

Sean is now a deputy head at an inner London school, and has a Master's degree. He now says that this experience had a permanent impact upon his sense of well-being and his self-perception. He says:

I felt that the experiences I had in primary school caused an insecurity that has stayed with me. I was very aware of the social dynamics in class. The Oblongs knew that things were different for them, and looking back, I felt that I had already been written off – this really affected how I felt about myself. At secondary school I was always in the low sets, and predicted Grade 'D' GCSEs, which, to me, proved my worthlessness at the time. Fortunately, I found a home in creative subjects, which I believe saved me. I was accepted to do 'A' levels in Art and Technology, and went on to successfully complete a degree, then a PGCE and a Master's degree. During my time in Higher Education, my formative experiences came back to haunt me, and I felt like an imposter. I worried that someone would find me out because I didn't deserve to be working at that level – that I wasn't really good enough. This has made me extremely mindful of labelling children too early and the importance of providing a well-rounded curriculum where children can discover what they can do rather than what they cannot. I have to say, that not all of the Oblongs have such a happy end-of-story to tell as I do. I wouldn't be where I am today if it was not for those creative subjects, which opened up a world that made sense to me.

Analysis

REFLECTION

How many Seans have you come across in your school experiences?

The problem is that you will never know. Many schools are using ability groupings as a way of coping with a curriculum that they feel forced to teach, but one that is not really suitable for such young children. Sean's story helps us to be mindful of the deep feelings that very young children experience, and how we as teachers can positively, or negatively, influence their self-perception and feelings of self-worth.

Mental health awareness: data check

Step into almost any staffroom in an English primary school and you will find that the conversations on the lips of the teachers and support staff will, sooner or later, stray onto the hot topic of *well-being and child mental health.*

REFLECTION

Are we, as a profession, getting better at talking about mental health?

This topic is at the forefront of current issues in both education and society in the UK today. Statistics released by the UK's Mental Health Foundation (MHF) in 2017 state that one in ten children are likely to have a mental health problem in any one year. Disorders that children can suffer from include anxiety, depression, ADHD and schizophrenia. Average that out, and this means that there are, potentially, three children in every class of 30 who are dealing with diagnosed – and undiagnosed – mental ill-health that will negatively impact on their ability to develop and sustain relationships, cope with everyday problems or, quite simply, to manage engagement with school and work on a basic, functional level (MHF, 2017). Data collated independently by teaching unions, the NASUWT (2017) and NAHT (2017), show that the upsurge in children presenting with mental health problems over past few years is at crisis level and the UK government has responded by promising more money for mental health first-aid training for teachers and other measures that we are yet to see come to fruition. By requesting data from NHS Trusts in England through the Freedom of Information Act, the NSPCC found that 123,713 referrals were made by schools seeking professional mental health help between 2014/15 and 2017/18, and that 56 per cent of these referrals came from primary schools. With the NHS under enormous pressure, children who are referred may well be declined help if their symptoms are not deemed severe enough for interventions. Alternatively, they might have to wait a very long time to be seen, so they remain untreated and in our classrooms (QCC, 2017; Frith, 2016).

We also know that child happiness is reported as being in decline (Children's Society, 2013) and that the children's charity, ChildLine, released statistics that show a huge increase in children as young as ten displaying suicidal feelings in the year 2016/17, compared with previous years (NSPCC, 2017). These are all very concerning facts for primary teachers, who might not even be aware of the extreme emotions that some of their pupils are experiencing. Many teachers are likely just to be doing their very best to contain children's emotions by implementing tight behaviour management strategies in an effort to keep the lid on the challenges that children suffering mental distress can present. While research and data should help us, as educators, to specifically focus our awareness and recognition of children with mental health difficulties, we must remember that many reasons for the increase in poor mental health are way beyond our control as class teachers, as the root causes may be linked to a number of different factors. What is perhaps worrying is that there seems to be a lack of questioning *why is it happening?* Why, in one of the richest countries in the world, are more children finding life so hard? Alison Roy, a child and adolescent psychotherapist, explains some of the reasons for us.

Figure 4.1   Year 2 children explore their feelings through visual art

Ask the expert: Alison Roy

I have a theory that every time you make an important choice, the part of you left behind continues the other life you could have had.

Jeanette Winterson

In my work over the last 15 years, with children's mental health services, I have come to recognise that there are a number of reasons why children experience poor mental health, and these are far from straightforward. The fact that so many children appear to be developing significant mental health problems is a puzzle, and in order to understand this we need to look beyond the child and at the context for these difficulties: If we only look at the 'child' part of the puzzle, we have an incomplete picture of a bigger problem, so we need to consider the difficulties and needs of others who are deeply connected to that child. Donald Winnicott, psychoanalyst and paediatrician, said: *There is no such thing as a baby, there is a baby and someone*. The notion of the child and the 'someone' helps us reflect on why we are seeing certain symptoms and recurring difficulties.

It is somewhat controversial to assume that the child expresses something of the difficulties originating from their most significant attachment figures. Research, however, suggests that this is, in part, an accurate assumption. Every child has their own genetic traits, personality and predispositions, but it is the environment in which the child grows up that incubates potential difficulties, even if these take some time to materialise. Some of the most chronic and complex mental health problems for children such as extreme aggression, suicidal thoughts and tendencies, self-harm, anxiety, eating disorders and depression may emerge in later childhood, but warning signs are often evident earlier, and either don't get noticed or resources aren't available to address them adequately.

Distressed adults with whom the child is closely connected can transfer feelings and fears directly to the child: these adults can then miss signs of the child's own suffering.

This isn't only significant regarding parents and carers, but is the same for other adults, who have an impact on the developing child and their personality, such as teachers. If these adults are overly and consistently anxious, feeling under threat or lacking in creative resources, there is little balance for the child and they are more likely to view the world as persecutory and overwhelming. They may also continually seek drama and intensity, which they equate with feeling connected and alive: this means there is little capacity for moderation and resilience, and this view of the world becomes a template for the child in how they approach and manage life and all its challenges.

How can we recognise the symptoms?

- Sudden changes in presentation and mood are important to look out for and can indicate a problem, although taking the time to notice is a challenge in itself. Most teachers are already extremely busy meeting general demands of the school and might miss some of the early signs of a mental health problem.

- It is often the case that children who present challenging behaviours in class are able to access some support. These children can express themselves by drawing attention to their difficulties in this way, and communicate their distress to others, albeit in socially undesirable ways. Those, however, who are socially withdrawn and 'quiet' can become invisible: their difficulties can go unnoticed until there is a crisis, by which time specialist intervention is required.

- More children report feeling isolated despite our apparently super-connected, virtual society: it is therefore important for parents and professionals to notice when children are withdrawing either into the virtual world, or deliberately away from contact with others.

How can we support children with mental health difficulties?

It is important not to think about the child in isolation when it comes to emotional and psychological well-being, for these can serve as a kind of barometer for the society or community where they are located. Children are very good at communicating distress and difficulty and in this respect they can tell us a great deal about what is going on, but we do need to learn to *listen* to them and recognise the difference between communication behaviours as expressions of individual liveliness, and other communications that indicate genuine distress. To do this we need to provide a safe space, an atmosphere where children can become relaxed and feel free to talk, and this can be achieved through engaging children in arts activity. For teachers who understand the value of arts education, this can be a time when they can get a more honest communication from children, one that is not driven by targets and fear of failure.

The importance of creative play in building vital relationships and attachments should not be underestimated. For example, collaborative arts projects, such as creative dance or making musical compositions, involve anticipating and responding to the actions of others and repeating patterns. This also involves close proximity, concentration, brushing hands, negotiating touch: these kinds of interactions are where building trust and resolving problems together are encouraged, which are vital for healthy social development. Without the space to concentrate in this way – in the presence of *another* – children are missing vital opportunities to support and encourage each other in more intimate and quiet environments, learn about proximity and distance to and with others and develop a shared understanding of a complex problem. Being able to read and interpret situations and the responses of others is key to managing adult life, and these skills are learned in childhood through play and creative activity. This kind of play is missing from many children's experiences in life and in the classroom, as the National Curriculum seems to have overlooked the central role of these key ingredients.

A secure child is one who feels reassured that they have significant adults who understand them well and intuit their needs. In this way, through creative connection and an openness to being playful, the adults can help the child make sense of the world without panic and drama – for the sense of threat has been removed. This is key in terms of the role of arts in education – creative play can often be a time when the significant adult (in this case the teacher) is relaxed and authentic.

My experience, as a professional supporting teachers and mental health staff, is that the opportunities for thinking and talking together about challenges are minimised over serious businesses of meeting targets and expected grades. Attending to the emotional needs of the individual child by facilitating secure relationships between professionals and children reduces the chances of severe mental health difficulties emerging and allows the early signs to be spotted. We ignore the strength of these relationships at great cost to the development of children and to society.

Analysis

REFLECTION

Do you recognise any of the examples given by Alison Roy?

In school, stress caused by an overemphasis on success in exams is a key factor for feelings of poor self-esteem and lack of self-belief in young children. Children with pre-existing mental health problems are doubly at risk because of the added pressure caused by testing. Schools minister since 2010, Nick Gibb, has put forward the idea that children should be forced to take even more exams, and at much earlier ages, so that they get used to it – and he believes that this in turn will help alleviate the mental stress caused by exams (Gibb, 2018).

REFLECTION

What do you think of this concept?

Do you agree that frequent, harder tests at younger ages will toughen children up and help them to feel less stressed about exams?

Would you be happy to see the main aim of the education system for primary children to become solely focused on the ability of individual children to pass tests? Of course, this is pretty much what we have seen emerging now in many primary schools, given the severe narrowing of the curriculum – but we, as practising professionals, are reluctant to fully admit it, and we are equally unwilling to fully let go of the concept of the primary teacher as a generalist, who values a multi-faceted curriculum, one that is geared towards the multi-faceted individuals who populate our classrooms.

As explained by Alison Roy above, there are myriad reasons why children feel or experience stress, whether consciously or subconsciously, and while many of these reasons are rooted outside of the school, it is often within the school environment that teachers are expected to pick up the tab. Time and funding are both in short supply to enable teachers to manage children's emotional lives, and as progress targets in core areas of English and maths are prioritised and arts diminished. Research, however, is beginning to make clear that the arts play a key role in enhancing and enriching an individual's life experience and that subjects associated with arts are central to us being able to lead well-balanced lives (Cutcher, 2013; APPGAHW, 2017).

A critical view

Stride and Cutcher (2015) suggest that while creativity is accepted as a key skill for the future, our linear and logical world continues to promote a marginalisation of the attributes facilitated by engagement in creative activity and enterprise. The high-stakes educational climate, which focuses so unwaveringly upon academic achievement in narrow fields, has forced the arts in state sector schools to become an unnecessary luxury. There are often misconceptions around why the arts are taught and why they are important. A critical review conducted by See and Kokotsaki for the EEF (2016) underlines this: the research looked at whether participation in arts had positive impact upon children's academic ability and found no conclusive evidence. Research in Australia by Vaughn *et al.* (2011), however, seems to directly contradict this point by stating that *arts education not only has intrinsic value, but when implemented with a structured, innovative and long-term approach, it can also provide essential extrinsic benefits, such as improved school attendance, academic achievement across the curriculum as well as social and emotional wellbeing* (p. 3), although this paper was not included in the EEF review.

REFLECTION

How do we know who is right, and is the point missed anyway?

While See and Kokotsaki's review understandably acknowledges a lack of concrete evidence that arts engagement enhances academic achievement, participation in the arts is well known for the wider benefits that occur within individuals, including their emotional health (Crossick and Kaszynska, 2016; Neelands *et al.*, 2015; Henley, 2012; Eisner, 2002). For example, we must ask whether we believe arts are on the curriculum simply in the hope that they raise achievement in the '3 R's alone. Surely, arts subjects should be included in any primary curriculum for their *own sake*: for the unique contribution they make to the richness of children's lives, to provide another language, to offer an alternative way for children to communicate their ideas, thoughts and feelings about things that are important to them, things that they cannot articulate through words – or tests.

Watch Elliot Eisner speaking about why we should teach the arts on this video: **https://www.you tube.com/watch?v=h12MGuhQH9E**

THEORY FOCUS

The 'healing properties' of the arts

Studies by Hamilton et al. (2003 and initiatives in schools such as Creative Partnerships (Sharp et al., 2006) highlight health and well-being benefits of participation in the arts. In recent years, research suggests that by engaging with arts activity children develop socially, emotionally and intellectually, with general health and well-being benefits becoming ever-more apparent. Particularly interesting is the inquiry report by the All-Party Parliamentary Group, *Creative Health: The Arts Health and Well-being* (2017), which recognises that *The act of creation, and our appreciation of it, provides an individual experience that can have positive effects on our physical and mental health and well-being* (p. 10). It acknowledges that it is time to realise that the arts *make a powerful contribution to health and well-being* (p. 5), providing many examples of the positive impact that arts participation has upon individuals of all ages, in terms of good mental and physical health. It states that

> When [. .] developing support for children and adolescents, particularly in the areas of prevention and early intervention, they need to embrace the healing properties of the arts in relation to anxiety, depression, stress and more severe mental health problems.

(p. 96)

Is it too much to expect schools to take this on board, and find space and time in a relentless curriculum for children to experience the 'healing properties of the arts' for every child? Read the report here: **www.artshealthandwellbeing.org.uk/appg-inquiry/**

THEORY FOCUS

Building resilience

Research by Stride and Cutcher (2015) studied building resilience through arts activity, and demonstrate that participating in art activity affords the

> ability to withstand or adapt positively to change (and this) is a necessary tool to navigate the world in which we live. Many constructs exist as a means of understanding the process of positive adaptability, such as emotional intelligence, intrapersonal intelligence and resilience.

(p. 2)

The key message in understanding the importance of emotional and mental health for learning is that all the finite knowledge in the world is only useful up to a point: if a person cannot relate to others, or if they lack emotional intelligence to be able to get along with other people, or do not have the resilience to cope when things go wrong, then how can they function or find their place in the world? Today's children need these qualities in abundance in order to be able to empathise across cultures, as our globalised world becomes ever smaller.

CASE STUDY

What does this mean for classroom practice?

Meera was in her third year of teaching in a Year 4 class. A new child, Sophie, had joined the group, having moved from another city. Sophie suffered from an anxiety disorder called 'selective mutism': Sophie spoke freely at home but was unable to engage in any conversation or communication once outside of this environment. Meera researched online so that she understood the condition and worked with the parents to find ways to help Sophie feel more relaxed at school. Sophie's parents expressed that Sophie loved drawing, so Meera decided to plan frequent art activities for the whole class that could be integrated into the usual curriculum. This way Sophie was supported and included in a natural way, which helped her and her peers to find new ways to communicate together.

Read more about *selective mutism* here: **https://www.nhs.uk/conditions/selective-mutism/**

REFLECTION

What are your own attitudes, confidence levels and understanding of the value of teaching arts subjects?

How will you justify making time and space for arts learning in your daily or weekly curriculum within your own class?

How could you influence planning to ensure that all children have regular access to good-quality arts experiences in your school?

A different kind of accountability

We have acknowledged the difficulties and pressures that teachers are under to prepare children for testing and have recognised the impact on children when the emotional side of teaching and learning is ignored. The issues, research and statistics that we have looked at here illustrate the need for us, as primary teachers, to facilitate the emotional development of *all* children through our curriculum and through our teaching. This helps us to remember that we must be very mindful of the enormous importance of building and understanding relationships, of making space to explore intense childhood emotions, and of allowing children to communicate their feelings in the wide variety of ways that working in and through the arts enables. We should remain conscious of the necessity to nurture growth in children's confidence through offering them a wide range of practical and creative experiences in which they can find their talents. By enjoying learning through new modes of personal expression we can help children find mental peace and give them the awareness of a sense of wonder which they will need for the uncertain world of the future. You, as the classroom teacher, have the responsibility to realise and implement good-quality experiences in arts education: to recognise the potential of prioritising children's emotional health and well-being through harnessing the power that creative expression brings to the overall educational experience. In the end, we are all accountable for children's sense of well-being while they are in our care.

CHAPTER SUMMARY

In this chapter, we have explored some of the reasons why children's mental health has recently become a critical issue for teachers. We have looked at evidence from major teaching unions and mental health charities, including the NSPCC. We have heard evidence from real-life examples of how a rigid regime of narrow learning does not afford opportunities for all, and that early experiences can affect us for years into our futures, either in a positive or a negative way. It is in our hands, as primary teachers, to value every child for the uniqueness that they bring, and to give every child the opportunity to show what they are capable of, in whatever medium that is.

KEY POINTS TO CONSIDER

- The effects of a narrow curriculum have negative repercussions for some children. Reflect upon the diverse viewpoints that acknowledge the pressures and consequences of a one-size-fits-all approach to learning.
- How do we recognise children with poor mental health? Consider ways to support all children by exploring emotions through arts engagement.
- Current research and theory support the well-being benefits of learning in and through the arts, including the importance of building personal resilience.
- Allow children space and time to grow emotionally as well as intellectually through arts education.

Further reading

Howard, C., Burton, M., Levermore, D. and Barrell, R. (2017) *Children's Mental Health and Emotional Well-being in Primary Schools*. London: Learning Matters.

Rooke, A. (n.d.) *Cultural Value: Arts and Mental Health: Creative Collisions and Critical Conversations.* AHRC. Available at: **https://ahrc.ukri.org/documents/projects-programmes-and-initiatives/arts-and-mental-health-creative-collisions-and-critical-conversations/**

Make a visit to The Art Room: **https://www.theartroom.org.uk**

Find out more about child mental health: **https://youngminds.org.uk**

References

Anttila, E., Jaakonaho, L., Juntunen, M., Martin, M., Nikkanen, H.M., Saastamoinen, R. and Turpeinen, I. (2017) *Comprehensive School: Finland's Largest Cultural Sector.* ArtsEqual. Available at: **www.artsequal.fi/documents/14230/0/PB+eng+Koulu+kulttuurikeskuksena/4ec2e095-cd17-4b0f-8c8e-54226645a61f**

APPG for Arts Health and Well-being (2017) *Creative Health: The Arts for Health and Wellbeing, Inquiry Report.* Available at: **www.artshealthandwellbeing.org.uk/appg-inquiry/** (accessed 16 August 2017).

Atkinson, M. (2016) The devastating decline of the arts in schools will hit the poorest children the hardest. *Times Educational Supplement.* Available at: **https://www.tes.com/news/school-news/breaking-views/devastating-decline-arts-schools-will-hit-poorest-children-hardest**

Children's Society (2013) *The Good Childhood Report.* Available at: **www.childrenssociety.org.uk/good-childhood-report-2013-online/**

College Board, National Coalition for Core Arts Standards in America (2012) *Child Development and Arts Education: A Review of Recent Research and Best Practices.* New York: College Board. Available at: **https://www.nationalartsstandards.org/sites/default/files/College%20Board%20research%20-%20child%20Development%20Report.pdf.**

Crossick, G. and Kaszynska, P. (2016) *Understanding the Value of Arts and Culture. The AHRC Cultural Value Project.* Swindon: Arts & Humanities Research Council.

Cutcher, A. (2013) Art spoken here: Reggio Emilia for the big kids. *International Journal of Art and Design Education, 9* (2): 318–30.

Eisner, E. (2006) *What Do the Arts Teach?*, Speech at 2006–7 Chancellors Lecture Series, Vanderbilt University. Available at: https://www.youtube.com/watch?v=h12MGuhQH9E

Frith, E. (2016) *CentreForum Commission on Children's and Young People's Mental Health: State of the Nation.* Available at: **https://epi.org.uk/publications-and-research/children-young-peoples-mental-health-state-nation/**

Gibb, N. (2018) Schoolchildren should take exams earlier to cope with mental health pressures. *The Independent,* 7 February. Available at: **https://www.independent.co.uk/news/education/education-news/schoolchildren-exams-more-early-mental-health-pressure-stress-education-nick-gibb-a8199291.html**

Hamilton, C., Hinks, S. and Petticrew, M. (2003) Arts for health: still searching for the Holy Grail. *Journal of Epidemiology and Community Health,* 57: 401–2.

Henley, D. (2012) *Cultural Education in England: An Independent Review by Darren Henley for the Department for Culture, Media and Sport and the Department for Education.* London: DCMS and DfE.

Hutchings, M. (2015) *Exam Factories: The Impact of Accountability Measures on Children and Young People.* National Union of Teachers. Available at: **https://www.teachers.org.uk/files/exam-factories.pdf**

Mental Health Foundation (2017) *Surviving or Thriving.* Available at: **https://www.mental-health.org.uk/publications/surviving-or-thriving-state-uks-mental-health**

NAHT (2017) The government's Green Paper on mental health is failing a generation. Available at: **https://www.naht.org.uk/news-and-opinion/news/pupil-well-being-news/the-gov ernments-green-paper-on-mental-health-failing-a-generation/**

NASUWT (2017) Schools need support to deal with mental health upsurge among pupils. Available at: **https://www.nasuwt.org.uk/article-listing/schools-need-support-mental-health-upsurge-pupils.html**

Neelands, J., Belfiore, E., Firth, C., Hart, N., Perrin, L., Brock, S., Holdaway, D., Woddis, J. and Knell, J. (2015) *Enriching Britain: Culture, Creativity and Growth.* University of Warwick, Warwick Commission. Available at: **www2.warwick.ac.uk/research/warwickcommission/future-culture/finalreport/**

NHS Health Development Agency (2000) *Art for Health: A Review of Good Practice in Community-based Arts Projects and Initiatives which Impact on Health and Wellbeing.* London: NHS Health Development Agency,

NSPCC (2017) *Not Alone Any More: ChildLine Annual Report.* Available at:**https://www.nspcc.org.uk/services-and-resources/research-and-resources/2017/not-alone-anymore-childline-annual-review-2016-2017/**

NSPCC (2018) School referrals for mental health rise by over a third. Available online: **https://www.nspcc.org.uk/what-we-do/news-opinion/one-third-increase-in-school-referrals-for-mental-health-treatment/**

Quality Care Commission (2017) *Review of Children's and Young People's Mental Health Services.* Available at:**www.cqc.org.uk/publications/themed-work/review-children-young-peoples-mental-health-services-phase-one-report**

See, B.H. and Kokotsaki, D. (2016) *Impact of Arts Education on Cognitive and Non-cognitive Outcomes of School Aged Children.* EEF. Available at: **https://v1.educationendowmentfoundation.org.uk/uploads/pdf/Arts_Education_Review.pdf**

Sharp, C., Pye, D., Blackmore, J., Brown, E., Eames, A., Easton, C., Filmer-Sankey, C., Tabary, A., Whitby, K., Wilson, R. and Benton, T. (2006) *National Evaluation of Creative Partnerships. Final Report.* London: Creative Partnerships.

Stride, Y. and Cutcher, A. (2015) Manifesting resilience in the secondary school: an investigation of the relationship dynamic in Visual Arts classrooms. *International Journal of Education and the Arts, 16* (11). Available at: **www.ijea.org/v16n11/**

Vaughan, T., Harris, J. and Caldwell, B.J. (2011) *Bridging the Gap in School Achievement Through the Arts.* Melbourne: The Song Room, p. 3.

West-Knights, I. (2017) Why are schools in China looking west for lessons in creativity? *Financial Times,* 27 January. Available at: **https://www.ft.com/content/b215c486-e231-11e6-8405-9e5580d6e5fb**

Winner, E., Goldstein, T. and Vincent-Lancrin, S. (2013) *Art for Art's Sake? The Impact of Arts Education.* Educational Research and Innovation, OECD Publishing. Available at: **http://www.oecd.org/education/ceri/arts.htm**

5
PHILOSOPHY AND LEARNING TO THINK

AIMEE QUICKFALL

KEYWORDS: PHILOSOPHY; THINKING; REFLECTION; CRITICAL THINKING; CURIOSITY.

CHAPTER OBJECTIVES

This chapter:

- explores what philosophy is and why it is important for a broad and balanced curriculum
- analyses the research around philosophy with children
- provides a practical guide to how philosophy can work in your setting
- gives examples of children who have benefitted from participating in philosophical discussion

LINKS TO THE TEACHERS' STANDARDS

Working through this chapter will enable you to meet all of the Teachers' Standards, in particular:

TS 1:   Set high expectations which inspire, motivate and challenge pupils

TS 2:   Promote good progress and outcomes by pupils

TS 5:   Adapt teaching to respond to the strengths and needs of all pupils.

Introduction

In this chapter we shall explore what philosophy is, and what it definitely isn't. We shall go on to look at the research in this area, plus some theoretical arguments for and against using philosophy with children. Following discussion of the evidence, we shall explore a model for using philosophical enquiry with a group of children or a whole class, and review case studies of children who have inspired and informed philosophical work in primary schools.

Why philosophy?

When I applied to do a philosophy degree, my friends and family asked a series of questions that I think are useful for us to consider together at the beginning of this chapter. They asked:

What is philosophy?

Strictly speaking, the study of philosophy and philosophical enquiry are two different things. *Philosophy* involves a good deal of consideration of the philosophers of the past and present and their ideas and arguments. *Philosophical enquiry* is about your own thinking (and that of your community). It can encompass thinking about thinking, thinking about how the world works, about what numbers are, about what is right and wrong and whether that can change. It teaches us to know ourselves; to know how we go about thinking and the limits of that process (Stokes, 2015). Philosophers think about ideas beyond general everyday pondering. They think *hard* (which is why they are so much fun at parties). Philosophical enquiry is about approaching an idea in a certain way, constructing an argument and testing it with thought experiments.

Do people like us do that sort of thing?

Yes, of course they do. It is my contention that all people should be philosophers and that we all are, but we are at different stages of our philosophical development. Some children are advanced, some adults are beginners. I also believe that early exposure to dangerous and deep thought is a very good thing indeed. Philosophy isn't social-class based, although it is sometimes seen that way. It isn't about your age, ethnicity, gender or beliefs. A group of PGCE Primary students made portraits of what they thought a philosopher might look like, before taking part in an enquiry session. Figure 5.1 shows a stereotypical response. As you can see, they imagined that philosophers were probably white, male, a little bit posh, constantly perplexed and sporting facial hair. Historically, there is some truth in this assumption, and we just have to think about some of the current debates around equal opportunities for BAME and gender-related issues to remember how deeply entrenched our assumptions are. Of course, you don't need to be a part of that demographic to be a philosopher or to take part in a philosophical enquiry: it is by nature, open to all.

Figure 5.1   Drawings of a 'typical' philosopher by a PGCE student

What equipment do you need?

One close relative of mine asked if I needed a camera. Why did he ask that? Actually, the only equipment necessary is your brain. That's all. You don't need to be able to read or write or do really hard sums.

How long is it going to take?

This is a really good question. The best and worst answer I can give is that it is never finished. Your philosophical journey lasts a lifetime. Which soundstiring, but look at it this way – no one would complain about having to carry on breathing all their life. Thinking deeply about the big, wonderful mysteries of life and the tiny, puzzling details is like breathing deeply, it will enrich your experiences and give you wider perspectives – and a richer life. In school, we can put children on this path. And if we start in primary school, the gains will still be there when pupils are well into their secondary education (Topping and Trickey, 2007).

Why is philosophy important?

Philosophical enquiry is more than a foundation subject, a bit like breathing is more than just a job on your 'to do' list. It should underpin the curriculum, not be a distinct subject in a package. It helps to keep everything broad and balanced, it suggests many possibilities and keeps our sense of wonder alive (Russell, 1912). For the individual child, philosophical enquiry has an impact on socio-emotional development, engagement in learning and progressing maths, reading and writing (Godard *et al.*, 2017; Tolmie *et al.*, 2010; Trickey and Topping, 2007). It builds confidence and communication skills (McCall, 2013; Siddiqui *et al.*, 2017). It includes the children in a community and teaches them how to respectfully disagree, make connections, identify weaknesses in evidence they are presented with and to think about their own thinking (Murris, 2000).

We shouldn't just think about the individual when we consider teaching to think (Kerslake and Wegerif, 2018). Whether a whole community or small group of children are involved, philosophical enquiry helps children to see each other in different ways (Murris, 2000). It highlights the strength of friendship, when children can disagree and still be friends (McCall, 2013). It teaches children that the oldest person in the room isn't necessarily in receipt of all the answers. And that the child that they thought was 'the cleverest' sometimes gets stuck. The best thing is when it teaches them that the child they thought had little to offer, in terms of learning, comes up with something so unique, so relatable and intelligent, that they are truly stunned, and their relationship with that child changes forever. Philosophical enquiry can, therefore, change the power relations in the classroom (Lipman, 1998; Matthews, 1984; Vansieleghem and Kennedy, 2011).

For the wider community and society, practising these skills in childhood can only enrich the present and the future (Glina, 2006). Being able and getting used to empathising with the viewpoints and ideas of others will make society less violent (Gregory, 2011). It can be dangerous to talk about children as if they can only have impact when they are grown-up and 'completed'; in short, philosophical enquiry can change their world right now.

THEORY FOCUS

What does the research tell us about philosophy with children?

Recent research commissioned by the Education Endowment Foundation (EEF, 2015, and also Gorard *et al.*, 2017) has reported that a one-hour session of philosophical enquiry in Key Stage 2 classes improved reading and mathematics outcomes on summative assessments by up to four months in a school year. The positive outcomes were even more impressive for children considered disadvantaged (the measure here was eligibility for free school meals). Teachers of the classes that took part in the research also noted that children had improved patience, listening skills and self-esteem (Siddiqui *et al.*, 2017). The research involved 3,000 children, from varied settings and backgrounds. Research also suggests that involvement in weekly philosophical enquiry sessions at primary school has a lasting positive effect, two years later in secondary education, even though the philosophical enquiry sessions have not continued (Topping and Trickey, 2007)

Cassidy and Christie (2013) have explored the dialogic advantages of using a philosophical enquiry model in six primary schools. Studies with established philosophical enquiry groups taking part in a one-hour session each week have shown that the sessions provide *a context for genuine collaborative engagement in learning where the actual process of learning itself is a shared one* (Cassidy and Christie, 2013: 1081). Learning activities which provide chances for children to engage in philosophical talk, e.g. exchanging ideas, having differences of opinion and constructing new understandings are *potentially the most powerful means by which meaningful new learning can take place in classrooms* (ibid.: p.1074).

In my experience, this research often surprises teacher trainees on PGCE Primary courses. Almost all of them report never having seen a session of philosophical enquiry or heard this being discussed in schools. They are usually familiar with a lot of recent research on cognitive load, behaviour management strategies and the impact of systematic synthetic phonics programmes and are aware of the importance of applying evidence to practice to improve outcomes for the children in their care. Why haven't they heard about the impact that a weekly hour of enquiry can have, with lasting differences? The trainees wisely point out the potential difficulties of fitting a session into the timetable, the risk of unwanted behaviour from the children, the opinions of senior management and inspectors, and the challenge of accessing training in order to deliver good-quality enquiry sessions as a practitioner. Once they understand the methods of enquiry and have tried it out in placement, many of them report back that they have continued to use this: it isn't as mysterious and tricky as it might at first seem.

REFLECTION

Why do you think philosophy is not a major feature of classroom practice?

What are the theorists saying about philosophy with children?

Developmental stages and readiness

Theorists argue that the age of the philosophical enquirer is key to whether the inquiry is successful, in fact some would suggest that if children are exposed to philosophy too early, it can cause confusion and distress (Wilson, 1992; Pohoata and Petrescu, 2013). Often these arguments rest on ideas of developmental stage theories, such as Piaget's (1972) four-stage model of child development. In this model, children enter the 'concrete operational stage' between the ages of 7 and 11, which means they can think in abstract ways without the need for apparatus, props or stories to support their thinking. It is argued that philosophical enquiry is abstract in this way, as the thinker can manipulate ideas and test their theories in their mind.

There are objections to the developmental stage critique of philosophy with children. Let's begin by questioning some assumptions. Do all adults reach the 'concrete operational stage'? Some would suggest not (Dasen, 1994) and that there is more to consider here than chronological age as a restriction to enquirer status. There is also an assumption here that the level of the trained philosopher is the standard we should be expecting children to reach before they can take part in philosophical enquiry, a kind of intellectual snobbery about the subject (Matthews, 1995). If children cannot practise the skills of debate, comparison, connection and synthesis then how would they ever become eligible to join the club?

There is a further assumption that trained philosophers never use props, stories, anecdotes or apparatus for thinking. In my experience, this is an incorrect assumption. Philosophers use stories all the time to illustrate their points. They use examples, imaginary and real, diagrams, sketches, symbols and pictures. And why shouldn't they? Does the use of a prop make you a weaker thinker or a more creative one? There is little evidence to suggest that reaching a concrete operational stage is a prerequisite for considering some of the most interesting questions. Children will ask fascinating questions using anything at their disposal such as stories, toys, sticks, mud, stars, clouds, even body fluids!

The subject knowledge barrier

Another argument against philosophical enquiry with primary age children is that they do not have enough knowledge to create arguments with true philosophical weight, as their understanding of the world is limited. This is different to the developmental stage objection, as seemingly this argument could apply to adults who did not reach a required level of knowledge too. The premise here is that when constructing a philosophical argument, a lot of background experience and information is needed. The example given (Murris, 2000) is the Ship of Theseus, which has been a favourite among undergraduate philosophy students in recent years. Theseus has a ship which is replaced plank by plank until none of the original parts remains. If all the old planks, nails and fittings are assembled to make another ship, which one is truly the ship of Theseus? The new one, replaced piece by piece, or the one with original parts that have been reassembled? This is a story about persistence of identity, and it can be applied to the regeneration of cells in a human body and whether loss of memories can change identity. Critics may argue that because children do not have the knowledge of how the parts of the ship could be replaced, and would not grasp the idea that the old pieces might retain the identity of the ship of Theseus, they would not understand the argument and may well end up being confused, upset and frustrated by the whole exercise. And to some extent, I agree.

Young children, faced with this narrative of ships and ancient Greeks, might not understand the concepts. Some children undoubtedly do understand the issues of identity that this story represents (Matthews, 1984, Murris, 2000). BUT if you build a castle with blocks, take it apart then reassemble the pieces to make a house, you can ask all sorts of questions. Where is the castle now? When the Queen returns from her holiday, will she recognise her home? Will it still be her home to live in? Using props makes the concepts accessible. The next question is whether children need to be able to understand that the castle/house is a metaphor for identity. In my opinion, this isn't the most important question. If they can argue why it is or isn't the same building, who owns it, who should live in it – then they are 'doing' philosophical enquiry; even young children can do this.

Children search for understanding – as practitioners, we encourage this search. If we decide that children do not have enough subject knowledge, *true authority to speak from their experience* (Haynes and Murris, 2013: 1085) or the right kind of thinking skills to engage in a search for understanding, then we are not engaging them in this most fundamental and important quest – to learn. Much of the criticism levelled at philosophical enquiry with children is an argument about what philosophy and philosophical enquiry really are, which should not necessarily stop anyone from having a go in the real world (Murris, 2000).

Philosophical enquiry in your classroom

Philosophical enquiry with your class is *most effective when it is participatory, proactive, communal, collaborative and given over to constructing meanings rather than receiving them* (Fisher, 2007: 626). The following example is a model that can be used for an enquiry session with children of primary age (and teenagers and adults!). I have used variations of this model for many years and as you grow in confidence you will want to adapt it, add and take away, but I always come back to this plan when setting up a new community. Other models are available but tend to follow similar steps (Haynes, 2002).

Before you start

Agree rules for your group: what is important to the community?

I have included a list of rules from one of the communities I worked with in Figure 5.2.

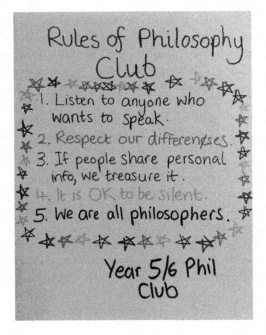

Figure 5.2   Rules of a Philosophy Club

It is important that children know that challenging ideas and disagreeing with others are all part of the discussion and should be welcome (Cassidy and Christie, 2013).

Talk about what philosophy means and who can be a philosopher

The answer is all of you!

Consider your role in the community

At first, you will find yourself explaining the process and facilitating the discussion, but as the group becomes more experienced, your role is to step back and allow the children to lead the sessions. My aim for the children is to stop them looking to me when the discussion gets tricky, and to look to each other for solutions and further development of the debate.

Before each session

Choose a stimulus

This could be a story, a picture, some music, a smell, a dilemma – children become skilled at choosing a stimulus for the sessions.

Consider roles for children

You may want to give roles such as *enquiry scribe* (to record the discussion in pictures/words or both) or *facilitator* (monitoring the rules of the community), particularly if you have children in the class who may dominate the session or find it hard to engage. These are strategies that will encourage all children to take part or listen. Both are valid and important roles.

Suggested models for the session

1. Play a game with a community objective – e.g. Listening skills

Circle time games are excellent for this. My favourite is 'Count Down'.

- The whole community stands in a circle. The only rules are that to sit down, you have to say the next number, and to end the game, everyone has to sit down.

- If two people speak at the same time, everyone has to stand up . . . so the first person says 'one', and sits down, then across the circle, the second says 'two' and sits down.

- This is surprisingly difficult and is a magnificent game for improving eye contact and listening skills in preparation for using those skills in a discussion. I once had a group who could do this facing out of the circle with their eyes closed. They were amazing and very well organised!

2. Share the stimulus

Give children time to react.

3. Individual thinking – word generation

This part of the session promotes paired thinking and encourages question generation:

- Ask the children to write down a word that comes into their mind when they see/hear/smell the stimulus.

- Working with a partner, use your words (and not the stimulus now) to generate a question for discussion. This takes practice and, to start with, the questions may be easily answered by asking an expert. Children quickly develop the skill of asking philosophical questions, but you can offer some examples. Children should write down their question, or an adult or scribe could do this for them.

4. Share questions, make connections

This is perhaps the most important part of the activity and can also be deployed when children have thought of their individual word.

Read the questions out and give thinking time. Are there any connections between the questions? This might be word choice or theme, but in time they will begin to connect questions that would lead to certain types of discussions. Pile up the questions in their connection groups.

5. Secret vote, choose a question

Read a representative question for each group. The children must close their eyes while they vote for the question that they wish to discuss. This cuts the risk that the question belonging to the most popular member of the class gets chosen. After a few sessions, most groups realise that the question choice is very important to the quality of the discussion, and you may decide as a group to abandon the eye-closing!

6. Begin the discussion with the question authors

Ask the authors of the chosen questions if they would like to explain what they mean by the question. It may be that their thinking when writing is different to the interpretation of others and it helps to start the discussion with some clarification.

7. The discussion begins

At first, and even after a lot of experience, this can be a nerve-wracking moment for the teacher, as the children go quiet sometimes. Hold your nerve – really deep thinking does need reflection and consideration, and silences and spaces are not a sign that things have gone wrong. Try to avoid jumping into the gaps. If the discussion needs a kick-start, the *facilitator* can re-read the question. Another strategy is to ask children what specific words in the question mean to them.

8. Finish

When communities are established, the end of the discussion is often very tricky, as the children do not want to end the debate. Ways to bring the discussion to a close include: asking each person to summarise their thoughts; asking the scribe to recap on the discussion from their notes; asking children to take their discussions out to play with them at break time.

Overcoming challenges

Time

Finding time for a session of philosophical enquiry can be tricky. Some ideas to try are:

- Highlight the benefits of philosophical enquiry to anyone in your school community who has influence over the timetable, including parents and governors.

- Make the stimulus for the session something that links to a topic or literacy text.

- Philosophy Clubs are worth trying – and are often very popular, once the children hear about the sessions from their friends. I would recommend having a limit on club members!

Behaviour management

There is often a concern that children will not cope with the enquiry session and that disruptive behaviour is more likely when children are in this philosophical mode where rules may seem 'looser' (Trickey and Topping, 2004). Every class has different dynamics. Over many years of experience, I have not found disruptive behaviour to be a problem but would never assume that I know your class better than you do. If things do get tricky, you can pare back the session. Sometimes I have run an enquiry to the *making connections* stage only, particularly with younger children. Always go back to the behaviour policy of your school and the rules of your community of enquiry.

Inclusion

Some children may struggle to access elements of the enquiry process. It is possible to run an enquiry without writing or reading, and if support is deployed effectively, ideas can be expressed and discussed in many ways. I have adapted sessions for a wide variety of learners, from children who would draw their ideas, to those who communicated in sign language, to the child who would 'phone in' from another room with his comments after listening to the discussion via a video link to an interactive whiteboard. A session of enquiry can be adapted in all of the most creative and supportive ways that you use for other subjects.

Impact

PGCE trainees often ask how they will show progress in a session like this, and how they will evidence the progress after the session has ended. The benefits of philosophical enquiry are well documented, but if evidence is required, the notes of your community enquiry made by your scribe can be displayed. Some groups video their sessions to share with parents, but I think the best measure of progress is the testimony of the children themselves. Often if you ask them how they have changed over the course of a session, they will find this hard to answer, but if you ask whether they changed their mind, or who managed to change their ideas, they will usually have a remarkable answer. These could be recorded, if you need to.

Inspections

I am often asked what Ofsted or senior leaders would think if they observed a philosophical enquiry session. Here is a story about what happened during a two-day inspection at my school:

CASE STUDY

Picture Book

My Year 6 class were no strangers to philosophical enquiry. We had been using strategies for thinking for a while and had enquiry sessions every week. But we didn't usually hold our sessions with an inspector in the room. For this one, we used a picture book called *Harry and Hopper* (Wild and Blackwood, 2012) which, if you haven't read it, please do - but be warned that a dog dies half-way through and it will make you cry! Picture books are brilliant for enquiry sessions because they *act as alternative philosophical texts that can help open the kinds of spaces in which children and adults can engage freely with philosophical thinking* (Haynes and Murris, 2013: 1088; also see Haynes and Murris, 2012).

I was pretty sure with an inspector in the room I would hold it together and we worked through the process of setting up our enquiry. However, the story worked its magic, and before I got to the end of the page, I was crying and my voice was wobbling all over the place. My class, who were kind and thoughtful (and very funny) as a community, rallied round and read for me. Then we came up with our key words and questions. The question they voted for was *If something makes you cry, is it wiser to avoid it in future?* which was asked by a boy, Sam, who would have been deemed 'a low achiever' in a Maths/English ability set classroom. Their discussion ranged from their favourite sports to seeing a parent just at weekends and being upset when they had to leave to pets dying. Again, when concluding the discussion, Sam showed his skill by summarising the points that had been recorded in pictures and words by our scribe. He shared that when his grandma had died the year before, it had hurt so much, but that it was worth that pain because he had known love and gained so much from knowing her and risking the heartbreak. Which obviously set me off again, and this time the inspector gave me a tissue and very fair and positive observation feedback.

CHAPTER SUMMARY

In this chapter we have made the case for employing philosophy for children as a strategy to encourage deep thinking, empathy, reflection and sense of community.

I hope this has encouraged you to have a go at philosophical enquiry with your own class. If you do, please don't be put off if it doesn't go smoothly the first time. This is a challenging activity and everyone will improve with practice. Once you are up and running, be an advocate for philosophical enquiry and tell your parents, colleagues, governors and community about what enquiry adventures you are on. You may find you have some budding (and some very experienced) philosophers in your midst already who would love to be involved. Good luck!

We have:

- explored what philosophical enquiry is and why it should be part of a broad and balanced curriculum.
- analysed some of the research around philosophical enquiry with children.
- rehearsed a practical model for philosophical enquiry in your own setting.

Further reading

Cassidy, C. and Christie, D. (2013) Philosophy with children: talking, thinking and learning together. *Early Child Development and Care*, 183 (8): 1072–83.

Education Endowment Foundation (2015) *Philosophy for Children: Evaluation Report and Executive Summary: July 2015.* London: EEF.

Godard, S., Siddiqui, N. and See, B. (2017) Can 'Philosophy for Children' improve primary school attainment? *Journal of Philosophy of Education,* **http://onlinelibrary.wiley.com/doi/10.1111/1467-9752.12227/abstract**

Siddiqui, N., Gorard, S. and See, B. (2017) *Non-cognitive Impacts of Philosophy for Children: Project Report.* School of Education, Durham University, Durham.

Support materials for your community

Buckley, J. (2013) *Pocket P4C: Getting Started with Philosophy for Children.* Chelmsford: One Slice Books.

Tomley, S. and Weeks, M. (2015) *Children's Book of Philosophy: An Introduction to the World's Greatest Thinkers and Their Big Ideas.* London: DK.

Wild, M. and Blackwood, F. (2012). *Harry and Hopper.* London: Scholastic.

Worley, P. (2015) *40 Lessons to Get Children Thinking: Philosophical Thought Adventures Across the Curriculum.* London: Bloomsbury.

References

Bronfenbrenner, U. (1979) *The Ecology of Human Development: Experiments by Nature and Design.* Cambridge, MA: Harvard University Press.

Cassidy, C. and Christie, D. (2013) Philosophy with children: talking, thinking and learning together. *Early Child Development and Care, 183* (8): 1072–83.

Dasen, P. (1994). Culture and cognitive development from a Piagetian perspective. In W .J. Lonner and R. S. Malpass (eds), *Psychology and Culture.* Boston: Allyn & Bacon, pp. 145–9.

Education Endowment Foundation (2015) *Philosophy for Children: Evaluation Report and Executive Summary: July 2015.* London: EEF.

Fisher, R. (2007) Dialogic teaching: developing thinking and metacognition through philosophical discussion. *Early Child Development and Care, 177,* 615–31.

Glina, M. (2006) A community of barbarians: the community of inquiry as a strong democracy. *Thinking, 16* (1): 5–22.

Godard, S., Siddiqui, N. and See, B. (2017) Can 'philosophy for children' improve primary school attainment? *Journal of Philosophy of Education,* **http://onlinelibrary.wiley.com/doi/10.1111/1467-9752.12227/abstract**

Gregory, M. (2011) Philosophy for children and its critics: a Mendham dialogue. *Journal of Philosophy of Education, 45* (2): 199–219.

Haynes, J. (2002) *Children as Philosophers.* London: Routledge.

Haynes, J. and Murris, K. (2012) *Picturebooks, Pedagogy and Philosophy.* New York: Routledge.

Haynes, J. and Murris, K. (2013) The realm of meaning: imagination, narrative and playfulness in philosophical exploration with young children. *Early Childhood Development and Care, 183* (8): 1084–100.

Kerslake, L. and Wegerif, R. (2018) *Theory of Teaching Thinking: International Perspectives* (Research on Teaching Thinking and Creativity). London: Routledge.

Lipman, M. (1998) Teaching students to think reasonably: some findings of the philosophy for children program. *The Clearing House: A Journal of Educational Strategies, Issues and Ideas, 71* (5): 277–80.

McCall, C. (2013) *Transforming Thinking: Philosophical Inquiry in the Primary and Secondary Classroom.* London: Routledge.

Matthews, G. (1984) *The Philosophy of Childhood.* Cambridge, MA: Harvard University Press.

Matthews, G. (1995) *Dialogues with Children.* Cambridge, MA: Harvard University Press.

Murris, K. (2000) Can children do philosophy? *Journal of Philosophy of Education, 34*: 261–79.

Murris, K. (2002) *Teaching Philosophy with Picture Books.* London: Infobooks.

Piaget, J. (1972) *The Psychology of the Child.* New York: Basic Books.

Pohoata, G. and Petrescu, C. (2013) Is there a philosophy for children? *Euromentor Journal, IV* (3): 7–12.

Russell, B. (1912) *The Problems of Philosophy.* London: Williams & Norgate.

Siddiqui, N., Gorard, S. and See, B. (2017) *Non-cognitive Impacts of Philosophy for Children, Project Report.* School of Education, Durham University, Durham.

Stokes, P. (2015) *The Naked Self: Kierkegaard and Personal Identity.* Oxford: Oxford University Press.

Tolmie, A., Topping, K., Christie, D., Donaldson, C., Howe, C., Jessiman, E. and Thurston, A. (2010) Cognitive gains at 2-year follow up. *British Journal of Educational Psychology, 77*: 787–96.

Topping, K. and Trickey, S. (2007) Collaborative philosophical inquiry for schoolchildren: cognitive gains at 2-year follow up. *British Journal of Educational Psychology, 77*: 787–96.

Trickey, S. and Topping, K. (2004) 'Philosophy for children': a systematic review. *Research Papers in Education, 19* (3): 365–80.

Vansieleghem, N. and Kennedy, D. (2011) What is philosophy for children, what is philosophy with children – after Matthew Lipman? *Journal of Philosophy of Education, 45* (2): 171–82.

Wild, M. and Blackwood, F. (2012) *Harry and Hopper.* London: Scholastic.

Wilson, J. (1992) Philosophy for children: a note of warning. *Thinking, 10* (1): 17–18.

6
DEVELOPING A SUPPORTIVE ETHOS FOR ALL LEARNERS

CARRIE WINSTANLEY

TO BE KIND IS MORE IMPORTANT THAN TO BE RIGHT. MANY TIMES, WHAT PEOPLE NEED IS NOT A BRILLIANT MIND THAT SPEAKS BUT A SPECIAL HEART THAT LISTENS.

F. SCOTT FITZGERALD

KEYWORDS: SUPPORTIVE; CHALLENGE; EQUALITY OF CHALLENGE; LEARNING; INCLUSION/INCLUSIVE; ENABLING; ADDITIONAL NEEDS; LEARNING ENVIRONMENT; VALUES; ETHOS.

CHAPTER OBJECTIVES

This chapter helps you to:

- understand the nature and importance of a supportive ethos
- think about inclusion, inclusivity and equity: what does this mean?
- consider equality of challenge for all
- audit and improve learning spaces to ensure that you support all learners

LINKS TO THE TEACHERS' STANDARDS

Working through this chapter will enable you to meet all of the Teachers' Standards, in particular:

TS 1:   Set high expectations which inspire, motivate and challenge pupils

TS 2:   Promote good progress and outcomes by pupils

(Continued)

(Continued)

TS 5:   Adapt teaching to respond to the strengths and needs of all pupils

TS 8:   Fulfil wider professional responsibilities

Part 2: Personal and professional conduct

Introduction

Developing a 'supportive ethos' is an essential foundation for all effective learning. As articulated in the introduction to this book, children need a sense of belonging in order to flourish and so social and emotional aspects of learning should not be neglected, as learners must be fully engaged in order to learn productively. Schools are social, emotional and intellectual places (Husu and Tirri, 2007) and there are many things that teachers can do to try and ensure that all their pupils are encouraged to participate fully in all aspects of their classroom experiences.

So, the key objective of this chapter is to help teachers consider how best to provide a genuinely supportive setting for their learners. Given that the book's readership is primarily those working in mainstream school settings, this chapter is focused on helping support the range of learners most frequently encountered in such schools. The underpinning principles, however, constitute fundamentally good practice for all. As reflected in Part 2 of the Teachers' Standards, people should not have their difference or singularity denied (Todd, 2001). As such, the points discussed here are applicable to any learning setting, with any 'type' of learner, of any age or background. Through this chapter, teachers will learn about developing and maintaining a supportive ethos which comprises a range of elements, including the principles and related practice needed for the creation of supportive and inclusive learning spaces; the careful design of supportive and inclusive learning spaces; and a focus on developing holistic, supportive approaches to including all learners.

Because schools are social, emotional and intellectual spaces and this chapter's focus is the wide-ranging foundation for positive learning, myriad links from this chapter can be seen to other parts of the book, where more detail can be found on, for example, positive behaviour management, holistic learning and equable and compassionate assessment practices, etc.

What do we mean by a 'supportive ethos'?

Every school as a whole, and each classroom in particular, has an ambience, an atmosphere, a climate, an ethos. The *feeling* of any space or place can be intangible but simultaneously palpable. We have all experienced times when entering a new space is a positive, relaxing event, and others where we are distinctly uncomfortable. Given that children and teachers spend a significant amount of time together in classrooms and that they are expected to learn, to communicate, to develop and ideally to flourish, we need to ensure that the ethos that they are living and working in at school is supportive and positive. An ethos is about much more than the physical indoor and outdoor spaces of the school, however, as it also encompasses how people behave towards one another. This is because *how* people communicate and relate to one another in turn reflects their values, attitudes and priorities. Before exploring some of the detail about *ethos* more deeply, it's worth thinking more generally about different types of atmosphere that we have all encountered throughout our own schooling as pupils, as well as while working alongside colleagues in their spaces, and in creating our own classroom climates.

REFLECTION

Do you strive for a particular classroom 'feel'? What is most comfortable for you?

Consider this spectrum of adjectives describing possible classroom atmospheres:

silent – quiet – humming – active – flowing – buzzing – noisy

Some are obviously going to be more conducive than others for different daily tasks such as individual quiet reading activities, group drama projects or, say, problem-solving in pairs. All of them are potentially positive descriptors that seem to suggest positive atmospheres. A much wider range of adjectives could be applied to the classroom. As you peruse this list, think about both the actual room you work in and your ideal classroom. Here is the more judgemental (scrambled) list of descriptors with 'loaded' language:

calm / boisterous / gentle / tranquil / peaceful / orderly / repressive / agitated / sparse / turbulent / raucous / chaotic / exciting / strict / meticulous / stimulating / relaxed / efficient / dull / well-organised / focused / directed / cluttered / lively / nourishing

Some of the words might split opinion, with different teachers and learners finding some atmospheres more conducive than others. Perhaps there are some ideas here that are more of an aim than a reality. This gap between actual and desirable atmospheres is explained by McLaughlin (2005: 312) as your 'experienced' ethos and your 'aspirational' ethos. There are ways to bridge this gap, however, because although the *ethos* can seem intangible, it is possible to break down its elements. This can help us to examine how ethos functions and consequently how it can be developed and improved. It is possible to organise these elements of ethos in different ways.

THEORY FOCUS

In 2000, a report on teacher effectiveness was commissioned by the government of the day (Hay McBer in DfES, 2000). It emerged as an influential yet controversial paper, claiming that an important role for teachers was in creating a classroom 'climate'. While considering the idea of classroom climate was not new, the report provided a nine-point list of the characteristics of a climate for effective teaching. As you review this abridged list below, consider whether you think that it

(Continued)

(Continued)

covers all the values that support social, relational and individual aspects in schools (as recommended by Husu and Tirri, 2007):

- *Clarity*: How lessons relate to broader subjects, school aims and objectives.
- *Order and discipline*: Civilised behaviour is maintained in the classroom.
- *Standards*: There are clear standards for pupils' behaviour and achievements and a clear focus on higher rather than minimum standards.
- *Fairness*: There is an absence of favouritism and consistent links between classroom rewards and actual performance.
- *Participation*: There are opportunities for active pupil participation (discussion, questioning, giving out materials, etc.).
- *Support*: There is a feeling of emotional support in the classroom and pupils are willing to try new things and learn from mistakes.
- *Safety*: The classroom is a safe place and pupils are not at risk from emotional or physical bullying etc.
- *Interest*: Classrooms are interesting and exciting places and pupils feel stimulated to learn.
- *Environment*: The classroom is comfortable, well-organised, clean and attractive.

Although the points noted above are all relevant for developing ethos, they are not sufficient to explain all its aspects. Various critiques have been made of the instrumental way classroom climate is considered in Hay McBer (see Campbell *et al.*, 2003) as it neglects some key areas. Some of the points were already well-established (such as elements of safety, as articulated by the psychologist Maslow in the 1940s), but others are lacking. For example, while 'systems' are significant in creating ethos, there is little emphasis on relationships in this model, nor much note of how language is used; both of these aspects are significant in providing a positive ethos (and are discussed later in this chapter). Others researching classroom climate emphasise the importance of inclusion, equity and ethical relations (Peaston, 2011; Todd, 2001), some focus on pupil voice (Hopkins, 2008), and others on connectedness (Rodgers and Raider-Roth, 2006).

Read more about Maslow's theory here: **https://www.simplypsychology.org/maslow.html**

The role of values

The other major omission from the list above is a clear statement about teachers' values, beliefs and principles. It is a much trickier area as it is inappropriate to prescribe or force values and principles. They can't be absorbed or genuinely adopted simply through a checklist of behaviours since they are part of an individual's belief system. We need to come to understand our values and then develop ways to embody them and regularly enact them, and for these values to serve as underpinning principles for our actions (Husu, and Tirri, 2007). One aspect of school where values, beliefs and principles become visible is through community relationships. The ways in which people communicate should reflect a positive and shared understanding of the rights and responsibilities of all members within and beyond the direct learning community. This means that as well as pupils, teachers and support staff, office and technical staff, parents and external agencies should all be included in understanding the community's values.

REFLECTION

What values do you subscribe to? How do these values sit within the school community that you are part of?

Here is an example of school values that may overlap with those in your own school context.

All members of the school community are expected to:

- respect difference;

- hold high expectations of positive behaviour;

- use positive language;

- engage with our activities, including reflection and development;

- adhere to a no-tolerance policy of bullying or discrimination;

- help maintain a positive school environment;

- strive to care for oneself and others.

What the values listed above are striving to help with is the task of drawing out *principles* of a supportive ethos.

These principles are all to do with providing opportunities for children to explore, find and exhibit their own abilities through a rich, diverse curriculum with carefully planned activities that offer just the right amount of challenge. It is important to recognise that creating a supportive while manageable ethos is not necessarily very easy. In the day-to-day whirl of classroom activity, it can be simpler to focus exclusively on practical necessities. But by simply holding a clear vision of what it means to be fully inclusive can be helpful. As stated by Husu and Tirri (2007):

> . . . *examining visions may encourage teachers to deal with the gap between their hopes and their practice. Learning to navigate the gap between vision and practice may be helpful in developing the contextual understanding of teaching.*

(2007: 394)

School values depend to a certain extent on the leadership of the organisation (Peaston, 2011), but individual teachers can still strive to create a welcoming ethos that supports learning, viewing it as important, enjoyable and achievable, but with consistently high expectations.

Figure 6.1   Teachers can ensure that they retain a welcoming ethos that promotes enjoyment of learning alongside high expectations

When leadership is authoritative and distributive in nature, this can help teachers remain ambitious and motivated for their pupils, no matter what type of school they are in or what demographics make up their local context. This concept is explained very clearly here:

> *Research into authoritative school 'climate' indicates that it is one in which there is a balance between a high expectations and structure on one hand and warmth and support on the other. This authoritative 'climate' has been cited as reducing student dropout rates, improving attainment and led to less bullying and victimisation in schools.*

(Scottish Government, 2018: 3)

Inclusion and inclusivity – theory and practice

Because the concepts – and hence the language – of inclusion, inclusivity and equity are often used in discussions around school ethos, it is also worth delving a little deeper here. In the world of education, specific additional meanings are attached to words such as 'inclusion' in different contexts, and this can cause confusion when discussing inclusive practices in non-specialist settings. Within the field of special and inclusive education, hard-fought theoretical and practical arguments underlie the different conceptions of these words. Although this book focuses largely on mainstream education, teachers still have to manage an extensive range of needs among the children in their care. Some of these needs can be described through a diagnosis of a recognised learning difference, condition or syndrome. While individual experiences of any such condition will differ, the cluster of needs that tends to arise can be anticipated usefully, with some potential problems averted.

THEORY FOCUS

Notions of disability and learning difficulty have shifted as society has changed and understandings have developed considerably. Models of dis/ability reflect and sometimes shape the creation of policies as well as people's understanding of inclusive practice; here we consider some of the ways that dis/ability and inclusion are understood theoretically. Influenced by fields like sociology, psychology, health, economics, philosophy and disability studies, these developments help us to think about the nature of dis/ability, and in turn about providing support. Here are a few of the key distinctive models:

- **Medical model.** People are disabled by impairments or differences that should be 'fixed' by medical treatments, even when there is no pain or illness. This model considers what is 'wrong' with the person and not what they need. It creates low expectations and can lead to people losing independence, choice and control of their own lives.
- **Social model.** Disability is caused by the way society is organised rather than by a person's difference. Barriers that restrict life choices should be removed so people with disabilities can be independent and equal in society, with choice and control over their own lives. People with disabilities developed the social model of disability because the traditional medical model did not explain their personal experience of disability or help to develop more inclusive ways of living.
- **Capabilities approach.** Superseding the binary approaches above, this notion highlights equality and justice. Its main feature is a focus on people's capabilities, that is what people are effectively able to do and what they are able to be. The approach evaluates people's dis/advantage in terms of their abilities to function in their own contexts and places the achievement of their well-being as central, so it is a holistic approach.

Read more about these ideas in Mitra (2006) and Terzi (2005).

What does this mean for classroom practice?

Here is a brief case study from a Year 2 teacher working with a child on the autism spectrum in her class.

CASE STUDY

When I heard that I was going to be teaching Child A I was nervous, as I'd heard that she hasn't made much progress with learning and that she was disruptive. I'd seen her unusual behaviours around school. However, she had a helpful Education and Health Care Plan. It was long, but once I'd read it properly, I met with the SENCO and the ed-psych which helped me understand it all better. We worked through scenarios that could cause her problems and so I was able to prepare the

(Continued)

(Continued)

classroom space in ways that would help her focus by being more comfortable. With the TA's help, we set up a workspace for her on the floor, with cushions and a low table as a desk as she finds chairs a bit problematic. We also continued with the visual timetable and provided headphones and a music player as that helps her manage the sensory things. So far, things are going well. Another thing I've tried to do is work with people who know her well to try and speak encouragingly about her and focus on her successes. My trepidation wasn't really necessary, but it was good to be prepared. We're all working on using more positive language to describe her – and others in the school who are sometimes a bit challenging. I think that will help people feel more confident and then be more helpful.

This scenario is quite a clear example of how adjustments to the classroom space can help promote a more positive and supportive ethos with a focus on enabling the pupil to express his/her capabilities. The teacher has also realised that the way the experience is discussed in the staffroom and with support staff also has an impact. Peaston, discussing children with similar difficulties, found the same, noting that *staff attitude was seen as vital, and a positive attitude was modelled and promoted by the leadership team* (2001: 11). In both instances, language is noted.

Just as the language we use to encourage learners impacts on their sense of inclusion, so the language we use to describe difference can serve to include or to alienate. How we talk with, and about, people with disabilities reveals our understanding of people's potential and also influences their own expectations. In their work on strategies for closing the learning gap, Hughes and Vass (2001) focused on the language, identifying helpful types for supporting learning and motivation. I've added here the no-blame approach (DfES, 2003).

Language of . . .	Function of the language	Phrases
. . . success	Signalling confidence to children	'I know you can'
. . . hope	Allowing children to ask for help positively – 'I'll try but I need some help'	'What will help you do it?' 'You will get this; let me help'
. . . possibility	Recognising that activities are challenging but can be achieved	'Yes, you did get it a bit stuck; let's see which bit is tricky for you'
. . . no blame	Avoiding saying 'You have messed up'	'What do we need to remember here?' 'Can I explain this a bit more clearly?'

Adapted from Hughes and Vass (2001) and DfES (2003).

Equality of challenge

As noted, there are many facets to equity and they are all relevant for building a supportive ethos. Some are statutory and protected and so there are checks on how effectively they are enacted.

The right to 'equality of challenge', however, is not enshrined in law. While there is some requirement through the inspection and school improvement regimes to incorporate challenge, it is up to
schools and teachers to work out how best to do that and what levels or types of challenge should
be provided.

A supportive ethos must encompass an enabling education. This requires that sufficient resources
are made available to allow the development of all children's talents to a high level, as well as supporting areas of difficulty. This is particularly important where there is a significant discrepancy
between a pupil's potential and their performance due to reasons such as EAL or a learning difficulty. In these instances, the support cannot only be for their areas of difficulties, but also for the
aspects where they could excel. This is the principle of equality of challenge (Winstanley, 2004) and
it demands that all pupils are provided with stimulating engaging work that matches their needs,
providing sufficient challenge for them to learn well but with enough support for them not to be
floundering.

REFLECTION

How exactly can teachers provide challenge?

Take a look at the table bedlow with the seven key ingredients of challenge and the quotation
below. Consider how you already use these elements in your teaching. Perhaps there are ways you
could focus on increasing those strategies that you employ less frequently. It is worth taking practical steps to ensure that all the pupils in your care have appropriate challenge as often as possible.
(For more detail on the ingredients of challenge, see Winstanley (2010).)

Ingredient of challenge	Ask yourself	Ideas to try
Cognitive engagement and cognitive dissonance	Are the pupils hooked into the ideas they're working on? Are the activities giving them the right level of puzzlement?	Children source a 'challenge of the week' so you can see what they find interesting and their perceived level of difficulty.
Risk of failure and chance of success	What is the attitude to making mistakes in class? Are there genuinely manageable and genuinely difficult activities?	Follow up some 'mindset' activities and have a 'celebration of learning from mistakes' board.
Independence and self-direction	How frequently can the pupils get on without support? What opportunities are there for independence?	Encourage individuals to undertake a sustained project of their own choosing.
Metacognition	Do pupils regularly review their own ways of working?	Post some key questions for nudging children to review how they learn.

(Continued)

(Continued)

Ingredient of challenge	Ask yourself	Ideas to try
Like-minded peers	Are groups mixed up for tasks, including across the year group or wider school?	Run a 'hobbies day' where everyone shares their passions across the school, finding like-minded children.
Novelty and passion	Have you taught something you absolutely adore in the last week? Are there any areas of your day where routine feels more like being stuck in a rut than a useful habit?	Challenge yourself and the children to change one habit for a few days and talk about the impact.
Learning beyond the classroom	When did you last take a lesson into a different space just because you wanted to (rather than needing particular equipment)?	Swap classrooms with a friendly colleague for one (relatively self-contained) lesson, just for the refreshing change.

The teacher is the key in providing challenge. It is the responsibility of the teacher to engage with ideas, such as the various ways challenges can be manifested, and then to make considered decisions about how best to support the learners in their care [...] The ingredients are to be integrated and combined in ways that successfully enhance pupils' education. For this to be meaningful, teachers need to engage with the principles of what they are undertaking and examine their own understanding, reviewing how they feel and what they do.

(Winstanley, 2010: x)

Learning spaces

Here we focus on practical matters associated with making indoor and outdoor learning spaces as supportive and inclusive as possible. Certain requirements need to be met for inclusivity and some of these are statutory, such as good enough illumination for pupils who need to lip-read and including attention paid to reflective surfaces and flickering lighting. As well as the look of spaces, it is worth also considering the sound and literal feel of a space by reviewing the surfaces along with the displays and demarcated areas. While it is not generally possible to change all the furniture and re-carpet the classroom, it is feasible to use fabric and props to introduce different textures and shapes, particularly 3D elements to the classroom. Some schools also allow children to be shoeless indoors or wear slippers – this can make for a more relaxed and calmer environment (Heppell, 2011).

For children who need minimal distractions due to ADHD or some forms of autism, quiet workstations or desks where they can use headphones are sometimes helpful. Being aware of the sensory experience of the classroom is helpful for teachers to understand children's behaviour and to find ways to minimise potential distractions. For example, it can also sometimes be preferable to avoid bells and alarms for regular activities such as signalling lunchtime, as these can be upsetting for some people and can cause or exacerbate anxiety. The smell of spaces can also cause discomfort, but simply adjusting the ventilation can eradicate the problem. Similarly, hard furniture or floors can be problematic for some children, but a cushion can relieve this issue. Relaxation over uniform regulations can also transform the experience of children who are impacted by sensory discomfort. Classrooms can easily become stuffy or some pupils may be seated in a draughty spot and this can also impact on their ability to concentrate. Although the majority of pupils in mainstream classrooms are able to manage without major adjustments, it is helpful for all learners to be in a comfortable environment. (For a really helpful sensory audit, see Attfield *et al.* (n.d.) at: **www. aettraininghubs.org.uk/wp-content/uploads/2012/05/37.1-Sensory-audit-tool-for-environments.pdf**.)

A good way to review the impact of the school ethos on your learning spaces is to participate, preferably together with a colleague, in a 'Learning Walk' around your school, or take photographs of various spaces for shared analysis at a staff meeting. A cursory search of the Internet unlocks myriad templates for auditing the school spaces in this way, but here is a generic exemplar that you can adapt to meet your needs.

REFLECTION

Take a 'Learning Walk' around selected indoor and outdoor spaces and try looking at all spaces through different lenses.

Lens	Sample questions
Engagement	How inviting is the space? What's the feel? How about the colour palette and textures? Is it comfortable, calming or stimulating as required?
Learning	Do the spaces support learning? Are activities child-initiated? Can children access resources? Are objectives and targets clear?
Inclusivity	Do images of people reflect the diversity of the school? Are all the words fully inclusive? Are displays fully visible to people of all heights (try looking with the lights on and off)? Do spaces and language support school values? Are there focused places like 'Buddy Benches' for children to go to if they need peer support?
Use	Is the function clear? How useful is the space? Are learners using it as intended? (If not, why not and can it be changed?) Are the spaces flexible? Do learners have ownership of the space? How does usage change at different times?

For more specific classroom audits, a guide or checklist should be bespoke to each school in order to reflect its practices and values, but most are likely to include ideas such as these:

- interesting displays of children's work;

- class rules/expectations/contract/charter co-created with pupils;

- topic or theme-based walls with key vocabulary and subject-specific words/operations;

- challenge ideas with provocations and questions;

- motivational displays with a variety of messages both extrinsic ('Golden Time'/'Team Points') and intrinsic positive affirmations ('We take pride in our work' 'Be determined and you will achieve');

- behaviour monitoring (a visual reminder of how the children are getting on – this must be updated repeatedly to reflect improvements);

- handy reminders – for curriculum issues like targets and also practical items about upcoming events;

- number lines and spellings and/or sounds and phonics;

- visual timetables;

- interactive displays.

Another recommended and supportive practice is to include 'working walls' or 'interactive walls'. These display work-in-progress and are necessarily incomplete and probably untidy, as they reflect the iterative progression of thoughts and unfolding of ideas.

Figure 6.2   An example of an 'interactive wall'

These displays should be at a good height for children to see and interact with, such as by adding writing, images or sticky notes, etc. They should always incorporate objectives and information about the task-in-progress, so that any viewer can see what is being undertaken in ways that build pupils' confidence. Over time, all children should have their contributions included, but this can be done in groups.

CHAPTER SUMMARY

In this chapter we have examined what it means to provide a supportive ethos in our schools so that all learners are emotionally comfortable and ready to learn. We have considered that the many interpretations of the term *inclusion* can lead to some misconceived perceptions about individuals in our classrooms. But we have also reflected on how, with a deeper knowledge and understanding of the theory surrounding this, we can make our classrooms a more inclusive place, where every child is challenged to rise to their full potential. All of these elements contribute to the creation and maintenance of learning spaces with a supportive ethos. In our schools *pupils should have support for their problems, freedom to develop socially, personally and intellectually but also have the opportunities to be challenged, stimulated and engaged* (Winstanley, 2009: 103).

KEY POINTS TO CONSIDER

A supportive ethos:

*   is essential to children's effective learning and well-being;
*   embraces difference and diversity;
*   is underpinned by clear values;
*   must be inclusive and promote equity;
*   provides equality of challenge for all learners;
*   is impacted by the quality, design and use of learning spaces.

Further reading

Peaston, H. (2011) *Mainstream Inclusion, Special Challenges: Strategies for Children with BESD*. National College for Leadership of Schools.

This research project is helpful in sharing the practical difficulties of creating a supportive mainstream ethos for children with a wide range of additional needs.

Wallace, B., Leyden, S., Montgomery, D., Winstanley, C., Pomerantz, M. and Fitton, S. (2009) *Raising the Achievement of All Pupils within an Inclusive Setting*. Oxford: Routledge.

Full of practical strategies for developing best practice based on research visits to a range of schools, this book is underpinned by ideas around a supportive school ethos.

Winstanley, C. (2010) *The Ingredients of Challenge*. London: Trentham.

This book looks in more detail at all the elements that make up challenge within a supportive school and classroom climate. It has many practical aspects, supported by theory.

References

Attfield, I., Fowler, A. and Jones, V. (n.d.) *Sensory Audit for Schools and Classrooms.* **www. aettraininghubs.org.uk/wp-content/uploads/2012/05/37.1-Sensory-audit-tool-for-environments.pdf** (accessed 2015).

Campbell, R.J., Kyriakides, L., Muijs, R.D. and Robinson, W. (2003) Differential teacher effectiveness: towards a model for research and teacher appraisal. *Oxford Review of Education, 29* (3): 347–62.

DfES (2000) *A Model of Teacher Effectiveness: Report by Hay McBer to the Department for Education and Employment.* **www.dfes.gov.uk/teachingreforms/leadership/ mcber/01.shtml**

DfES (2003) *Improving the Climate for Teaching and Learning in the Secondary School*. London: DfES.

Heppell, S. (2011) *Shoeless Learning Spaces.* **http://rubble.heppell.net/places/shoeless/** (accessed 2017).

Hopkins, E.A. (2008) Classroom conditions to secure enjoyment and achievement: the pupils' voice. Listening to the voice of Every Child Matters. *Education 3–13, 36*(4): 393–401.

Hughes, M. and Vass, A. (2001) *Strategies for Closing the Learning Gap*. Stafford: Network Educational Press.

Husu, J. and Tirri, K. (2007) Developing whole school pedagogical values – a case of going through the ethos of 'good schooling'. *Teacher and Teacher Education, 23*: 390–401.

McLaughlin, T. (2005) The educative importance of ethos. *British Journal of Educational Studies, 53* (3): 306–25.

Mitra, S. (2006) The capability approach and disability. *Journal of Disability Policy Studies, 16* (4): 236–47.

Peaston, H. (2011) *Mainstream Inclusion, Special Challenges: Strategies for Children with BESD*. National College for Leadership of Schools. Online only available at: **https://dera.ioe.ac.uk/3760/1/download%3fid=149406&filename=mainstream-inclusion-special-challenges-strategies-for-children-with-besd-full-report.pdf** (accessed 2011).

Rodgers, C.R. and Raider-Roth, M.B. (2006) Presence in teaching. *Teachers and Teaching: Theory and Practice, 12* (3): 265–87.

Scottish Government (2018) *Developing a Positive Whole School Ethos and Culture – Relationships, Learning and Behaviour.* **https://www.gov.scot/publications/developing-positive-whole-school-ethos-culture-relationships-learning-behaviour/** (accessed 2018).

Terzi, L. (2005) Beyond the dilemma of difference: the capability approach on disability and special educational needs. *Journal of Philosophy of Education, 39* (3): 443–59.

Todd, S. (2001) 'Bringing more than I contain': ethics, curriculum and the pedagogical demand for altered egos. *Journal of Curriculum Studies, 33* (4): 431–50.

Winstanley, C. (2004) *Too Clever by Half: A Fair Deal for Gifted Children.* Stoke: Trentham Books.

Winstanley, C. (2009) Providing challenging opportunities in the classroom. In B. Wallace, S. Leyden, D. Montgomery, C. Winstanley, M. Pomerantz and S. Fitton, *Raising the Achievement of All Pupils within an Inclusive Setting: Practical Strategies for Developing Best Practice.* London: Routledge, pp. 101–30.

Winstanley, C. (2010) *The Ingredients of Challenge.* Stoke: Trentham Books.

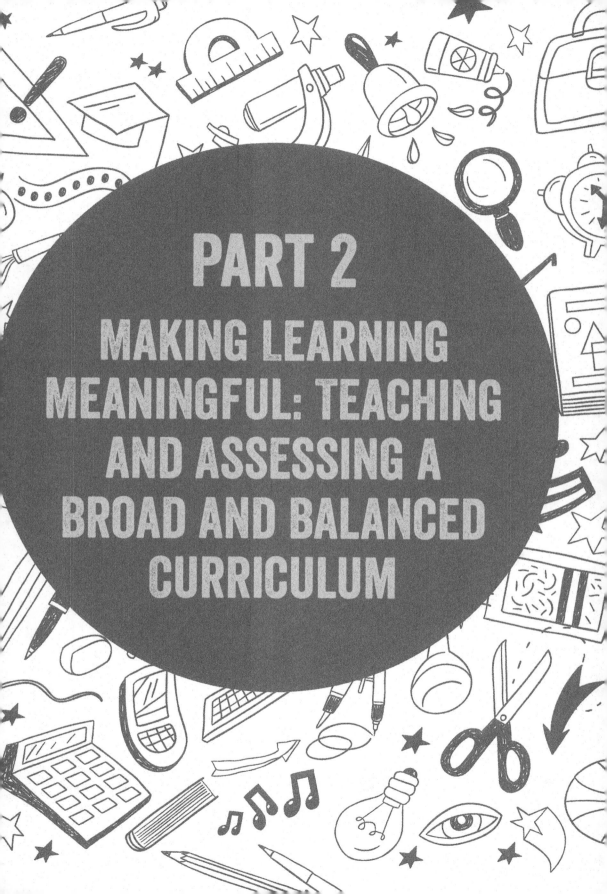

PART 2

MAKING LEARNING MEANINGFUL: TEACHING AND ASSESSING A BROAD AND BALANCED CURRICULUM

7

LEARNING TO ENQUIRE: THE ROLE OF THE HUMANITIES

TONY EAUDE

THE HUMANITIES PREPARE STUDENTS TO BE GOOD CITIZENS AND HELP THEM UNDERSTAND A COMPLICATED, INTERLOCKING WORLD. THE HUMANITIES TEACH US CRITICAL THINKING, HOW TO ANALYSE ARGUMENTS AND HOW TO IMAGINE LIFE FROM THE POINT OF VIEW OF SOMEONE UNLIKE YOURSELF.

(NUSSBAUM, 2017: 4)

KEYWORDS: HUMANITIES; CULTURE; BREADTH AND BALANCE; WHOLE CHILD; GLOBAL CITIZENSHIP; ENQUIRY; FIELDWORK; CRITICAL THINKING; YOUNG CHILDREN.

——— CHAPTER OBJECTIVES ———

This chapter helps you to:

- broaden your understanding of the humanities beyond History, Geography and Religious Education, to include areas such as literature and philosophy
- discuss how 'the humanities' contribute to the education of the whole child, so that children recognise what it means to be human and the role of culture
- explore the ways of working and thinking associated with the humanities, such as enquiry, observation, interpretation of contested ideas and critical thinking
- consider the implications for primary school teachers in a context where the humanities are often marginalised

---
LINKS TO THE TEACHERS' STANDARDS

Working through this chapter will enable you to meet all of the Teachers' Standards, in particular:

TS 2: Promote good progress and outcomes by pupils

TS 3: Demonstrate good subject and curriculum knowledge

TS 4: Plan and teach well structured lessons

TS 5: Adapt teaching to respond to the strengths and needs of all pupils

---

Introduction

Alexander (2010) describes how almost all school systems across the world have made the distinction between what he calls Curriculum 1, often called the 'basics', and Curriculum 2 – the rest, including the humanities and the arts. Alexander argues that what is included in each may vary slightly, for instance with science and technology sometimes in Curriculum 1, but that Curriculum 2 has always been seen as 'desirable but inessential'. In recent years, Curriculum 2 is often marginalised and allocated little time in primary schools in a climate where skills in literacy and numeracy are emphasised so strongly.

I shall suggest that the humanities, broadly defined, and the ways of working associated with them are essential to a broad and balanced curriculum, the education of the whole child and how children learn to participate as citizens of a democratic society.

What do we mean by the humanities?

Let us start by reflecting on the questions below. It will help if you try to think not just in terms of separate subjects but what skills and attitudes children need to learn in order to thrive in a world of diversity and change.

REFLECTION

What do you think 'the humanities' consist of?

Which subjects do you include in the humanities? Are there any about which you are not sure?

Which skills or attitudes do you think the humanities involve and help to develop?

I imagine that most primary teachers will think immediately of History and Geography, and perhaps Religious Education and citizenship. In Eaude (2017), I considered the humanities in primary schools, drawing on Small's (2013) work to suggest that this view is too limited. The several definitions of the humanities in Grigg and Hughes (2013: 2) all emphasise not being too constrained by traditional subject boundaries.

Small, writing from a university perspective, discusses how the humanities have usually been seen as a crucial element of being an educated or a cultured person, but indicates that quite which subjects or disciplines are involved is not fixed and open to debate. So, while history and the study of religion are usually included, so are literature, languages and philosophy, and while geography is sometimes, it is often seen more as a social science.

From this, and how young children learn, I argued that one should not restrict one's view of the humanities in primary schools to History, Geography and Religious Education but adopt a loose definition including learning a foreign language, literature and philosophy – and perhaps drama. You may be surprised to see literature and philosophy included, as the former is often considered as part of 'literacy' in how most schools teach the 2014 National Curriculum, and think that philosophical thinking is beyond young children (see Chapter 5). Why these are included is discussed below.

What do children learn by studying the humanities?

In reflecting on what the humanities can offer children, I and three colleagues suggested that it is more useful to think in terms of skills, attitudes and ways of working than of subjects, recognising that each subject or discipline has specific types of knowledge and ways of working. This led towards the following conclusion. Please read it carefully before you continue!

THEORY FOCUS

We want children to:

- understand concepts related to human culture such as time, space and belief in how human beings can understand themselves and their relationship with the natural world, places and each other;

- develop skills and habits associated with critical thinking such as assessing, interpreting and applying information;

- explore their own identities, values and beliefs and be interested in, and engage with, other people's;

- participate in democratic processes, learning to discuss their ideas and speak appropriately for themselves and others;

- learn to understand, and empathise with, people who are different as well as those who are similar, challenging stereotypes and becoming more humane and compassionate individuals.

(Adapted from Eaude *et al.*, 2017: 390)

Let us think about these. You may have noticed that the word 'knowledge' does not appear. Young children learn most deeply when they are engaged and interested in tasks that they find interesting and meaningful. This does not mean that knowledge does not matter, but the humanities should involve:

- learning more than propositional knowledge, such as lists of kings, queens and battles, the names of countries and rivers and what members of different religious groups wear and how they worship;

- understanding concepts associated with particular subjects, or disciplines, such as time, space and belief – as in History, Geography and RE – and many more related to human culture, how people understand themselves and their relationship with the world and each other;

- procedural knowledge – know-how, involving ways of working such as enquiry, fieldwork and interpretation of what children encounter; and

- personal/interpersonal knowledge – knowledge of oneself and other people and how these interact.

The humanities are more about ways of working which lead to deeper understanding of the concepts involved and of oneself and other people than collecting content knowledge. The skills and

Figure 7.1   Encouraging children to question promotes critical thinking

habits associated with critical thinking are applicable across the whole curriculum – and throughout life. These matter particularly in a world where information is available at the touch of a screen but where it is hard for children and adults to know to what extent such information should be trusted. Critical thinking skills include assessing, interpreting and applying information, which are essential when dealing with complex situations and questions. But critical thinking also, in Bailin *et al.*'s words (1999: 281), involves *the kinds of habits of mind, commitments or sensitivities (which) include such things as open-mindedness, fair-mindedness, the desire for truth, an inquiring attitude and a respect for high-quality products and performances.*

Such qualities help children in exploring identities, values and beliefs, i.e. who people (including oneself) are, their backgrounds, how they act and what they value and believe. These questions are among the most important and puzzling ones in life, not least because they do not have easy answers. In helping children to consider these, the humanities make a significant contribution to children's spiritual, moral, social and cultural development (SMSC), as discussed in Chapter 3.

REFLECTION

How do you think that the ways of working associated with the humanities benefit young children?

Eaude (2018) argues that the humanities are essential in developing the whole child and influencing how they think about, and interact, with other people. As indicated by Nussbaum in the quotation at the start of this chapter, the humanities are essential in enabling and encouraging democratic citizenship in a diverse world. This involves children participating, for instance by engaging in debate about controversial issues such as the sustainability of the planet, the reasons for xenophobia and the role of religion; and being able to express their views coherently and confidently. Such an approach may also encourage children to take action to help others and improve the area where they live.

You may think that young children will not be able to cope with such difficult issues. Very young children may need complex ideas and situations to be simplified, but they can learn to question and interpret from a younger age than adults tend to think and are constantly developing their identities, values and beliefs. Older children in Key Stage 2 can cope with and enjoy addressing complex and controversial issues and often show startling insights. How teachers can help them to do so is discussed below.

One of the most cogent arguments for the humanities is that they help children to understand and empathise with people who are different and those who are similar (see Nussbaum, 2010). Understanding one's own and different cultures and societies is essential in a globalised world. Being exposed to accurate information and expected to discuss and justify one's views can help to challenge and alter children's stereotypical views and behaviour and enable them to become more humane and compassionate.

The active ways of working such as fieldwork and observation help to engage most children. While the formal curriculum may determine much of the content of what teachers are expected to teach, teachers have some flexibility is deciding whose history and geography to choose and which aspects of Religious Education to focus on. For instance, studying the migration of different ethnic groups may help engage children, especially in diverse communities where they and their families have experienced this. Discussing what religious commitment involves enables children to understand that religions are not homogeneous. In addition, children from a background of faith are helped to understand their own and other people's religion better while others are helped to recognise what religious commitment involves in a world where this is often a source of both motivation and conflict. Such areas of study and ways of working help to motivate many children who are disengaged from more passive, 'academic' types of school learning, especially when what is taught does not reflect their own experience or interests.

Figure 7.2   Engaging in practical observation activities increases children's motivation to learn

The approach set out above enables children to recognise that many questions do not have simple answers and that people may understand the same situation in very different ways, depending on their cultural assumptions. Working in this way helps children's understanding to become more nuanced and can help to counter stereotypes and prevent them developing extremist views.

How do the humanities fit into the primary curriculum?

Consider the following statement from the Government White Paper in 1985.

THEORY FOCUS

Many children are still given too little opportunity for work in practical, scientific and aesthetic areas of the curriculum which increases not only their understanding in these areas but also their literacy and numeracy . . . Over-concentration on the practice of the basic skills in literacy and numeracy unrelated to a context in which they are needed means that those skills are insufficiently extended and applied.

(Cited in Alexander, 2010: 243)

This situation has probably got worse since 1985 with the current emphasis on literacy and numeracy skills taught out of context. This raises the question of how teachers can provide a meaningful context for children to learn such skills and whether the humanities can contribute to this.

REFLECTION

How does children's learning in the humanities relate to other areas of learning, especially literacy and numeracy?

Teaching the humanities is not just about transmitting factual knowledge and covering the formal curriculum in History, Geography and RE. It involves children enquiring and interpreting situations, preferably ones that are meaningful to them.

Let us explore how one might go about teaching the humanities and embedding this in a broad and balanced curriculum by considering this case study.

CASE STUDY

A group of seven and eight year olds are doing a local study of the area around their school. They go out observing, making notes and drawing. Among the buildings they see are a church, a community centre and a mosque. Among the shops are ones that have been there for many years and some which have just opened. Subsequently they create maps and models and discuss and read about how the area has changed in the last few years. Some interview their parents and grandparents. The whole class makes a presentation, involving a song that they have composed, a short play they have written and models they have constructed.

This type of project helps children to understand themselves and their families in relation to the community in which they live. The children participate a wide range of different activities which cross subject boundaries, undertake fieldwork, ask questions, develop concepts related to history,

Geography and RE, and explore identities, values and beliefs, their own and others. The children are enabled to understand concepts such as how people and places change over time and how identities and cultures affect people's beliefs and practices, drawing on their own and their families' experience. They also use and develop knowledge and skills associated with literacy, including interviewing people, reading and learning in other subject areas such as design, architecture, music and drama. In doing so, they work together using a wide range of skills and understand more deeply how people live now and have lived.

This case study shows how the children learned about their local community with the teacher trying to ensure that children were not constrained by subject boundaries, while learning the knowledge and ways of working associated with different subjects, or disciplines. The learning was embedded in a meaningful local context. This matters especially for young children, as they find abstract thinking more difficult than do adults. However, let us consider another example with a group of older children.

CASE STUDY

A visitor watches a history lesson with a class of 11 year olds about the aftermath of the Second World War in Germany as a part of a topic on the impact of war on societies. The teacher introduces the lesson with a story about how a particular family was affected. The children are encouraged to talk and write in relatively short bursts to keep some with a low attention span involved. At one point, the class is divided by a rope representing the Berlin Wall to help them understand what it might feel like to be separated from friends. The children debate, role-play, write, draw and think, so that the session proves to be more than just a history lesson.

Figure 7.3 Journey to hope: capture children's learning about the Second World War through creative displays

Is this the only way to teach the humanities?

There is no one way of teaching the humanities successfully. Sometimes a lesson within a specific subject area may be appropriate, but it is important to be prepared to cross subject boundaries. Sometimes, a cross-curricular project may work better, over time, but children must be introduced to, and use, the knowledge, concepts and skills associated with different disciplines, especially towards the older end of Key Stage 2. But this case study illustrates some tools which teachers may use to engage children with a topic outside their immediate experience.

Stories are often one of the best ways of introducing complex ideas about people and how they feel, think and interact with other people and the world around them. Similarly, literature provides an accessible way for children to learn how other people feel and respond in situations which may be familiar or in a completely different world. And drama is a particularly powerful way of understanding one's own feelings, what it is like to be someone from another time, society or faith, and how people who are different from oneself may feel – as well as building children's sensitivity and empathy and so helping to undermine stereotypes. In doing so, it is usually best to start by looking for and emphasising similarities if one is not to overemphasise difference.

Discussion of issues related to how humans act and interact, often controversial, is an essential part of a good humanities education, preferably with the children doing most of the talking and asking most of the questions and the teacher guiding the discussion. Philosophy for Children (P4C) provides one good basis for children learning ways of thinking together and listening and responding to and challenging other views in a thoughtful and respectful way. While it may be used as a separate lesson, especially at first, P4C is most effective when these ways of working are adopted in discussion in all aspects of the curriculum.

What are the implications for the teacher's role?

The case study also indicates how children are expected to act, draw and write their thoughts so using a range of ways of representing experiences which makes it more likely that the historical concepts are embedded. Part of the teacher's skill is to decide when to change activities so that the children remain interested, while also giving time and space for enquiry and reflection. This raises the following question.

REFLECTION

How much should one allow children to explore for themselves and how much should the teacher structure activities?

Both case studies above indicate that the teacher ensured that the children maintained their curiosity and a sense of agency. Children are naturally curious until they learn not to ask. It is important for teachers to encourage children's questions and follow children's lines of enquiry, at least to some extent – to be *enabling, enhancing and empowering* in Catling's (2003) words. This highlights the importance of pedagogy – and how teachers make the judgements which enable children's learning to become deeply embedded.

THEORY FOCUS

Discovery provides a large problem space; expository teaching a more delimited one. Each has its risks. Too large a problem space and a child may never hit on a solution; define it too narrowly and a student may simply memorize a solution.

(Olson, 2001: 113)

Olson's ideas suggest to me that, rather than seeing themselves mainly as instructors, the teacher's role is to provide a structure and environment which encourages and enables children to enquire. For instance, teachers need not talk too much, but ask questions which encourage children to think and understand that there are other ways in which they can interpret their experience.

Teaching in this way can be hard for the teacher, but it is important that children learn to work in this way if they are to become confident in thinking about difficult issues. Enquiry-based learning can lead teachers into areas which they may not be familiar with and about which they may not be very knowledgeable. Children may ask questions that teachers can't, or are unwilling to, answer. Even very young children ask profound questions which adults may not be able to answer – such as why people look different and where God came from. And older children may raise controversial issues such as those to do with racism or religion.

Teachers are often wary of raising complex and contested questions with young children. Inexperienced teachers need to be careful about how they introduce and discuss these but this is not a good reason to avoid them. And addressing such issues often engages children's interests and can be one of the most fulfilling aspects of being a primary teacher.

Of course, teachers require a sound basis of knowledge about History, Geography and Religious Education if they are to teach these successfully, and especially if they are to help older primary children understand and discuss difficult and controversial issues. But being able to structure such knowledge in ways that children will find comprehensible and engaging is key. Qualities such as enthusiasm, open-mindedness and flexibility are often more important than a great depth of subject knowledge if children are to be enabled to enquire for themselves. And it may take a long time to create the relationships and the environment where children feel able to work in the ways discussed above and where teachers feel confident enough to empower them to do so.

How should one approach planning and assessment?

---- **REFLECTION** ----

What are the implications for teachers' planning and assessment?

Adopting an enquiry-based approach means that teachers must plan carefully but flexibly, so that they can structure the activity, but be prepared to exercise *disciplined improvisation* (Sawyer, 2004: 13) and judgement. Lessons must be planned not to cover too much content and time and space must be set aside for questions, reflection and discussion.

While teachers have to know what they hope to achieve, learning objectives must be fairly broad and not too tightly defined, as otherwise they may constrain curiosity and enquiry. Teachers must also think carefully about how children are grouped, with groups which are mixed in terms of background and ability often helping to bring a range of perspectives and skills, which will not happen if all the children have similar backgrounds and viewpoints.

Much of what has been discussed cannot easily be tested, but this does not mean that children's achievement and progress cannot be assessed. For instance, a portfolio of work can be both a source of pride and help children, parents/carers and teachers see progress over time, and the education of the whole child entails assessing children's attributes and qualities, not just the facts they have been able to memorise.

---- **CHAPTER SUMMARY** ----

This chapter has suggested that the humanities are an essential part of the education of the whole child and a broad and balanced curriculum. It has encouraged you to think more in terms of what the humanities can help you to achieve from the point of view of children's identity, values and beliefs rather than as subjects where the main emphasis is on factual knowledge. The ways of working and thinking, such as enquiry, observation and interpretation, and critical thinking skills, are particularly important in a complex and changing world. Such ways of working are engaging for most children, but especially many of those disengaged from school learning. Young children need to be able to cross subject boundaries, but also learn the knowledge, concepts and skills associated with specific disciplines. Teaching in this way requires time and space and can be hard with a very full curriculum and intense pressure on children to score highly in tests. It entails careful but flexible planning and assessing children through their work and approach over time rather than just through tests.

KEY POINTS TO CONSIDER

- 'The humanities' stretch across subject boundaries, including History, Geography and Religious Education, but also other areas related to human culture, such as citizenship, literature and drama.
- The humanities are to do with ways of working and interpreting how people in different eras and cultures think and act.
- The humanities (and the arts) are often marginalised in a curriculum dominated by literacy and numeracy.
- Finding the time and space to help children engage with complex ideas is not easy but is very important if they are to become active, thoughtful and well-rounded citizens.

Further reading

Eaude, T. (2017) Humanities in the primary school – philosophical considerations. *Education 3–13*, 45 (3): 343–53.

An article which discusses many of the ideas in this chapter, especially what the humanities 'are' and what they 'do' in relation to young children.

Grigg, R. and Hughes, S. (2013) *Teaching Primary Humanities*. Harlow: Pearson.

A detailed guide to teaching History, Geography and Religious Education in primary schools which is practical but takes account of the complexity of the issues involved.

Pickford, T., Garner, W. and Jackson, E. (2013) *Primary Humanities: Learning through Enquiry*. London: Sage.

A simple practical book about enquiry-based learning and the implications for teaching in History and Geography.

References

Alexander, R. (ed.) (2010) *Children, Their World, Their Education*. Abingdon: Routledge.

Bailin, S., Case, R., Coombs, J. R. and Daniels, L. B. (1999) Common misconceptions of critical thinking. *Journal of Curriculum Studies*, 31 (93): 269–83.

Catling, S. (2003) Curriculum contested: Primary geography and social justice *Geography, 88* (3): 164–210.

Eaude, T. (2018) Addressing the needs of the whole child: implications for young children and adults who care for them. *International Handbook of Holistic Education*. Abingdon: Routledge, pp. 61–9.

Eaude, T., Butt, G., Catling, S. and Vass, P. (2017) The future of the humanities in primary schools – reflections in troubled times. *Education 3–13, 45* (3): 386–95.

Nussbaum, **M.** (2010) *Not for Profit: Why Democracy Needs the Humanities*. Princeton, NJ: Princeton University Press.

Nussbaum, **M.** (2017) Martha C. Nussbaum talks about the humanities, mythmaking and international development. *Humanities*, *38* (2): 4.

Olson, **D.R.** (2001) Education – the bridge from culture to mind. In D. Bakhurst and S. G. Shanker (eds), *Jerome Bruner: Language, Culture, Self*. London: Sage, pp. 104–15.

Sawyer, **R.K.** (2004) Creative teaching: collaborative discussion as disciplined improvisation. *Educational Researcher*, *33* (2): 12–20.

Small, **H.** (2013) *The Value of the Humanities*. Oxford: Oxford University Press.

8

DRAWING INSPIRATION FROM CHILDREN'S VISUAL CULTURE

ROBERT WATTS

IT IS NOT LIKELY THAT I SHALL CARRY GENERAL AGREEMENT ON THE PURPOSE I ASCRIBE TO EDUCATION, FOR HERE THERE ARE AT LEAST TWO IRRECONCILABLE POSSIBILITIES: ONE, THAT MAN SHOULD BE EDUCATED TO BECOME WHAT HE IS; THE OTHER, THAT HE SHOULD BE EDUCATED TO BECOME WHAT HE IS NOT.

(HERBERT READ, EDUCATION THROUGH ART, 1943)

KEYWORDS: ART EDUCATION; VISUAL CULTURE; IMAGES; CINEMA; TELEVISION; COMPUTER GAMES.

───── CHAPTER OBJECTIVES ─────

This chapter

- explores notions of visual culture and its relationship to art education
- reviews the range of images children currently encounter in school and at home
- provides ideas for learning experiences that draw inspiration from children's visual culture.
- offers a rationale for teachers to draw on children's visual culture in order to motivate learning in art and across the curriculum

Introduction

The scene is a traditional English classroom. Light streams through tall windows onto panelled walls as uniformed boys take turns to read aloud from their books. The teacher, an elderly man seated at his desk, is unaccountably irritated by the pace of the lesson and rapidly asks one boy, then another to continue reading before he impatiently assumes the task himself. He stumbles over several simple words, pauses and looks up. 'Shall we watch the video?' he asks the boys. 'We'll watch the video.'

Readers who remember *Little Britain* will recognise this scene. It's a sketch from the television series in which Mr Cleaves, played by Matt Lucas, finds various ways to illustrate both his incompetence as a teacher and his indifference to his pupils. In this instance, the comedy lies in the notion that he should consider a filmed adaptation of a novel to have the same educational value as the novel itself. As viewers we appreciate that the commitment required of us to engage with a book may be far greater than that demanded by a film or TV programme. It might take us several weeks to complete a novel, compared with a couple of hours slumped on the sofa in front of *Netflix*. Moreover, we believe there is less to learn from watching the movie. We miss out on the author's use of language, their attention to detail, their description of characters' internal lives. We laugh at Mr Cleaves because we know that real teachers would never say *we'll watch the video*, because time spent watching screens is time wasted.

Or is it? This chapter invites teachers who aspire to provide a broad and balanced curriculum to draw inspiration from children's visual culture. In recent years digital technologies have significantly broadened the range of visual material available to children, enabling them to access a rich and diverse variety of cinema, television and other media. However, the ways that children typically engage with this material – often alone, on hand-held devices and at random times – means that what were once shared, communal experiences are now individual and often isolated. Children engage with more visual material than ever before but rarely share their responses to it. Furthermore, there is little evidence to suggest that teachers either recognise the educational potential of this material or take advantage of opportunities to incorporate it into their teaching.

This chapter argues that, by embracing the richness and diversity of children's visual culture, teachers could raise their pupils' levels of engagement in their learning as well as their levels of attainment, not only in visually orientated subjects such as art and design, but also across the whole curriculum.

Visual culture – what is it?

The term 'visual culture' emerged during the 1990s in the work of authors who questioned traditional boundaries between art and popular culture (e.g. Walker and Chaplin 1997). It was first explored in an educational context in the 2000s, when several US authors sought to define visual culture in ways that emphasised an inclusive approach towards images. Freedman (2003), for example, proposed that visual culture *provides context for the visual arts and points to the connections between popular and fine arts forms* (2003: 1), while Amburguy (2003) conceived it as *a way of calling attention to visual qualities as important components of cultural practices* (2003: 45). In other words, while art remained a significant part of visual culture, other sources of images such as the cinema, television, computer games and even advertisements were also worthy of attention. These authors argued that, although images drawn from such sources may lack the status afforded to works of art, the extent to which they were woven into people's everyday lives lent them a similar significance.

Given that authors have written about visual culture for two decades, why should it now form a focus for teachers aiming to provide a broad and balanced curriculum? There are several reasons. Firstly, new technologies have revolutionised the ways that children engage with visual culture. Recent research shows almost three-quarters of 11 year olds own smartphones with cameras, while half share images on Facebook, Instagram or Snapchat and 90 per cent regularly access images online (Statista, 2017; Graham, 2016; Ofcom, 2016). Secondly, the traditional image of family members clustered around a television is outdated, as children increasingly view programmes alone. A recent report on children's media use concluded that children now watch one-third less broadcast television than they did in 2010 and are more likely to 'binge-watch' television series, often viewing alone on tablets, phones and other devices (Ofcom, 2017). Thirdly, in a reaction against the test-driven culture of primary schools, teachers are growing more aware of the role of pedagogical approaches that value children's perspectives such as *Philosophy for Children* (Fisher, 2013), while researchers of children's experiences have increasingly adopted child-centred methodologies intent on foregrounding children's perspectives on matters affecting them (Greig *et al.*, 2007; Kellett, 2010). New technologies mean that children's visual culture plays an increasingly significant part in their lives – and it makes increasing sense to make it a part of their experience in school.

REFLECTION

What are your perceptions of how children's visual culture is changing?

What childhood memories do you have of your own visual culture?

How did these experiences of visual culture influence your development?

What kinds of images do children encounter in school?

If we were to return for a moment to Mr Cleaves' antiquated classroom, we would notice its walls feature little in the way of displays. In contrast, creating displays of children's work is a well-established practice in primary schools (Hodgson, 1988), and today's teachers widely recognise the value of providing stimulating visual environments (Bryce-Clegg, 2014). Children also encounter images in picture books from an early age and are often highly skilled at interpreting meanings from images. Arizpe and Styles (2003), for example, describe how children notice complex details of illustrations and use their observations to deepen their understanding of the meanings of a text. The role of artists' work in primary schools is a little more complex, however, and it is useful to reflect briefly on the ways in which children encounter it.

As long ago as the 1940s, teachers were able to introduce their pupils to contemporary artworks, thanks to the School Prints initiative (Gooding, 1980). The project aimed to provide children with access to 'real' works of art, in the form of a series of lithographs by leading British and European artists of the time, including Picasso, Matisse and Lowry. Herbert Read helped to commission the artists and, despite post-war austerity, hundreds of schools bought prints to display in classrooms. The Arts Council was formed at around the same time, amid a growing conviction that art was for everyone, not just a gallery-going elite. We can only imagine children's responses to the School Prints, which were almost certainly unlike anything they had seen before. Very few would have had artworks in their homes and even fewer would have visited galleries; illustrated books were still relatively rare and televisions rarer still. The significance of the School Prints project is that it marks the beginning of the belief that teachers should be responsible for broadening children's experience of art and visual culture.

The presence of artists' work in primary classrooms grew stronger in the 1990s, when the National Curriculum for art and design identified 'knowledge and understanding' as an attainment target alongside 'investigating and making' (DES, 1991). The curriculum proposed that children should make connections between their own and artists' work and prompted teachers to draw inspiration from a range of artists, craftspeople and designers from diverse cultures. In practice, however, teachers were inclined to plan lessons based upon a narrow range of work by white, male, European artists from the late nineteenth and early twentieth centuries such as Monet and Van Gogh (Downing and Watson, 2004). In a parallel movement, museums and galleries developed educational programmes designed to make their collections accessible to children.

What links these initiatives is that each is underpinned by an implicit belief that children should value certain aspects of visual culture in much the same way that adults do. When asked to explain the meaning of the lithograph he created for School Prints, Picasso said: *The children will understand*. While this response reflects Picasso's belief that children have an instinctive appetite for art, it fails to take account of the problem that many children find it difficult to appreciate artists' work. Artists make art for many reasons, but rarely to please children. Whereas children's authors and illustrators create stories and images designed to entertain their young audiences, artists are rarely concerned whether children will appreciate their work. This presents teachers with the problem of finding strategies to raise levels of engagement with artworks, and many succeed, as evidenced by the annual *Take One Picture* exhibition of children's work at the National Gallery. Nonetheless, it remains a challenge for teachers.

REFLECTION

What images have you chosen to support learning in your own classroom?

What opportunities did children have to respond to these images?

Why do teachers sometimes prioritise artworks over other images?

What kinds of images do children encounter at home?

New technologies have not only changed the ways in which children encounter images but have also provided them with access to a more diverse range of visual material. While the recent shift in their viewing behaviour does not necessarily mean that children's tastes or interests have changed significantly, it poses challenges both for parents wanting to monitor their offspring's viewing habits and for educators aiming to understand children's experiences. The increased affordability of smartphones and tablets means children are more likely to be watching their own screens without adult supervision. In this context, it is understandable that much of the recent research into children's media use has focused on issues surrounding its impact on children's mental health and online safety (e.g., Zilka, 2017) rather than on its potential for learning.

My own interest in children's visual preferences developed from a study I carried out in which I asked 50 children aged 10–11 to find and photograph images they thought were beautiful (Watts, 2018). When children shared images during group interviews, I was surprised not only by the diversity of the subject matter but also by their ability to analyse and reflect upon their preferences. Images, it seemed, were important to children; they helped them to articulate their perceptions of the world and their understanding of their experiences.

My research was helped by the fact that builders had recently demolished a wall in our house. The re-design meant that a journey from the stairs to the kitchen that had hitherto taken me past the living room door now involved a walk through an open-plan space. Whereas previously I had only overheard muffled sounds of the TV programmes and computer games my children watched and played, I now regularly caught glimpses of them onscreen as I passed through the room. Some of the images were bewildering, some banal – but others were more distracting. Certain scenes were striking.

The demolition of the wall began to take on a somewhat symbolic significance as I began to realise that there was more to children's visual culture than I had previously acknowledged. I knew the movies they watched were often funny, exciting and entertaining, but I found I had underestimated their depth, diversity and visual complexity. Curiously, aspects of their most striking scenes were strangely familiar. Some reminded me of paintings.

The following section of this chapter explores three examples of images drawn from children's visual culture and explores how each offers teachers a starting point from which to explore children's knowledge and understanding. The images are drawn from the cinema, a computer game and a TV programme, and each depicts figures engaging (or hidden) in landscapes. Each image is accompanied by a painting with similar visual and atmospheric qualities. It might seem like an unlikely journey, but a lesson that begins by talking about *Toy Story* can conclude with a story from the Old Testament, another that begins with screenshots from the online game *Fortnite* can evoke a romantic landscape by Samuel Palmer, while a lesson inspired by the mysterious world of *Stranger Things* can be enriched by looking at Peter Doig's atmospheric paintings of mysterious landscapes. In each case, teachers can say to children: *We want to hear what you have to say about the images that intrigue you – and then perhaps* you'll *be interested in some of the images that intrigue us!* Some will need little prompting to make connections and many will be surprised to learn how contemporary artists, illustrators and animators draw on a rich tradition of visual culture.

REFLECTION

What are your perceptions of the changing nature of children's media use?

What do children find engaging about images they encounter outside of school?

What do you remember about how images impacted on you as a child?

Raising levels of engagement through focusing on children's visual culture – three examples to explore in the classroom

Toy Story 3

Many readers will know that the idea underpinning the three *Toy Story* movies is that children's toys, once out of sight, spring into lives of their own. In the final part of the trilogy the toys' owner, Andy, is now 17 years old and leaving home for college. He packs away his toys – Woody, Buzz Lightyear, Mr Potato Head and others – in the loft, but a series of mishaps leads to them being thrown into a garbage truck and eventually dumped onto a conveyor belt headed for a huge incinerator (Figure 8.1).

The action freezes, the wisecracks dry up and, one by one, the expressions on their faces harden. In a gesture suggesting acceptance of their fate, the toys slowly reach out to hold each other's hands. No two faces have quite the same expression. While some stare blankly into the abyss, others try to hide; Buzz Lightyear grits his teeth and looks towards Woody, whose eyes are wide open and mouth contorting in terror. By focusing on a single frame, children will see how beautifully the scene is drawn.

Figure 8.1   Toy Story 3. Disney/Pixar. **https://toystory.disney.com/**

It's a sobering scene for adults, let alone nine year olds. Like much contemporary children's cinema, *Toy Story 3* is layered with material intended to appeal to viewers of various ages. Humour, obviously, plays a key part, with some jokes squarely aimed at children and others knowingly targeted at adults, but the visual depths of the movie also resonate with young and old. Much of the emotional punch of the movie lies in its unsentimental depiction of the outmoded, unwanted toys, but the 'incinerator' scene taps in to a deeper, almost primal instinct. Children won't need you to tell them that this is terrifying stuff.

Begin by watching the scene together or looking at online images of it. Watch it again, this time without the sound – removing the dialogue, music and sound effects will help children focus their attention on its visual qualities. Freeze-frame the scene and ask the children to describe what they see. Remain receptive to a range of responses to the image but listen for those that allude to three aspects: character, colour and composition. When these themes arise, question children closely about them. Try to vary your language according to children's ages and abilities – ask each question twice, once using complex language, then again in simpler terms:

How did the designers succeed in making the scene so frightening?

(Why is this part of the film so scary?)

Can you describe how each character's expression reflects their feelings?

(How do the faces look different?)

How does the use of colour affect the mood of the image?

(How do the colours make you feel?)

Do the figures dominate the composition? Why not?

(Do the toys look big or small in the picture?)

Encourage children to think beyond the image and reflect on the deeper meanings it evokes. Several interesting themes arise from the image (and the movie) that children could explore through discussion: friendship, the passing of time, what is real and not real. Children might appreciate, for example, that the toys are *not* real but that the depiction of their relationships *is* realistic.

Once children have explored the plight of Woody and friends – they survive the scene, by the way – you might find they are ready to engage with work by artists who use different techniques to achieve similar effects. At two metres across, John Martin's painting *The Destruction of Sodom and Gomorrah* (Figure 8.2) looms over visitors to the National Gallery like a huge cinema screen.

Figure 8.2   John Martin (1789–1854), The Destruction of Sodom and Gomorrah (1852), oil on canvas, 136.3 x 212.3 cm, Laing Art Gallery, Newcastle upon Tyne, England. Wikimedia Commons.
https://commons.wikimedia.org/wiki/File:John_Martin_-_Sodom_and_Gomorrah.jpg

Martin's depiction of a storm raining down from Heaven anticipates the apocalyptic scenario depicted a century and a half later in *Toy Story*. Can children imagine the effect the painting had on viewers when it was first exhibited? Look closely at the painting, which depicts God's punishment for the immorality of the people of Sodom and Gomorrah, and you'll see the only survivors, Lot and his daughters, escaping the destruction. Look even closer and you'll see a bolt of lightning headed for Lot's wife, she who ignored God's warning not to turn to look at the scene and was turned into a pillar of salt. Happy endings, children will learn, were harder to come by in those days.

Fortnite

Few things date faster than new technologies and, by the time the ink dried on the page you are now reading, or the pixels appeared on your screen, the online battle game *Fortnite* may be a distant memory. At the time of writing in 2018, however, it is a constant presence in children's visual culture. Parents, educators and media commentators all express concern at the exponential growth of *Fortnite*, with player numbers rising from one million in August 2017 to 125 million by June 2018 (Statista, 2018a). They argue that the game is addictive, aggressive and can be disruptive to children's learning. As such, the idea that teachers might draw inspiration from *Fortnite* is, it must be said, contentious. However, while the game could be seen as the latest in a long line of boy-toys, figures from the US (Statista, 2018b) reveal, surprisingly, that a quarter of users are female, and the huge popularity of *Fortnite* means teachers should be curious about its appeal. Some might consider exploring ways of incorporating some of the visual aspects of the game into their teaching.

Fortnite is set on an island. One hundred online players parachute avatars on to the island, knowing only one will survive. A storm gradually descends, drawing players into an ever-decreasing circle of activity and tension builds as they conceal themselves in derelict buildings, gathering weapons and anticipating attacks. The visual environment of *Fortnite* is compelling. The scene illustrated below (Figure 8.3) is aesthetically pleasing, yet there is a sense of imminent danger lurking within the moonlit landscape.

Figure 8.3   Fortnite. Epic Games. https://www.epicgames.com/fortnite/en-US/home

And while the threat that faced Woody and his friends in *Toy Story 3* was apparent and imminent, the danger that lurks within and beyond this image – the abandoned car, the neglected house and the silhouetted trees – is subtler and more unsettling. We can anticipate scaling the hill, descending into the valley, conscious of what might lie in wait for us. The game's designers have heightened the sense of drama with a limited palette of deep blues, greens and purples, while the bright moon illuminates some surfaces as others are plunged into shadow.

A child playing *Fortnite* would *see* each of these things but might not consciously *notice* them. However, by isolating a single image from the rapid action of the game, we can encourage children to pause and reflect on its qualities, in the way we might lead them through a gallery of a hundred paintings before pausing to really *look* at one. Curiously, aspects of the *Fortnite* environment evoke certain genres of painting. Samuel Palmer was a Victorian artist whose work captured the essence of the English countryside, instilling it with a gentle, spiritual dimension, and *The Lonely Tower* (Figure 8.4) is a beautiful depiction of a moonlit landscape, with trees and hills silhouetted against a soft evening sky.

Figure 8.4   Samuel Palmer (1805–81), The Lonely Tower (c.1880–1), watercolour, 16.5 × 23.5 cm, Huntington Library, San Marino, California, USA. **https://www.the-athenaeum.org/art/detail.php?ID=243872**

While the quiet, reflective atmosphere of the painting is far more reassuring than the *Fortnite* environment, the pictorial devices Palmer employs to communicate his vision – the composition, the silhouettes, the moonlight – are strangely similar to those used by the game's designers. One significant difference, however, is that Palmer has included in his painting a number of figures, people who appear to integrate harmoniously with the landscape. If *Fortnite* is war, then *The Lonely Tower* is peace.

A second screenshot of *Fortnite* (Figure 8.5) illustrates its connection with another artistic tradition.

*Figure 8.5 Fortnite. Epic Games. **https://www.epicgames.com/fortnite/en-US/home***

*Figure 8.6 Caspar David Friedrich (1774–1840), Wanderer above the Sea of Fog (1818), oil on canvas, 94.8 x 74.8 cm, Kunsthalle Hamburg, Germany. Wikimedia Commons. **https://en.wikipedia.org/wiki/ Caspar_David_Friedrich#/media/File:Caspar_David_Friedrich_-_Wanderer_above_the_sea_of_fog.jpg***

In the eighteenth century a number of painters, writers and philosophers began to reappraise the appeal of vast, uninhabited, mountainous landscapes of the kind depicted in the game. The term 'beauty', they argued, did not do justice to such landscapes, and instead they conceptualised them as *sublime*. Caspar David Friedrich's painting *Wanderer in a Sea of Fog* (Figure 8.6) perfectly encapsulates the notion of the sublime.

Its mountains and diminishing clouds evoke a sense of infinite space, while the lone figure who has scaled one peak now stares across at the next and beyond into the distance. While Friedrich encourages us to imagine what it would feel like to *be there*, we are simultaneously relieved that it is the wanderer, and not *us*, in the landscape.

Children will quickly notice the similarities between the painting and the *Fortnite* screenshot and, with a little prompting, they will recognise that the game's designers are drawing on artistic traditions that date back centuries. The hooded avatar stands, back to the viewer, staring out into the hostile landscape. Mountains fade into the mist, creating a sense of infinity. The landscape falls away to each side, exaggerating the curve of the earth's surface – it's as if we are floating in a dreamlike state above the scene. While warm colours often create a welcoming atmosphere, the hues of this landscape are scorched, creating a sense that time is running out, not only for the hooded figure but also for the planet itself. This might be the most sinister sunset children will ever see.

Conclusion: drawing inspiration from children's visual culture

In a recent (2018) interview on BBC Radio 4's *Desert Island Discs* the Olympic diver Tom Daley described a happy childhood in which, when not plummeting ten metres into swimming pools, he often sat alone at a desk in his parents' garage, absorbed in drawing, painting and making things. Sadly, this image is increasingly unrepresentative of contemporary childhood. Children are now primarily consumers, not creators. The range of images accessible to them via the click of a mouse, the swipe of a screen or the flick of a TV remote is almost endless and, for much of the time, images are a distraction rather than an inspiration. As teacher Kevin Jones recently observed, *Images flow at our children like never before. They need to learn to read and interrogate the visual world, to find space to see feelingly and with wonder, to contact and reflect* (2015: 25). Jones identifies a key challenge facing primary teachers. But by embracing children's visual culture, teachers can grasp new opportunities to help children to 'see feelingly' – to be *absorbed* by images.

Whichever curriculum area we teach, we want children to be absorbed, like the young Tom Daley in his garage. We want them to be immersed in their learning, to use their imagination, to think new thoughts. It is widely recognised that a key characteristic of successful learners is that they make connections between different experiences, and as teachers we should look for connections rather than contrasts between different forms of visual culture. When we look at a painting in the National Gallery we don't simply switch on the part of our brain labelled 'Seventeenth-Century Dutch Masters' – we place the experience in the context of a broader range of experiences that might help us to empathise with the people it depicts or admire the skill of the artist or appreciate the beauty of the subject. Similarly, we need to understand more about what children find engaging and absorbing outside of the classroom and offer experiences that connect with their interests. We should provide children with opportunities to articulate responses to their visual culture – and to understand that the artists, illustrators and designers who create the images they love are often inspired by art of the past.

Let's conclude with one last visit to Mr Cleaves' classroom. *That boy at the back. Yes you! What's that you're hiding under the desk?* What else could it be but an early artefact of children's visual culture – a copy of *The Beano*. In the 1950s the comic sold two million copies every week, providing a generation of children with a shared experience that helped them to define themselves in relation to their peers and, to use a phrase of the time, their 'betters'. *The Beano* represented the classroom as a battlefield, one centred around conflict between the apparently irreconcilable priorities of teachers and pupils. Clearly, teachers of the time were less interested in Herbert Read's notion that they should educate their pupils *to become what they are* and more interested in educating them *to become what they are not.* They had narrow-minded expectations of how their pupils should succeed, strongly-held convictions about the need for conformity – and a total lack of interest in understanding what really motivated children.

Today teachers have a greater awareness of the value of child-centred approaches to teaching, of individual styles of learning and of children's diverse needs. But those who aspire to provide a broad and balanced curriculum should also create opportunities for children to explore, share and articulate responses to their own cultural experiences. By paying attention to children's perspectives we show them that we want to understand what engages, inspires and motivates them. A focus on children's visual culture offers an accessible, valuable way of providing a broader, more balanced curriculum in primary schools and reflects a genuinely child-centred approach to teaching and learning.

CHAPTER SUMMARY

- New technologies mean that children's visual culture plays an increasingly significant part in their lives.
- Children are interested in looking at visual images in a range of contexts other than 'real' art – while the creators of these images often draw inspiration from artists' work.
- Teachers should use images from children's visual culture to inspire their learning in art and design and across the primary curriculum.

Further reading

Eisner, E. (2002) *The Arts and the Creation of Mind*. New Haven, CT: Yale University Press.

A great starting point for reflecting on the purposes of art and the nature of creativity

Fisher, R. (2012) *Teaching Thinking: Philosophical Enquiry in the Classroom*. London: Continuum.

An inspirational text for teachers intent on helping children to articulate their thoughts through discussion.

Pipes, A. (2008) *Foundations of Art and Design*. London: Laurence King.

An original and insightful book that draws intriguing connections between the qualities of a diverse range of visual images.

References

Amburgy, P.M. (2003) Visual culture as cultural stories (three approaches to teaching visual culture in K-12 school contexts). *Art Education, 56*: 44–7.

Arizpe, E. and Styles, M. (2003) A gorilla with 'grandpa's eyes': how children interpret ironic visual texts. In E. Arizpe, E. and M. Styles (eds), *Children Reading Pictures: Interpreting Visual Texts*. Oxford: Routledge Falmer pp. 77–96.

Bryce-Clegg, A. (2014) *Early Years Display: Hundreds of Ideas for Displays which Actively Involve Children*. London: Featherstone Education.

Department of Education and Science (DES) (1991) *National Curriculum: Art for Ages 5 to 14*. London: HMSO.

Desert Island Discs (2018) (radio). BBC Radio 4, 5 October, 9:00. **https://www.bbc.co.uk/programmes/b0blhfpj**

Downing, D. and Watson, R. (2004) *School Art: What's in It?: Exploring Visual Arts in Secondary Schools*. London: National Foundation for Educational Research.

Duncum, P. (2002) Visual culture art education: why, what and how. *International Journal of Art & Design Education, 21* (1), pp.14-23.

Fisher, R. (2013) *Teaching Thinking: Philosophical Enquiry in the Classroom* (4th Edition). London: A&C Black.

Freedman, K. (2003) *Teaching Visual Culture: Curriculum, Aesthetics, and the Social Life of Art*. New York: Teachers College Press.

Gooding, M. (1980) The school prints. *Arts Review* July.

Graham, R. (2016) *Safer Internet Day 2016 – Staying Safe Online*. Available at: **www.comresglobal.com/safer-internet-day-2016-staying-safe-online** (accessed 5 October 2018).

Greig, A., Taylor, J. and MacKay, T. (2007) *Doing Research with Children* (2nd edition). London: Sage.

Guardian, The (2018) *Editorial: The Guardian View on Contemporary Art in Schools: A Joyful Idea Reborn*, 14 January. Available at: **https://www.theguardian.com/commentisfree/2018/jan/14/the-guardian-view-on-contemporary-art-in-schools-a-joyful-idea-reborn** (accessed 5 October 2018).

Hale, L. and Guan, S. (2015) Screen time and sleep among school-aged children and adolescents: a systematic literature review. *Sleep Medicine Reviews, 21*: 50–8.

Hodgson, N. (1988) *Classroom Display: Improving the Visual Environment in Schools*. St Albans: Tarquin.

Jones, K. (2015) Opinion: learning from our children. *Tate Etc., 34*. Available at:**http://www.tate.org.uk/context-comment/articles/opinion-learning-our-children** (accessed 27 June 2017).

Kellett, M. (2010) *Rethinking Children and Research: Attitudes in Contemporary Society*. London: Bloomsbury.

Ofcom (Office of Communications) (2016) *Children and Parents: Media Use and Attitudes Report.* Available at: **https://www.ofcom.org.uk/__data/assets/pdf_file/0034/93976/Children-Parents-Media-Use-Attitudes-Report-2016.pdf** (accessed 5 October 2018).

Ofcom (Office of Communications) (2017) *Box Set Britain: UK's TV and Online Habits Revealed.* Available at: **https://www.ofcom.org.uk/about-ofcom/latest/media/media-releases/2017/box-set-britain-tv-online-habits** (accessed 5 October 2018).

Ogier, S. and Ghosh, K. (2018) Exploring student teachers' capacity for creativity through the interdisciplinary use of comics in the primary classroom. *Journal of Graphic Novels and Comics, 9* (4): 293–309.

Read, H. (1943) *Education Through Art.* London: Faber & Faber

Statista (2017) *Share of Children Owning Tablets and Smartphones in the United Kingdom from 2017, by Age.* Available at **https://www.statista.com/statistics/805397/children-ownership-of-tablets-smartphones-by-age-uk** (accessed 5 October 2018).

Statista (2018a) *Number of Players of Fortnite Worldwide from August 2017 to June 2018 (in millions).* Available at **https://www.statista.com/statistics/746230/fortnite-players/** (accessed 2 November 2018).

Statista (2018b) *Distribution of Players of Fortnite in the United States as of April 2018, by Gender.* Available at **https://www.statista.com/statistics/865625/fortnite-players-gender/** (accessed 2 November 2018).

Walker, J.A. and Chaplin, S. (1997) *Visual Culture: An Introduction.* Manchester: Manchester University Press.

Watts, R. (2018) A place for beauty in art education. *International Journal of Art and Design Education, 37* (1): 149–62.

Wyse, D. and McGarty, L. (2010) *The National Gallery Initial Teacher Education Cultural Placement Partnership: A Research Evaluation.* University of Cambridge, Faculty of Education. Available at: **https://www.repository.cam.ac.uk/bitstream/handle/1810/263274/National%20Gallery%20Initial%20Teacher%20Education%20Cultural%20Placement%20Partnership%20A%20Research%20Evaluation.pdf?sequence=1** (accessed 5 October 2018).

Zilka, G. C. (2017) Awareness of eSafety and potential online dangers among children and teenagers. *Journal of Information Technology Education: Research, 16*: 319–38.

9

WRITING AS AN ART FORM: AN AUTHOR'S PERSPECTIVE

MICHAEL ROSEN

THE WORLD IS TOO MUCH WITH US; LATE AND SOON,
GETTING AND SPENDING, WE LAY WASTE OUR POWERS;—
LITTLE WE SEE IN NATURE THAT IS OURS;
WE HAVE GIVEN OUR HEARTS AWAY, A SORDID BOON!
THIS SEA THAT BARES HER BOSOM TO THE MOON;
THE WINDS THAT WILL BE HOWLING AT ALL HOURS,
AND ARE UP-GATHERED NOW LIKE SLEEPING FLOWERS;
FOR THIS, FOR EVERYTHING, WE ARE OUT OF TUNE;
IT MOVES US NOT. GREAT GOD! I'D RATHER BE
A PAGAN SUCKLED IN A CREED OUTWORN;
SO MIGHT I, STANDING ON THIS PLEASANT LEA,
HAVE GLIMPSES THAT WOULD MAKE ME LESS FORLORN;
HAVE SIGHT OF PROTEUS RISING FROM THE SEA;
OR HEAR OLD TRITON BLOW HIS WREATHÈD HORN.

WILLIAM WORDSWORTH

KEYWORDS: CONTEMPLATION; REFLECTION; DAYDREAMING; IMAGINATION; PROSODY; RHYTHM.

CHAPTER OBJECTIVES

This chapter:

- offers a view of writing as an art form in itself, from the perspective of an author: to understand the creative processes that are essential for writing
- questions where does writing come from?
- supports teachers in developing imaginative approaches that encourage children's writing in the classroom: to provide a range of practical starting points for creative writing with pupils
- provides practical guidance for encouraging high-quality writing by creating a writing friendly environment
- provides a critical methodology through the 'five questions' approach

LINKS TO THE TEACHERS' STANDARDS

Working through this chapter will enable you to meet all of the Teachers' Standards, in particular:

TS 1: Establish high expectations which inspire, motivate and challenge pupils

TS 2: Promote good progress and outcomes by pupils

TS 3: Demonstrate good subject and curriculum knowledge

TS 5: Adapt teaching to respond to the strengths and needs of pupils

Introduction

This chapter explores what it is to be an author from the viewpoint of a writer. The current National Curriculum focuses very much on the technical language and functionality of English grammar which, while important, cannot be taught to the exclusion of application, creativity and joy of expression. In this chapter, we learn that, to an author, the writing process functions in much the same way as any artist operating in any medium might work – in this case the medium is words on the page. Author and wordsmith, Michael Rosen, provides an insight into this process, and shares his experience of working with children that enables creativity and originality in writing, as well as giving us some practical suggestions for classroom use. He gives away some of his secrets to help us consider how children might be enthused to write their own engaging texts. He helps us think about how we can encourage and inspire the next generation to be writers and authors, by acknowledging and experimenting with these ideas within our own practice.

Where does writing come from?

It's quite common for writers to be asked where their 'inspiration' comes from. The idea that the starting point for writing is a single moment of inspiration goes back at least as far as the Romantic poets, who were very keen on ideas to do with the imagination and nature (such as was the poet Coleridge for example), and people who they imagined were nearer to 'nature' than those who were dulled or damaged by *getting and spending*, as Wordsworth suggests in his classic poem. In this context, they were reacting to what they saw as the over-analytic approach of the Enlightenment, which had based its ideas on 'Reason'. Do you recognise this in relation to the current curriculum?

The challenge of this approach to creativity today, particularly in the context of education and the classroom, is that it can lead us into demanding of children some kind of 'magical moment' of inspiration for their own work, or that writing is something mystical. Some poets have contributed to this sense of mystery and have even written about it in rather beautiful ways, for example as in the poem by Ted Hughes, 'The Thought-Fox'. Read the poem here: **https://www.poetryarchive. org/poem/thought-fox**

Clearly, there's no harm, as such, with all this, and indeed some children may relish this idea of mystery and the sudden spark of an inspiration. From my own experience, I can say that there are times when I'm in *daydream* mode – that there is indeed what feels like a moment, when I feel I've landed on an idea, or a feeling, or a memory that may well contribute to a story or poem. That said, I'm not sure that I would describe it as either mysterious or as an inspiration. I prefer the idea that it is a *discovery* – more of a Eureka moment – and that the discovery has happened because I've gone *exploring*!

My keyword here, then, is *daydreaming*. Some people prefer 'reverie' or 'contemplation' or 'reflection'. These words describe that state of mind and sense of being when anyone in all walks of life thinks about themselves, what is going on around them now or in any part of their past. This can be a major source for writing. You won't find the word 'daydreaming' on any National Curriculum document though. Education in the present environment is, as we know, very tied to ideas around the quantities of 'knowledge' that must be taught (DfE, 2013), the number of hours per week pupils are receiving instruction, learning objectives and learning outcomes. Daydreaming doesn't, won't and can't figure in any matrix where such processes are being prioritised and measured, but it doesn't mean it's not important.

REFLECTION

How do you view 'daydreaming'?

Can we use pupils' daydreaming in our teaching?

I think, no matter what the regime, there is space for daydreaming, both in the arts and in the writing process. If time has been allocated for writing, then there can and should be time for daydreaming. As described in *What Is Poetry?* (Rosen, 2016), it is comparatively easy to be structured and even instructional (!) and still incorporate daydreaming.

Try this out: create a moment on a regular basis in class when the pupils are invited to daydream for 30 seconds or a minute, solo, perhaps eyes shut, in silence and then record as much of the 'stream of consciousness' (James, 1890) that they had just experienced. We can make clear that these notes do not have to be grammatical or be spelled or punctuated according to the demands of the National Curriculum (DfE, 2013). They are, we say, *private notes*. They don't have to be shared with anyone. They are, we add, the raw material for writing.

We further explain that these notes can be 'played' with. This is crucial. They are not for squeezing into prescribed forms. We invite the pupils to see what they can do with the notes. If this takes place in an environment in which pupils experience an ever-widening range of texts – stories, poems, drama, TV and film scripts, speeches, instructions, polemic, etc. – then I know from experience that the pupils will find forms using what Wolfgang Iser has called our 'repertoire' of texts that sit in our minds (Iser, 1978).

One crucial point here is that, while playing this kind of writing-game, pupils experience the power of transformation that they possess. We all possess it. We don't all formalise it and 'catch' it in writing, but in education we should have time and space to realise this.

The found word

Just as the artist Marcel Duchamp introduced us to the 'ready-made' in 1913, by combining a bicycle wheel and a stool to create a sculpture, another way to look at writing is to see it as the critic Roland Barthes did in *S/Z* (1974), which is that we write with what he called the 'already'. He meant that any form of writing uses and assembles and reassembles hundreds and thousands of sounds, words, motifs, symbols, plot-lines, ideas, language from what has 'already' been written. This is of course a very unromantic way of looking at writing. It makes writers sound like people working in a junk shop, assembling bits of second-hand junk! But in a way, I think he's right, it is in the same tradition that an artist might use the *found object* to make a new piece of art. Hardly anything on the page you're reading right now is 'original'. And even if I made up an expression or word like 'flop-hopping' or 'mimm-wock', you could piece together the sounds I'm borrowing to make up these words and even, as with Lewis Carroll's 'Jabberwocky' as an example, make suggestions as to what they might mean. You would be using your 'already' to work this out.

REFLECTION

How might you use this rich idea with your pupils?

Collectors and scavengers

I suggest that rather than be over-concerned about the kind of 'vocabulary' which we pre-designate as 'wow words' or 'great vocab' or some such, we should devote time to assisting the pupils in being *collectors and scavengers* of words already out there, already at their fingertips. They sit in the midst of thousands of language situations. They sit among close family and a widening circle of relatives and friends. They spend time with their own friends in school and out. They bombard themselves with material from TV and online. They meet officialdom in the form of doctors, local authority and so on. All this constitutes a wide range of language, rich with different registers, dialects, modes of address and language types. The songs they like are full of figurative language and classic poetic forms and devices. What we suggest – and we can model this – is to tell pupils that they are all 'collectors and scavengers' of this material.

This is no less and no more than what all writers do in some form or another. It's not mysterious. It is a simple matter of treating language as something collectible. We regard it as the means by which we record and remind ourselves of ways in which language can evoke and express many different things in memorable ways. Because it is ourselves who've collected it, there is a way in which these words and phrases become 'ours'. We have pride that we 'discovered' it.

As with the daydream, these can and will offer us raw material for writing. We can use what we collect for contemplation and reflection. We can play with what we have found, changing words round, repeating them, using them for ideas of story motifs, symbols, plot-lines. I have seen several writers' notebooks, for example Roald Dahl's, David Almond's, Cressida Cowell's and of course my own. They are full, scrappy, diverse, fun, odd, provocative, nonsensical, paradoxical material – and much more.

See an example of David Almond's writing process and notebooks here: **http://davidalmond. com/on-writing/**

Looking and listening

Related to this idea of being 'collectors' are the more familiar ideas around 'looking and listening'. Again, this can be quite structured if we want it to be. We can go somewhere, or take part in an activity, which we pre-set as a writing moment. In this moment, we are going to *look and listen,* we say. These pre-set moments can (and should be) varied. There is no superiority between looking closely at a woodland floor and looking in the slop-bucket at the end of a school dinner. Poetry or storywriting has no in-built league table of what is a good or a bad thing to write about. The key thing is that we look and listen closely to places, people and situations – whatever and wherever they might be.

Using 'trigger questions'

Within this looking and listening closely, we might use some trigger questions to help us make notes for our writing: What are the names for all the things we can see and hear? What sensations do we connect with all that we can see and hear? What emotions do we connect with all that we can see and hear? What are the things we can see and hear like? (This last question takes us into the area of figurative language.) What if something I am looking at or listening to could speak and think? What would it say? (This personifies what I'm looking at or listening to.) If what I'm looking at and listening to is silent, what noise would it make if it could make one? This starts to play with 'synaethesia', when we make objects or processes, which we usually express as having one feeling, cross into another feeling: a table, for instance, could be making a kind of music, a piece of music could 'smell' in a certain way, and so on.

Once we've done a few kinds of this 'observing closely' using 'trigger questions', we can create or evoke situations in which the pupils won't need the trigger questions because they will be able to think up their own.

We should never forget that writers do this sort of thing *all the time*. It follows that we can find passages and examples of such writing and look closely at how the writer did this. We can then borrow and adapt these ways of writing for ourselves.

Warning: observing closely does not need to result in an adjective-adverb overload. We have many ways of describing things, processes and people without having to overdose on adjectives and adverbs. If we bear in mind that one of the best ways of making writing interesting is to surprise our readers, then it's often the appearance of a lone strange adjective or adverb that will do the trick rather than an effusion of them.

REFLECTION

How do you encourage and develop pupil confidence in writing?

What can you do to help children look, listen and become word-scavengers?

How can you give children a sense of ownership in their written work?

How do we start?

Another way to look at writing is to ask ourselves: How do we start? Where do we start? How do we get going? So far, I've described something quite patient and slow. It's quite possible to contrast this with 'quick' or spontaneous ways of starting.

1. We can encourage pupils to 'grab' the moment. This may well involve the kind of writing that goes on away from the classroom. We suggest that if and when they get an idea that they think might 'be good for a song' or good for a story, they do all they can to 'grab' it and get writing immediately. Of course, it's not always possible, but if we set up the idea of doing it, it's surprising how possible it can be. We need to 'affirm' this kind of writing, both for the process and what gets written. The writer D.H. Lawrence set great store on the idea of the spontaneous.

2. Writing is of course just one art form. In our multimodal world, we don't need to think of it as isolated from other art forms like, say, film, painting, music, dance, drama, cartoons, ceramics and so on (UKLA, 2004). All of these can be great starting points for writing. We can, for example, look closely at a picture or at a part of a picture and then record our thoughts. We might need the help of trigger questions along similar lines to the ones already suggested. Then we can take these notes and *play* with them: make patterns with them on the page, repeat parts of what we've written so that they set up rhythms and choruses.

Ideas laboratory

Having a playful approach to writing is paramount in stimulating pupil response (Rumney *et al.*, 2016). Stories and poems and dramas offer hundreds of starting points too. We can invent prequels and sequels. We can enter a 'crunch' moment in a story or poem, hot-seat someone (a character) in that moment, do an improvisation and turn that into a soliloquy, a song, a poem, the beginning of a story. We can summarise a story into a sentence or two. What if we change any of the people in that sentence by turning the males into females? What if we change the action in the sentence into something different? What if we change the time frame of the story? What if we change the setting of the story? What if we introduce another element into the story – a sub-plot? The imitate-and-adapt method is the one most used by film-makers! You can practise it with the shortest stories of all: nursery rhymes. Let's take 'Little Jack Horner' as an example. He could become, let's say, a famous sportswoman training for the Olympics. It's just before a big race. She's been told of the exact regime she needs to do before the race. But someone has left a lovely bit of her favourite cake in the changing-room. She eats it. She knows she has broken the regime. She goes out and runs. She wins the race. She congratulates herself ('I'm good!'). The coach tells her she won thanks to the training regime. She says nothing to the coach about eating the cake.

The musicality of language

The technical word for the sound of literature is 'prosody'. We can use the word 'music' or 'musicality' as well: all writing depends on and uses the music of language (Fanany, 2009). Sometimes this will be the rhythm or contrasting rhythms. Sometimes it will be the chiming or clashing ways we can write, using the consonants and vowels of the language so that sometimes they are the same (alliteration and assonance) and sometimes they clash (a sequence of percussive sounds followed by some smooth-flowing sounds). Part of writing is to find ways of writing that 'sound right'. The best way to learn this is to be immersed in many different kinds of writing. We can make this quite conscious by looking at the way writers do it. If you look at the first two or three pages of *A Christmas Carol* you can see how Dickens will, at one moment, write long-flowing sentences, and the next he uses short, sharp phrases with a lot of repeated sounds and words. This serves his purpose for one moment where he wants to be discussing things in a rather showy-off, self-conscious sort of a way, and the next where he wants to conjure up a busy, winter street scene. When children understand how writers use these kinds of strategies, they will develop confidence to use them in their own writing and allow themselves to become immersed in the musicality of language. In the following case study, we can see how one school embeds immersive writing into the curriculum.

─── CASE STUDY ───

Kate Frood (OBE), Headteacher at Eleanor Palmer Primary School in London explains how children are inspired and motivated to write in her school.

At Eleanor Palmer we have always maintained core principles about curriculum design, and we believe that holding on to those principles is key for us. Generally, this works by planning

(Continued)

(Continued)

each term to be shaped around a single overarching topic, and this is framed by a whole-school curriculum that ensures rigour, coverage and a knowledge-rich pathway. And whilst most all of our writing will link to the topics, there is space and value placed on children's personal motivations and interests. As a teaching team we talk about 'hooks'. For example, how do we engage the children? How do we encourage them to want to write and take ownership? These elements are absolutely essential. We also consider purpose and audience, even if the audience is just the child themselves! Why are we writing? Who is it for? And as far as possible we aim for authentic contexts within our connected curriculum. There's lots of Heh, why don't we . . .? in our school, so that the children have a sense of excitement and ownership over the many ways they can communicate through writing.

'Secret Strings' game

We can develop this kind of excitement to write, as described by Kate, by discovering even more strategies, such as by playing the 'Secret Strings' game. Every passage of writing contains 'secret strings'. These are the strings of prosody and imagery which link one part of a passage to another, maybe from one word to another, maybe from one sentence to another or across a whole passage or poem or song or scene in a play or across the whole piece of literature. The strings can simply be about the specific sounds that consonants and vowels make. It can be about the rhythms that words make. It can also be about the links between imagery and 'pictures'. Maybe the writer has repeated different ways of describing something like 'the dark'. Maybe the writer has used contrast – comparing dark with light, sky with sea, for example. These are secret strings too, or what we might call 'patterns of imagery'. Ask pupils to be 'detectives' and ask them to find the 'secret strings', having told them how it can be the sounds or the images that are linked. The only test is, *If you can find a string, say why it's a string. You can't be wrong: you can only be right in different ways.* This idea of secret strings can feed back into our writing. After all, if we can spot secret strings in other people's writing, we can put them into ours. We can use them to inform us about what 'sounds right'. Short sentences? Long ones? Repeated image? Rhythm across two or three phrases? Contrasting rhythms? Patterns? And so on.

Revealing and concealing

One of the most important motors for reading and writing is a process much overlooked by almost everyone except for writers. Some people call it 'reveal-conceal'. If you want people to read what you write, one way to encourage them is to create many moments when readers feel that interesting things are being 'revealed' but – almost without knowing – other things are being 'concealed'. Sometimes it's quite obvious. For example, if I say, 'Once upon a time . . .', this reveals that it's the beginning of the story but at the same time I'm not telling (withholding) what's coming next! It's an invitation to something that you sort of know a bit about (it's a story) but I haven't told you yet what's in the story. Now let's apply that across writing as a whole and find other ways of revealing-concealing. We have a variety of ways of teasing a reader that something may or may not happen later. There! I've used one of them, right there: the word 'later'. Used carefully, any of the words that talk of sometime ahead in the story or poem, without saying yet what it is, will be reveal-conceals. Sometimes we use the word 'would' with it. 'Later, she would wonder what really happened that day . . .'

Again, anything which is not immediately explained or only partially explained is reveal-conceal. I might suggest that a place or a person is more than what they first appear: a house might have the curtains open but no lights on; a person may be doing something for no apparent reason; a car which should have been going one way is in fact going another, and so on.

We can make these reveal-conceals happen through the narration or through dialogue or through what the narrator tells us about how people are thinking. In dialogue, we can have one person who 'knows' and another who does not. What? Where? Why? How? When? the person asks. The person who knows might say something or might withhold. Or again, we can set up one of the most powerful reveal-conceals of all: *dramatic irony*. In my earlier scenario based on 'Little Jack Horner', I finished on a bit of dramatic irony: the coach thinks our sportswoman succeeded because of the coach's regime . . . but 'we' know otherwise. This leaves us with a 'conceal' in which we can speculate about what might happen next, or indeed a 'moral' of the story about what coaches say and do and so on.

Interior monologues are great for reveal-conceal because it is a technique by which we 'identify' with the main protagonist (or the once being talked about at that moment) and so any danger, fear, wonder, hope, etc. that the protagonist feels is, in a sense, ours too. When we're writing, all we need to do is have our protagonist (our 'hero') express a doubt, or a worry, or an expectation, a prediction, a false prediction, a few, a wonder about what might or might not happen and we are in the midst of reveal-conceal.

There are hundreds more of these – many more than are usually described by the kind of criticism that is taught in schools, which is often limited to something along the lines of *How did the writer evoke tension?*

Patterns of expectation

Of course, writing should never be an activity which happens in isolation from reading (Graham *et al.*, 2017; Cumming, 2007), so another way to be a story or poem detective is to spot the reveal-conceals and then 'steal' these techniques for your own writing. Ask yourselves, why did I want to know more about 'x'? What had the writer written that made me wonder more about 'x' or what would or might happen next? (For older pupils try the first two or three scenes in *Macbeth* as an example! Or indeed any first two or three pages of a book written for children.) Sometimes this will involve matters to do with *how did the writer get me to care what might or might not happen to the central character? How did the writer get me to sympathise with this central character?*

Stories and poems also set up what we might call 'patterns of expectation' (Clarke, 1979). Some of these come from the fact that we have read a story something like that before. Something gets lost? Well, probably it'll get found. Somebody is in danger? Well, the story will probably tell us that they got out of danger. Somebody has done something foolish or naughty? They'll probably have to 'pay' for it later. Each of these situations, though, gets us guessing about how they might get out of the difficulty or how they might be 'punished' in the story. The whole time we are reading, we are making speculations and predictions based on what we *already know* about the people in the story *and* what we know of stories like the one we are reading. This is excellent raw material for helping us decide how to write. We need to play with our readers' expectations. We can imagine ourselves writing: 'At this point you probably think that Evie is going to . . .' We might even write that, then write the next scene and go back and cut out that sentence: 'At this point you probably think . . .' Your story can and should be inviting the reader to be thinking that – without telling them that they are!

We can study this kind of prediction game by stopping a story in the middle of its telling and asking everyone to predict. The key thing here is to *not* tell anyone if they're right or not. Read on. And then compare the predicted endings (or predictions of what's going to happen next) with what actually happens in the story. We can then say we can do this sort of building up expectations in our writing. It's the will it-won't it, side of reveal-conceal.

When we study all these reveal-conceals, we discover that these are ways in which we can feed back into our writing about why I might write like this, or like that? We can ask ourselves, am I giving the reader enough reveal-conceals to keep the reader hooked? And indeed, each reveal-conceal is a 'hook' that drags a reader through a text. If the hooks are no good, we lose our reader.

REFLECTION

How might you use the *musicality of language*, *Secret Strings* and *reveal-conceals* to inspire the children in your class?

How do we create a writing-friendly environment?

Writing will not flourish unless we create a writing-friendly environment. The main ways we can do this is through publication and performance, which makes it sound grander than it is. But just as any artwork is made to be viewed, or piece of music is made to be heard, what I mean by *publication* is any means by which we can enable the pupils' writing to be seen by other pupils, friends, family and the world at large. This might be through wall-displays, booklets, books, magazines, using the school bulletin, creating blogs, printing off writing 'pamphlets', creating 'guides' to places that the pupils have visited, and indeed any writing outlet at all is valuable. This involves re-thinking the ideal outcome of pupils' writing as not being the good bit of work in an exercise book, but a piece of writing that will be seen and read anywhere. This builds in expectation, purpose, a sense of audience and feedback: all the great motors for writing of all kinds.

The same goes for *performance*. Here I mean writing things that can be performed in class, in assemblies, creating soundtracks for videos, PowerPoints, or blogs, films, sound tracks, plays, poetry cabarets, late-night spooky readings and so on. Again, this builds in expectation, purpose, audience and feedback.

Together, when pupils see that their writing has a home and a place and is part of processes that involve readers and viewers, the whole matter of 'getting it right' takes on another meaning – and it's the same meaning that 'real' writers use: how will I interest and affect 'real' readers?

By doing this we immerse the pupils' writing into the world of writing at large.

Critical language? Five key questions

An argument that it's possible to raise with what I've said so far is that the pupils won't have a critical methodology to support their writing. What follows is based on 'interpretation' rather than 'retrieval' and 'inference' which, I think, are too narrow a basis for encouraging reading, writing and knowledge about texts. I suggest that we can build this through five key questions – which of course can and should be adapted and re-worded in age-appropriate ways.

1. The 'affect' question:

   In the face of any piece of writing, we ask the pupils is there any part of the piece (or all of it) that made you 'feel' something, that you were 'affected' by, that made you have emotions where you felt sad, or happy, or giggly, or fearful, or jealous, etc.? Discuss this in pairs. Say why and how you felt this.

2. The 'experiential' question:

   Is there any part of the piece or the piece as a whole that reminded you of something that has happened to you or to someone you know? Say why and how you feel about this. Discuss this in pairs.

3. The 'intertextual' question:

   Is there any part of the piece or the piece as a whole that reminded you of something that you have ever read, seen on telly, seen in a film, heard in a song, heard someone 'tell' before? How? Why? Discuss this in pairs. Share this with the whole class.

4. The 'transactional' question:

   Are there any questions you would like to ask anyone in the piece, or the author of the piece? Collect these in pairs and then with the whole class. Can we in the class answer any of these questions? Would anyone like to 'be' the character or the author and try to answer the question in a role-play? If we can't answer the question will it help to do an improv? Will it help to go online or look in a book for answers?

5. The 'cohesion' question

   See the section on Secret Strings above. An example might be: Are there any 'strings' which link one part of a sentence, paragraph, passage, song, play, etc. to another?

Together this set of questions provides the pupils with a critical apparatus which may be partly, mostly or in some cases an entire means by which to analyse text, theme, method and context of a piece of literature. For older pupils it can be a platform on to which we introduce the more formal terms. For younger pupils it may be a means and end in itself. For any age it can be part of a mixed diet of approaches.

If you use these five approaches (in different ways at different times, as suits you), you will build up a repertoire of critical language and an understanding that can feed straight back into writing – both creative and critical. It also reminds us that writing is about feelings and ideas attached to beings that we recognise. These feelings and ideas are intertwined with who we are, our culture and our outlook, and it is imperative that in schools we can and should develop these as a matter of urgency for the next generation of writers.

CHAPTER SUMMARY

In this chapter we have been reminded that writing is an art in itself, and that it is interdependent with other literacy skills of all types, gaining real experiences and becoming an observant collector of words from life all around us. We have also reflected on how we can encourage children to become enthusiastic writers through a range of supportive strategies in and out of the classroom.

KEY POINTS TO CONSIDER

- It is important to consider how an author gathers information and ideas for writing
- Daydreaming is not necessarily a bad thing!
- There are many strategies for developing starting points, and how to make our classrooms 'writing friendly'.
- Imaginative approaches to encourage children's writing in many contexts can be implemented.
- An understanding of how to create a critical methodology through the 'five key questions' approach is important.

Further reading

This also means creating reading-friendly environments through a thorough and thought-out reading-for-pleasure policy. These are all vital and should be adapted to suit their purpose for all schools, all teachers and – more importantly – for all pupils and parents.

If we want to create an environment in which children want to and can write, it has to be a reading-for-pleasure environment too.

https://www.pearson.com/uk/educators/primary-educators/subjects/primary-english/tips-from-michael-rosen.html

There is another here:

https://www.teachers.org.uk/reading-for-pleasure

And there is an ongoing programme here:

https://researchrichpedagogies.org/research/team/reading-for-pleasure

Read more about the 'found object' and Marcel Duchamp:

https://www.moma.org/learn/moma_learning/themes/dada/marcel-duchamp-and-the-readymade/

References

Barthes, **R. and Balzac**, **H.D.** (1974) *S/Z*. New York: Farrar, Straus & Giroux.

Clarke, **I.F.** (1979) *The Pattern of Expectation, 1644–2001*. London: Jonathan Cape,

Cumming, **R.** (2007) Language play in the classroom: encouraging children's intuitive creativity with words through poetry. *Literacy, 41* (2): 93–101.

DfE (2013) *The National Curriculum in England, Key Stages 1 and 2 Framework Document*. London: Department for Education.

Fanany, **R.** (2009) The musicality of language: an application of musical analysis to speech and writing, *Journal of Music and Meaning*, 7. Available at: **www.musicandmeaning.net/issues/show-Article.php?artID=7.4**

Graham, **S.**, **Xinghua**, **L. and Bartlett**, **B.** (2017) Reading for writing: a meta-analysis of the impact of reading interventions on writing. *Review of Educational Research, 88* (2): 243–84.

Iser, **W.** (1978) *The Act of Reading: A Theory of Aesthetic Response*. Baltimore, MD: Johns Hopkins University Press.

James, **W.** (1890) *Principles of Pedagogy: Stream of Consciousness*. Available online at:**https://psych classics.yorku.ca/James/Principles/prin9.htm**

Mithen, **S.** (2011) Musicality and language. In R. Gibson and M. Tallerman (eds) *The Oxford Handbook of Language Evolution*. Oxford Handbooks Online.

Rosen, **M.** (2016) *What Is Poetry?* London: Walker Books.

Rumney, **P.**, **Butress**, **J. and Kuksa**, **I.** (2016) *Seeing Doing Writing*. Sage Open. Available at **https://journals.sagepub.com/doi/pdf/10.1177/2158244016628590**

UKLA (2004) *More than Words: Multimodal Texts in the Classroom*. London: QCA.

10

LEARNING TO THRIVE WITH NATURE

TESSA WILLY, RICHARD DUNNE AND EMILIE MARTIN

THE ABUNDANCE OF THIS PLACE,
THE SONGS OF ITS PEOPLE AND ITS BIRDS,
WILL BE HEALTH AND WISDOM AND INDWELLING
LIGHT. THIS IS NO PARADISAL DREAM.
ITS HARDSHIP IS ITS POSSIBILITY.

(EXTRACT FROM 'A VISION' BY WENDELL BERRY)

KEYWORDS: HARMONY; NATURE; NATURAL WORLD; PRINCIPLES; CONNECTEDNESS; INTERDEPENDENCE; ENQUIRY; PURPOSE; LEARNING; CROSS-CURRICULAR.

CHAPTER OBJECTIVES

This chapter supports you to:

- recognise that all the components comprising our world are inextricably interrelated and interdependent
- understand that as we are a part of nature, so nature is a part of us – helping us to understand our own nature and how we can build and sustain these relationships

- recognise that the most effective and enduring teacher that children have is nature itself giving meaning and purpose to real-life learning
- appreciate the value of enquiry in our learning and the importance of asking and answering questions throughout life, in order to engage learners and inspire curiosity.
- understand that through enquiry we can engage children in real-life learning and inspire and sustain their creativity, making them excited and motivated about their learning
- demonstrate through school and classroom exemplars how theory can be manifested in practice, developing understanding and improved future practice.

LINKS TO THE TEACHERS' STANDARDS

Working through this chapter will enable you to meet all of the Teachers' Standards, in particular:

TS1:   Set high expectations which inspire, motivate and challenge pupils

TS3:   Demonstrate good subject and curriculum knowledge

TS8:   Fulfil wider professional responsibilities

Part 2: Personal and professional conduct

Introduction

In recent years, for a number of reasons, including the changing habits of how and where children live and play, the changing nature of our local area and increased perceived risk, children have experienced an increasing disconnect with nature (Louv, 2005, 2011). Waller *et al.* (2017) recognise the associated problems with this while others argue that it has been overplayed, that habits and habitats have indeed changed but we are still connecting with nature – just in different ways. What we need to do is to acknowledge nature, celebrate it and, most importantly, do so explicitly and accessibly.

As our habits change, connecting children with nature needs to be more carefully planned and deliberate and a tangible part of the curriculum. The role of school and the teacher is therefore crucial to help children discover aspects of the natural world that they might not otherwise come across and learn about. As teachers we have a responsibility to redress the developing imbalance in children's association with the natural world and help create opportunities where they can learn not just *about* nature but also *from* nature.

Many charitable organisations and educational movements have grown up to counterbalance this deficit and bring nature back into children's learning, such as the educational work of the National Trust as well as Forest, Water and Beach Schools. However, we shouldn't have to create a type of school nor rely on a charity to bring nature into children's experience and learning. It should be accessible for all children whether they live in a rural or urban, wealthy or deprived area.

In this chapter we will explore some of the myriad ways of making this possible, using a case study of one particular school, embracing and embedding connectedness with nature in its very core.

Learning to learn with nature through harmony

The early years of school embed learning through play and discovery and much of this takes place outside, interacting with a more natural world. As children get older there is an increasing reluctance to allow them outside in order to learn. This is partly due to a fear of losing control when they are not bound by the four walls of the classroom, and possibly more to do with our lack of confidence as we worry what to *do* with them outside and how they will learn without the stimulus and support of books, writing implements, the interactive whiteboard and so on. What we tend to forget is that the outdoors and nature itself are the most inspirational and boundless stimuli there are, encouraging them to nurture their instinctive childhood curiosity to explore all that is around them.

This is not to say that every lesson and experience that a child has must be outside whatever the circumstances and being uncomfortable is not always conducive to learning, but it is fair to say that we should be using the natural world much more frequently and effectively in our learning. This is not advocating going outside just for the sake of it but is about making learning meaningful and purposeful and showing children how we are a part of nature in all facets of our lives. As in all teaching, striking the most effective balance is key.

Giving children the opportunities to explore the natural world empowers them and facilitates child-initiated learning. In this way, they are able to make links between different areas of their knowledge and understanding and ask questions. Children naturally create what we would term 'cross-curricular' or integrated learning, by recognising the interrelatedness of knowledge that mirrors the interrelationships and interdependence of the natural world in which they exist. This is very different to the often rigid structure of the curriculum from Year 1 in English schools.

REFLECTION

Why do you think children today connect less with nature?

What impact do you think a greater connection with nature might have on their physical, social and emotional development?

What would be the benefits of a greater connection with nature for their academic development?

If we, as teachers, are to make deliberate and considered provision for children's engagement with Nature and nurture their connection to it, we need to give careful thought to the way we plan to enable this kind of meaningful, purposeful learning. As we have already mentioned, child-led discovery, play and outdoor learning are key parts of the early years of a child's education. It is a statutory requirement of early years settings to provide opportunities for outdoor play.

When HMI inspectors visited Reception classes as part of Ofsted's 2017 review of the curriculum, they reported that practitioners generally acknowledged that *the broader experiences and opportunities they offered children formed part of their curriculum* (Ofsted, 2017). These broader experiences included outdoor learning. This perspective on outdoor learning is interesting. It casts outdoor learning as something that is not merely a bolt-on in good weather but part of the fabric of what we believe children should learn. When outdoor provision is integrated effectively into learning, it can become a cross-cutting thread that is woven through the entire curriculum. This is an altogether more holistic pedagogy, a way of bringing together learning in different areas of the curriculum.

The structure of the Early Years Foundation Stage curriculum (DfE, 2017) itself no doubt encourages teachers to exercise greater freedom in the way they structure learning and in how they choose to deliver the curriculum. Framing the EYFS curriculum in terms of 'areas' such as 'Understanding the World' allows for a more flexible approach to planning which promotes cross-curricular, joined-up practice that is led by the children's interests and can be shaped by their surroundings.

This stands in stark contrast to the structure of the National Curriculum for England (DfE, 2013) from Year 1 onwards. Instead of areas, the curriculum is framed in terms of subjects. By its very structure, this document promotes a more discrete approach to teaching.

A question for teachers further up the school, then, is not *how can I bring nature into learning*? but *how can I use nature as the foundation for learning*? By thinking about the natural world as a frame for learning across the curriculum, it is possible to bring a coherence to learning that allows children to make links between the knowledge, understanding and skills they have acquired in different subjects, and to use this to further their learning.

This requires a different way of thinking about how we organise learning – and a different starting point for planning. By making nature the core focus, it gains a higher profile and becomes embedded in all learning. Here are some ideas to help you to embed this approach in your own practice:

> *Choose a feature of the natural environment that you and your students have access to or are familiar with. What trees are in your school grounds? Is there a river close by? Now look at the curriculum for your year group and see how you could build cross-curricular learning around it.*

Reconnecting with nature

The impact of our – and our children's – disconnection with the natural world shows itself in diverse and sometimes unexpected ways. When the 2007 edition of the *Oxford Junior Dictionary* was published, a clutch of nature-related words was omitted. The victims of this vocabulary cull included words such as acorn, bluebell, conker, dandelion, fern, kingfisher, lark, mistletoe and otter.

The decision to omit these words was grounded in the understandable view, which is nonetheless disheartening, that *the dictionary needed to reflect the consensus experience of modern-day childhood* (MacFarlane, 2016).

What does this tell us about the experience of modern-day childhood itself? The dictionary's omissions from its Junior edition prompted Robert MacFarlane and artist Jackie Morris to collaborate on *The Lost Words*, a compendium of poems and illustrations inspired by words that were cut from the children's dictionary. The text on the back cover of *The Lost Words* makes clear that this is not simply a collection of children's verse but an attempt to prevent the extinction of these words altogether, to counter *an alarming acceptance of the idea that children might no longer see the seasons, or that the rural environment might be so unproblematically disposable* (MacFarlane, 2016).

It is true that for many young people – and adults – today, an interaction with nature does not form part of their daily experience. But if we, as educators, accept that a core part of our role is to support children as they explore curriculum content, ideas and ways of doing and being that might be unfamiliar to them, do we not also have duty to facilitate for them a deeper connection to the natural world which may in itself be unfamiliar to them?

In a bid to reconnect children to the natural world, Ashley C of E Primary school in Walton-on-Thames has developed a curriculum built around principles of harmony that are evident in nature and which maintain the balance and health of the natural world. This unique curriculum development work, inspired by the ideas of HRH The Prince of Wales and set out in his book *Harmony: A New Way of Looking at Our World* (HRH Prince of Wales *et al.*, 2010), focuses on seven principles of harmony:

- The Principle of the Cycle
- The Principle of Health
- The Principle of Interdependence
- The Principle of Adaptation
- The Principle of Geometry
- The Principle of Oneness
- The Principle of Diversity

Central to this work is the idea that we can learn valuable lessons from nature as well as simply learning about nature. To use an example from the school's curriculum, it is about moving beyond 'learning about penguins' to 'learning from penguins about how they work together to ensure their survival'. Is it also about exploring how we can apply what we learn to our own lives.

By basing learning on these principles, the school aims to help children see how things are, how things work together and how we are part of a complex and self-regulating system. The school sets out to create a mindset among its students which governs how they choose to live, recognising the consequences of the things we do and the choices we make every day. Other schools are now embedding and developing this work in their own contexts, notably Surrey's South Farnborough Infant School, and St John's Primary School, Dorking.

CASE STUDY

Harmony principles in practice: diversity in wildflowers

At Ashley School, learning - and therefore, teaching - is organised into 'enquiries'. At the start of each half-term, children in every class are posed a question to stimulate enquiry. It might be *Why are bees so brilliant?* or *What can we learn from the stars?* Each enquiry is linked to a principle of harmony and this provides a framework for the children's learning over the course of the following weeks. It is then the job of their teachers to plan opportunities for cross-curricular learning that allows the children to explore ways in which this central question could be answered.

The children in Year 1, for example, are asked at the start of the summer term, *Which is my favourite wildflower and why?* This enquiry is linked to the harmony principles of Diversity and the Cycle. In order to answer the enquiry question, the children first learn about the life cycle of flowering plants. They learn to tell the story of this cycle by observing what happens in the natural world around them. They learn how the design of each flower helps attract pollinators and the role that pollinators - in turn - play in perpetuating the life cycle of flowering plants.

The timing of this learning is important. In the summer term there is an abundance of wildflowers in the school grounds for the children to learn from and learn about. Through detailed observation and sketching, they find out for themselves what different flowers look like and learn to identify them. They look at the different parts that make up each flower and pose their own questions about their form and function. They compare flowers from different plants, counting the number of petals, comparing colours and studying petal shape. They explore the geometry of the different forms we see in four, five and six-petalled flowers. By the end of the half term, they have become experts in wildflowers.

The children learn about the strength that comes from diversity: different flowers attract different pollinators in diverse ways. They are encouraged to see diversity in their own community and to value this as something that helps build resilience.

The enquiry, like all enquiries at the school, culminates in a 'Great Work'. Using the seeds harvested from the wildflower meadows that the previous Year 1 cohort planted, they sow their own wildflower meadows in the school.

Their meadow will, in turn, support the learning of the subsequent Year 1 classes. In this way, they are not only learning about cycles in nature, they have also become part of the cycle of learning that links one cohort of children to the one that follows in their footsteps.

Analysis

The learning that evolves from this enquiry is both relevant and meaningful and helps the children to connect with nature through their developing understanding of it. It is also current and topical: it is happening out there now, so they can see and interact with what they are learning about. This embeds their learning and enables them to apply it in the future in other contexts. Teaching with purpose about the real world can empower children and spark their curiosity and desire to know more about the natural world.

REFLECTION

Have you taught a similar enquiry before and are you able to see the impact on your children's learning? Could you think of a similar enquiry that you might do with your class that is relevant to your own setting? Consider how this might help them to connect more effectively with nature.

We are what we eat

Ask the expert: an interview with Patrick Holden, CEO of the Sustainable Food Trust

Q: Why, from a food and farming perspective, is it important that we help our children and young people reconnect with nature?

A: I grew up in London but my childhood experiences of nature on farm visits and holidays inspired me to get back to the land and become a farmer. I am convinced that the best way to preserve our rapidly diminishing biodiversity is to produce food by working in harmony with nature. We will only achieve this if we give our children impressions of nature throughout their formative years. These impressions inspire us, enhance our sense of well-being and make us feel more connected with the natural world.

Q: How can an understanding of the principles of Harmony contribute to healthier food production and farming practices?

A: The application of Harmony principles lies right at the heart of all sustainable farming systems. I'll give you two examples. Firstly, the Principle of the Cycle. You find this in the beautiful form of crop rotation, which builds up the fertility of the soil over three or four years and leads to a harvest of healthy vegetables, grains and other foods. A second wonderful example is the Principle of Diversity. Sustainable and organic farmers nearly always use mixed farming systems. These will include several different species of livestock many different crops and will support a host of farmland birds, small mammals, insects and wildflowers which exist in harmony with food production.

Q: What key messages about the interrelation of nature, food and farming do we need to convey to young people through education today?

A: Our education system must communicate to our children that they hold the key to striking a better balance between food production and nature conservation. They are agents of change, both in their role as food buyers and in their role as citizens and voters by making their messages heard by policy-makers.

Analysis

This interview highlights the importance of childhood experiences of nature. These experiences – children's interactions, explorations and understanding of the natural world – allow them to

Figure 10.1 By collecting and sowing wildflower seeds, children engage with the cycles at work in Nature

develop a greater sense of their own connectedness to nature. We are not moved to defend that from which we feel detached. When education facilitates this connectedness to the natural world (particularly for children who live in our towns and cities) and nurtures children's sense of empowerment, they are better equipped to work and live more harmoniously with nature.

REFLECTION

How have your own experiences of nature - or lack of them - affected your sense of connection to the natural world?

Nature as our teacher

REFLECTION

How do we encourage and nurture children's curiosity? How might enquiry-led learning help children to understand the world in a holistic and comprehensive way?

A critical view

Caring for the environment is perceived to come at a cost to us. Organic food, free-range meat, growing our own are often more expensive and time-consuming than buying the cheapest, most available food. Many people therefore are forced to eschew it and in so doing discourage children from benefitting from a better relationship with nature. Similarly, not buying food or flowers which have been flown in from other countries can be seen to have a deleterious impact on the local farmers abroad who have grown it, causing greater poverty in other parts of the world. This is a complex balance between what is 'right' or best for the natural environment and for us as humans. Further, there is a dilemma between having access to nature and keeping nature bounded and safe – the more that people have access to nature, the less natural it becomes. These are contentious issues and encouraging children to find out more about them through debate, discussion and critical thinking can allow them to see these complexities. They can begin to weigh up the arguments and, crucially, start to come up with some of their own solutions. It can also of course encourage them to look to nature for answers – how are contradictions such as these dealt with in the natural world and how does nature resolve such issues? They will then have even more to learn from nature as our teacher: enquiry is the key to helping them find some answers.

REFLECTION

How can we enable children to understand that nothing is simply black and white nor binary? How can we help them to see things from a variety of perspectives, understanding and appreciating different opinions? Why it is so important to have these discussions and debates?

THEORY FOCUS

Exploring the outcomes of a Harmony curriculum

During the academic year 2017-18. Alan Pagden and Nicola Kemp from Canterbury Christ Church University carried out a multi-sited ethnographic study of three schools that are 'doing things differently' in terms of their curricula. In the case of Ashley C of E School, which was one of the three case studies, this difference lay in its work to integrate principles of Harmony into the curriculum and the life of the school. The following is taken from conversation with Nicola Kemp about the research carried out at the school.

Q: To what extent were the children at the school involved in the research?

A: We started with a focus group with Year 6 children and asked them what they thought we should ask and who we should ask to find out what is special about their school. We used these questions to frame our research and each time we visited the school we reported back to the children. Their input informed the whole data collection process.

Q: What evidence was there that the children were developing a sense of their own sustainability leadership?

A: The children were clear that the ethos of the school was about *deeper stuff . . . than the aca-demic side*, as one child put it. For the children, this 'deeper stuff' could be understood as 'life skills'. They were all very aware of how different elements of what the school offers (the formal curriculum, the school site and the environmental management systems) were preparing them for life beyond the school and they were also able to articulate the purpose of this as understanding that 'we can make a difference ourselves'. When the Year 6 children spoke about their residential trip to Chamonix, which is focused on sustainability leadership, they revealed an understanding of sustainability in terms of caring for themselves, others and the environment:

> *It's not just knowing about stuff for ourselves, it's about sharing it with other people, so they get more of an understanding about what's going on with that and what we can do to help it.*

> (Year 6 child)

Q: To what extent did teaching and learning and the nature of the school's curriculum contribute to this understanding?

A: It was clear that the children's understanding could not be attributed to one particular element or aspect of the school but derived from the holistic multi-layered experience which has been developed over many years. We saw and heard about examples of influence across the school community from the school cook and gardener to parent volunteers, from the class teachers to the senior leadership team. Everyone is encouraged to develop leadership capability and to be rel-atively autonomous and this relies upon trust relationships within the school community.

CASE STUDY

Children as researchers: using Harmony principles to develop a cohesive curriculum

The children in Year 5 at Ashley C of E Primary school spend the first half-term of the school year exploring the enquiry question: 'What journey does a river take?' As with all medium-term plan-ning at the school, the teachers take as their starting point the Harmony principle that underpins the learning – in this case the principle of the Cycle – and use this to bring together content and skills from across the curriculum.

From the geography programmes of study in the National Curriculum for KS2, the children learn about:

(Continued)

(Continued)

- the topographical features of landscape in the local area (the River Thames is close by);
- the parts of a river along its course and the water cycle;
- our use of water as a resource and what happens to it before it comes out of the taps in our homes; and
- the distribution of fresh water as a resource, what happens when there is too little (drought) or too much (flood) of it and our duty not to waste or degrade it

From the Science programmes of study the children learn about:

- reversible changes, drawing on their understanding of the water cycle, and comparing these to irreversible changes plus mixtures and solutions; and
- the role that filtering, sieving, evaporation and condensation can play in the purification of drinking water.

Learning in maths, English, music and art are also linked to the focus on rivers and cycles.

This case study shows us how it is possible to reorganise the content of the curriculum to present teaching and learning in a more cohesive, cross-curricular way. By adopting this approach, nature – and the Harmony principles we see at work in nature – frames learning and brings together content and skills from subject disciplines across the curriculum.

How can you develop Harmony principles in your practice?

The development of a Harmony curriculum at this school is already well-established, but for schools or even individual teachers wishing to introduce Harmony principles to their own practice, a smaller-scale approach will initially be much more manageable. A good starting point in developing your own understanding of Harmony principles and how you can integrate them with your teaching is to focus on one principle over the course of two or three lessons. You might consider the Principle of Oneness when you teach an RE unit, or explore the Principle of Geometry through leaf sketches in a series of Art lessons that bring together skills such as observational drawing, colour mixing and painting with watercolours. From this starting point, it is possible to build up to a half-term's learning theme around one of the principles, adding another the next year or whenever it feels right to move forward.

Harmony principles in practice

No matter how big or how small the first steps towards Harmony learning are, what is certain is that this approach requires teachers to embrace a new way of planning.

Usually the process of planning and delivering a curriculum of learning starts by referencing the National Curriculum and pulling curriculum objectives into a planning document. This is a very logical thing to do, but it means that the National Curriculum objectives drive the learning and, if planned in subject separate ways, the learning quickly becomes very disjointed and disconnected. It can all feel rather piecemeal and even pointless from a student perspective.

(Dunne, 2019)

Instead, nature's principles of Harmony become the starting point for planning. This allows us to put well-being and sustainability at the heart of learning. From there, map a journey through the learning that includes NC objectives, but do not let these dominate. Teachers have to think carefully about how each objective will be presented and applied and the context for the learning.

By planning teaching and learning in this way we can help our young people draw inspiration from nature that will inform the way they live and the decisions they make. Using nature's principles as a common theme or framework for learning brings cohesion and purpose, which leads to meaningful outcomes.

REFLECTION

How might you embed some of the principles of Harmony in your everyday teaching?

Which cross-curricular topics that you do could incorporate learning from as well as about nature?

How can you help the children that you teach connect more with nature as an everyday, regular event?

CHAPTER SUMMARY

In this chapter we have examined the Principles of Harmony and looked at how we can use these to immerse children in developing an understanding of nature. We have argued that enquiry should be central as a pedagogical tool to engage children with key themes which underpin the way we live our lives – and need to in the future.

This is an exciting time for those involved in education: there is a real opportunity to rethink how we structure the education we offer to our children, and reflect on the experiences of nature this education provides them with.

Harmony is not a subject. It does not require anything additional to be crammed into the school timetable, which is often already splitting at the seams. Harmony calls, instead, for a far more radical rethinking of the way we approach learning, one which makes nature the teacher and which promotes a greater connectedness with the natural world to ensure its – and our – long-term collective well-being.

┌─────────────────── **KEY POINTS TO CONSIDER** ───────────────────┐

We have:

- recognised that we are all a part of nature and are interconnected and interdependent;
- considered that nature is a part of us which can help us to understand ourselves and our relationships with others better;
- recognised that the best and most enduring teacher that children have is nature itself giving meaning and purpose to real-life learning;
- appreciated the value of enquiry in learning and how important it is to be always asking and answering questions in order to motivate learners, inspire curiosity and sustain creativity;
- demonstrated through school and classroom exemplars how theory can be manifested in practice, developing our own understanding and improved future practice as teachers.

└──┘

Further reading

HRH The Prince of Wales (2010) *Harmony: A Vision for Our Future* (Children's Edition). London: HarperCollins.

HRH The Prince of Wales, Juniper, T. and Skelly, I. (2010) *Harmony: A New Way of Looking at Our World*. London: HarperCollins.

Find out more about Harmony Schools at: **https://www.psta.org.uk/outreach/schools**

References

Aynsley-Green, A. (2018) *The British Betrayal of Childhood*. London: Routledge.

Catling, S. and Willy, T. (2018) *Understanding and Teaching Primary Geography*. London: Sage.

Children's Society (2017) *The Good Childhood Report*. Accessed at: **https://www.childrens society.org.uk/sites/default/files/the-good-childhood-report-2017_full-report_0.pdf** (last accessed 16 November 2018).

DfE (2013) *The National Curriculum in England: Key Stages 1 and 2 Framework Document*. London: Department for Education.

DfE (2017) *Statutory Framework for the Early Years Foundation Stage: Setting the Standards for Learning, Development and Care for Children from Birth to Five*. London: Department for Education.

Dunne, R. (2018) Why we need an education revolution. *Learning for Well-Being Magazine*, Issue 5. Well-being Foundation, pp. 1–8.

Dunne, R. (2019) *Harmony: A New Way of Looking at and Learning About Our World*. Bristol: Harmony Project.

Gill, T. (2009) Now for free-range childhood. *Guardian*. Accessible at: **https://www.theguardian. com/commentisfree/2009/apr/02/children-safety** (last accessed 16 November 2018).

Harari, **Y.** (2018) *21 Lessons for the 21st Century*. London: Jonathan Cape.

Hicks, **D.** (2017) Walking lightly on earth. *Primary Geography*, Spring Issue. Sheffield: Geographical Association.

HRH The Prince of Wales, **Juniper**, **T. and Skelly**, **I.** (2010) *Harmony: A New Way of Looking at Our World*. London: HarperCollins.

Kumar, **S.** (n.d.) Learning from Nature. *Resurgence and Ecologist*. Available at: **https://www.resur gence.org/satish-kumar/articles/learning-from-nature.html** (last accessed 19 November 2018).

Lane, **E.** (2017) Pryd a mwy or shared meal and more. *Primary Geography*, Summer Issue. Sheffield: Geographical Association.

Louv, **R.** (2011) *The Nature Principle*. New York: Chapel Hill.

Louv, **R.** (2005) Last child in the woods: saving our children from nature-deficit disorder. *Journal of Leisure Studies and Recreation Education, 21* (1): 136–7.

MacFarlane, **R.** (2016) *Landmarks*. London: Hamish Hamilton.

MacFarlane, **R. and Morris**, **J.** (2016) *The Lost Words*. London: Hamish Hamilton.

Ofsted (2017) *Bold Beginnings: The Reception Curriculum in a Sample of Good and Outstanding Primary Schools*. London: HMSO.

Spielman, **A.** (2018) *HMCI Commentary: Curriculum and the New Education Inspection Framework*. Available at: **https://www.gov.uk/government/speeches/hmci-commentary-curriculum- and-the-new-education-inspection-framework**

Waller, **C.**, **Griffiths**, **H.**, **Waluda**, **C.**, **Thorpe**, **S.**, **Loaiza**, **I.**, **Moreno**, **B.**, **Pacherres**, **C. and Hughes**, **K.** (2017) Microplastics in the Antarctic marine system: an emerging area of research. *Science of the Total Environment, 598*: 220–7.

11

BALANCING THE EQUATION

PINKY JAIN

MATHEMATICS IS NOT ABOUT NUMBERS, EQUATIONS, COMPUTATION OR ALGORITHMS. IT'S ABOUT UNDERSTANDING.

(WILLIAM THURSTON, 2009)

KEYWORDS: MATHEMATICS; CONTEXT-BASED LEARNING; PROBLEM-BASED LEARNING; CROSS-CURRICULAR; METACOGNITION; INTER-DISCIPLINARY; EXPERIENTIAL LEARNING.

━━ CHAPTER OBJECTIVES ━━

This chapter:

- explores reasons why we currently teach and structure mathematics in school the way we do
- considers the reasons for discrete subject teaching in mathematics and questions whether this is the only way
- examines the role of mathematics and the knowledge it contains in developing richer and more sustainable understanding in children
- considers how we can meet the aims and content of the National Curriculum for mathematics and still ensure that children are prepared for all the demands of future education and work, but more importantly have a love for learning mathematics

---

━━ LINKS TO THE TEACHERS' STANDARDS ━━

Working through this chapter will enable you to meet all of the Teachers' Standards, in particular:

TS 1:   Promote good progress and outcomes by pupils

TS 2: Set high expectations which inspire, motivate and challenge pupils

TS 3: Demonstrate good subject and curriculum knowledge

TS 4: Plan and teach well-structured lessons

TS 5: Adapt teaching to respond to the strengths and needs of all pupils

Introduction

You may be thinking what place a chapter on mathematics has when considering a broad and balanced curriculum. We feel it is essential to consider the teaching of mathematics and what a subject that holds such a high status can offer to ensure a broad and balanced experience for children in school. How did we get to the twenty-first century where we have witnessed phenomenal development in technology, health, living standards and the ability to share ideas, but have seen such little change in the systems that we use to impart and develop knowledge, specifically in mathematics? Over the years, schools have seen many changes in curriculum, philosophies and how decisions are made for schools – away from the autonomy that schools had in the late 1960s, the centralisation of schools in the 1980s and 1990s to the current landscape where there is a real mixed economy of quasi-autonomy in academies and central control in maintained schools. On the whole these changes have impacted policy and strategy for developing the school system and the content taught in schools, and it could be argued that though there has been system-wide change, it has had limited influence on the way we teach. If we scratch beneath the surface, then we will see very little difference between how we teach mathematics today and how it was taught back in Victorian England. We must consider if the current pedagogical strategies are fit for purpose from the view of not only future needs (which none of us can proclaim to predict), but also from the perspectives of the children we are teaching and the real essence that is mathematics. Askew (2012) suggests that:

Policy initiatives in England, and elsewhere, tend to treat the teaching and learning of mathematics in primary schools as a technical problem: we already know from current practices the solution to engaging children and raising standards. If teachers can be better 'trained' to 'deliver' mathematics using existing techniques then all will be well. While teaching arithmetic to Victorian clerks might have been a technical problem, teaching mathematics is too complex to be reducible to a prescriptive set of techniques. We need to work with a view of mathematics teaching as an adaptive challenge. That means trying out new ways to teach and in particular allowing pedagogies to emerge rather than imposing them.

(2012: xvi)

In this chapter, we will explore this challenge through considering:

- the historical background to our current state of thinking with some consideration of the implications and impact that government policies have had on narrowing the curriculum;

- Primary practice and how discrete subject teaching limits children's ability to make connections and develop understanding, in addition to looking at the idea of how mathematics teaching, when combined with effective interdisciplinary links, can enable children to make real meaning of what they are learning and the world around them;

- links from the primary National Programmes of Study for mathematics to areas where contextual learning can take place;

- the tension that teachers feel between the need to ensure that children have the skills to achieve high outcomes in national tests such as the times tables test or the SATS at Key Stage 2 and teaching in a more integrated manner;

- how we can move from teaching mathematics in such a *prescriptive manner* to a more organic approach which allows for the true essence of mathematics to be shared and, more importantly, understood.

There is much talk about the anxiety that children feel in relation to mathematics (Moustafa *et al.*, 2017; Dowker *et al.*, 2016; Maths Anxiety Trust, 2019) and the limited uptake of the subject by different groups of children for further studies. This makes us consider the role that our pedagogical choices in primary schools have in shaping the wider societal view of mathematics, as we are at a unique juncture where we need not only to consider a different approach to teaching mathematics, but also how we perceive the subject itself as a society.

Looking back to move forward

REFLECTION

Why do we teach mathematics as a subject on its own?

Why does mathematics dominate so much of the school timetable?

To examine these questions, we need to briefly consider the state of British education and how we have developed our values and philosophies over a period of time. By going on this journey, we should be able to establish how the ingrained view we have about mathematics as a subject, its characteristics and purpose, has evolved.

From the time of the Industrial Revolution in Britain, the shape of the education system has been dominated by the needs of the future that children will be entering. This notion of preparing them for the future is a challenging one as it requires a level of prediction which we cannot achieve. Askew (2012), Claxton (2008) and many other observers of education all tussle with this notion of predicting the future and preparing children for it.

> There is much talk of 'equipping' pupils for the future that they will be 'entering' when they leave school. But the future is not a place that exists, simply waiting for pupils to enter it. The pupils of today are the creators of future societies, not visitors to them.
>
> (Askew, 2012: xvii)

Toffler (1970) observed profoundly that we have applied the same thinking to the development of education as we have done to economic development.

... the whole idea of assembling masses of students (raw material) to be processed by teachers (workers) in a centrally located school (factory) was a stroke of industrial genius ... The inner life of the school thus becomes an anticipatory mirror, a perfect introduction to industrial society. The most criticised features of education today – the regimentation, the lack of individualisation, the rigid systems of seating, grouping, grading and marking, the authoritarian role of the teacher – are precisely those that make mass public education so effective an instrument of adaptation for its place and time ... Young people passing through this educational machine emerged into an adult society whose structure of jobs, roles and institutions resembled that of school itself.

(Toffler 1970: 355)

It is this notion of industrial-scale education and how to manage it that has had the most profound impact on mathematics. The need to quantify and ensure that all children have been taught all that is needed to be future-ready has led to a reductive view of mathematics. It has been sectioned into small parts which can be taught in a linear manner and the quality of the learning can be assessed and quantified to meet external demands such as league tables and SATs results, while greater focus on content and not how it has to be taught has dominated our thinking. This can be seen in the current changes to the way in which schools are being encouraged to teach mathematics to support our climb in the PISA tables to 27th in 2015 (OECD, 2019) and match the outcomes of other nations who have a higher position. There has been significant financial investment from central government in learning from some of these other jurisdictions which are higher in the PISA tables such as Singapore and China with projects like the Shanghai Teacher Exchange, textbooks being encouraged in schools with central funding, and whole-class teaching models being emulated from the Singapore-China approach (Gibb, 2017; Boylan *et al.*, 2018). The rate of top-down change has left mathematics to become a process-driven mechanical subject. Though we must be mindful to appreciate that there is not a big problem in primary mathematics (Askew, 2012), it has become a subject taught in a linear segmented manner, focused on a very narrow measurable content. It is not taught as an evolving multi-dimensional organic subject that changes. Harel (2008) states that is more akin to a 'living organism':

It grows continually as mathematicians carry out mental acts and their mathematical communities assimilate the ways of understanding and ways of thinking associated with the mathematicians.

(2008: 273)

REFLECTION

Should mathematics be taught in a linear, segmented manner? Should we make room for a more 'organic' development of children's mathematical knowledge?

In conclusion, we started with the question 'why do we teach mathematics as a subject on its own?' The answer lies simply within history, in that it has enabled us to support industrial growth, technological growth and societal demands. In short, mathematics has leant itself to be taught in a mechanical manner and, as yet, we have not stopped to examine the methods we use to teach mathematics and make any radical changes. The other question that was asked at the beginning of this section was 'why has mathematics dominated the school timetable?' In part, it is because it is an easy way to measure output and performance, or, as Claxton (2008) states, we have become habituated to this way of education and we are not able to see beyond what we deem as the norm as it is ingrained in our culture and thinking. It is difficult to be an alien in a world which has been built around us and by us. Claxton (2008) encourages us to consider stepping outside this world and reconsider the world of education afresh in light of cognitive science and the knowledge growth we have experienced and have to offer.

To teach just maths, or not to teach just maths?

In the previous section, we established that the nature of schooling and the methodologies used for teaching mathematics have changed little in their essence. It would be a very safe bet, when generically describing schools across the world, that a vast majority of them teach subjects such as mathematics, science, art and others as separate, individual, distinct areas of knowledge, with each being given some time within a weekly timetable. There may be a range of variations in the way that time is allocated and distributed among each subject. However, it is almost certain that there will be a hierarchy of importance given to subjects such as mathematics and science before other areas of knowledge, and that the teaching of each of these will require children to switch from one subject to the next. This boxing of subjects is a very common approach – one that has been in practice for many years – and the vast majority of people will have experienced this way of learning. We need to consider if this way of teaching works.

REFLECTION

Is teaching mathematics as an isolated subject the best way to develop understanding?

In order to examine this, it is helpful to consider a small case study.

Jess (age nine) sits in the playground on a warm sunny day looking perplexed. A teacher approaches Jess and questions her as to what is worrying her, and Jess replies with the following statement:

Jess: We have been doing space as a topic and my teacher said you can fit 1,300 Earths into Jupiter. I don't understand how she knows that.

Let us consider this for a moment. Now, we could argue that this is a simple mathematics question which can be answered by a few calculations, albeit a little complex for Jess as she is only nine years old and may not have the necessary computational skills to be able to establish a way forward mathematically. Also, as spheres are involved, things could get a little interesting. Besides using mathematical calculations, there are other ways of answering this question such as instinct, approximation and estimation, using computer modelling, or our past experience with learning about planets and their comparative size, to work out the reasonableness of the claim and approximate whether 1,300 Earths do indeed fit into Jupiter. However, the challenge is not how we would answer this question, but whether Jess is able to satisfy her curiosity using the skills that she has. We could just say it is a fact but we must wonder what impact this might have on Jess and her understanding. This question raises interesting challenges that if all we have to rely on is our mathematical knowledge and what we have been taught, then some of the most interesting questions about the world around us cannot be answered or even comprehended without us having advanced mathematics in our armoury. This could mean that when children who are instinctively curious about the world and want to consider such questions as they often do, then they will struggle to answer these and may lose heart and, devastatingly, stop trying to think about the things that they are curious about. It would be fair to say that relying only on mathematics is a limiting approach and one that most children, thankfully, don't do. Let us explore how the conversation continued.

Teacher: How do you think she could have worked it out?

Jess: *(after a long pause):* Well, I think we should, like, figure out the size of Jupiter and half that size, and figure out the size of Earth and half that size, then make it that size. But then you have to quarter it so that you can hold it. Well, maybe she made a model. A bit like when we did our miniature gardens – and if you find out the size of Jupiter and half it and half it and half it and half it again, basically so that you can hold it in your hand . . . *(paused for a while clearly thinking about the problem, then said)* then you can do the same with Earth, you keep on halving it but you need to do it the same number of times so that it is fair, like in a game you need to be fair. So, let's say I halved Jupiter 20 times, you have to remember 20 in your head, and do the same again with Earth to make it a fair test.

Teacher: How does all of this help?

Jess: Then you cut open the top so that you can put the Earths in, and put the top back on. But the top will be curved, so you can make a tower at the top. But you have to count how many Earths as you are putting them in. Then you can fit 1,300 Earths inside the Jupiter you made and count them. You would need lots of them like a ball pool full, and you would need to pile them carefully.

Teacher: Does this give you an answer?

Jess: Well yes because you have counted the number of baby Earths you have put inside Jupiter.

This conversation illustrates many things which make us challenge the way we teach mathematics and answers the question why teach mathematics at all. Benjamin (2013) suggests that we learn mathematics for three reasons – calculation, application and lastly inspiration. Looking at the example above, the question posed by Jess is not answerable by her level of skills in calculation. However, she has been able to connect ideas by applying her experiences and observations to reason an approach which will give her some sense of comprehension and support her curiosity. She is inspired and motivated by the sheer questioning and the need to understand the world around her. It could be argued that the true form of mathematics is to do just that. Davis and Hersh (1990: 7) state:

Mathematics could be 'about' anything as long as it is a subject that exhibits the pattern of assumption-deduction-conclusion.

Mathematics allows us to represent, understand and puzzle all that is around us. It allows for modelling and representing the world in a way that we can hold and wonder to express different ways of thinking about the world. Furthermore, Askew (2012) argues that reducing mathematics to simply calculating answers is limiting the possibilities and reducing the ability of allowing children to understand the world. As we have seen in the conversation above, being able to connect a range of seemingly unconnected ideas together allows a challenging problem to be solved in a beautiful and simple manner. But if we only focus on mathematics as a subject to be taught in an unconnected manner and without being a true expression of the world around us as it is currently, then we are losing the flexibility to think, reason and understand.

Figure 11.1   Mathematics can be a true expression of the world around us (Architect Frank Lloyd Wright inspired by geometrical shapes that appear in nature)

What is the way forward?

Robinson and Aronica (2009) offer the possibility that ensuring greater breadth and balance in the curriculum will potentially give each child the opportunity to find what they call their *element* or sense of relevance, which is key to ensuring that children are learning mathematics in its truest form. The notion that we only learn mathematics as something that will be useful to us in the future is to take away the ability to inspire, motivate, puzzle the world around us and to use mathematics as a way to identify and communicate what it means to ourselves. There is a real beauty to the world and exploring this through the use of mathematics is what we should be encouraging children to do.

As we have seen in the case study above, the only way that Jess was able to explain the question to satisfy her curiosity was to use a broad range of ideas that fall within a multitude of disciplines from art (making models), science (fair test), mathematics (sense of proportion), design and technology (making miniature gardens) to English (communicating through language and processing her ideas and thoughts) to be able to come to some reasonable conclusions about the question that was perplexing her. This begins to illustrate how limiting it is to talk about subjects as discrete blocks of knowledge, and to not endeavour, through our teaching and experiences that children have when gaining knowledge, to make connections and explore ideas in a fluid and dynamic manner. It is dangerous to continue to only consider knowledge in small discrete blocks, as we see how beautifully Jess has been able to connect ideas and answer quite a complex question which is currently beyond her calculation capability, but not beyond the use of her imagination and experiences. This opportunity to reason, explore and make connections is the very essence of what we consider to be mathematics. So, we must question and challenge why we continue to teach in such a limiting manner.

THEORY FOCUS

Research carried out by Boaler (2015), Askew (2012), Skemp (1976, 1987), Shellard and Moyer (2002) and many other researchers on mathematics education state the following key features as being crucial for good mathematics teaching:

- allowing the learner to engage with mathematical concepts through experiencing mathematics;
- working cooperatively to explore, explain and analyse;
- making connections with different aspects of not only mathematics, but also the world around them;
- teaching concepts, not process;
- allowing a range of contextualisation tools to be used, by which we mean resources and examples that help structure and provide imagery for concepts within mathematics;
- the use of modelling in the form of concrete pictorial abstract exemplifications of mathematical ideas.

This leads us to look at our question: *Should we teach mathematics as a discrete subject as is the case currently?* From the body of evidence presented here, teaching mathematics as we do in a discrete manner means that we are missing the opportunity to allow the deep understanding and connectivity that is needed between areas of knowledge and does not allow children to go with their curiosity and to develop a true appreciation and comprehension of the world around them.

The importance of balance

So far we have established that we have the opportunity to reconsider and reimagine how we teach mathematics – to move away from the process-driven discrete teaching which has been developed to fulfil a need that was present in the past but is no longer the case for the new landscape in which we find ourselves. Also, to ensure we fully allow and support children to embrace real mathematics, we need to change the current perspective we have in schools. This is all well and good, but how do we meet and balance the demands of being measured on outcomes of a very narrow content with the wider and on the whole, most teachers would agree, more meaningful outcomes that can only be achieved by teaching mathematics in a more interdisciplinary way. Note that the phrase used here is *interdisciplinary* and not cross-curricular, as the latter emphasises, and further embeds, the notion that subjects are independent and discrete and all we need to do is make connections and links between them. There is more to broadening the curriculum than just establishing cross-curricular links, as we saw in the example given earlier. There was fluidity in the knowledge used to understand and solve the problem addressed by Jess. Therefore, let us finally consider how we can balance the desire to employ a more connected and organic approach to support deeper understanding with the need to achieve high academic outcomes. That is to say, how can we balance the tension between form and function? How can we teach the content prescribed, but in a more integrated manner to meet the *aims* of the primary mathematics curriculum?

Figure 11.2   We can match the aims of the National Curriculum with a more integrated method of teaching

The first step to achieving this would be to move away from thinking within subjects and towards finding mathematics in everything that we do. The table below shows a possible approach to lessons which involves focusing on interesting investigations that allow children to engage and develop their mathematics in an integrated manner and use a range of ideas. The table lists 'disciplines' as a way of highlighting links. Do note, however, that there are no actual boundaries between disciplines when it comes to resolving questions such as those listed. Lessons should be seen as a fluid movement between ideas that come from many possible areas of knowledge.

Lesson purpose	Links to other disciplines	Examples of links to National Programmes of Study for Mathematics
How many balloons does it take to fill a room?	Art Science Design and Technology	**Number place and value** • Counting • Identifying more or less • Comparing values • Addition • Multiplication **Geometry** • 3D shapes • Ordering shapes • Distinguishing between regular and irregular shapes **Measurement** • Length • Width • Height
Investigating maze design	Art History Design and Technology	**Geometry** • 2D shapes • Position and direction • Lines of symmetry **Number place and value** • Equivalence
Investigating if our foot is indeed the same length as our wrist to elbow, and finding other such facts and if it is the same for all people	History Science Art	**Geometry** • Reflection • 3D shapes • Parts of circles • Straight lines • Angles **Number place and value** • Fractions **Ratio proportion** • Relative sizes **Statistics** • Averages
Looking for examples of patterns in music	Music Science	**Number place and value** • Fractions • Sequences • Comparison **Geometry** • Patterns • 2D shapes

(Continued)

169

(Continued)

Lesson purpose	Links to other disciplines	Examples of links to National Programmes of Study for Mathematics
When going for a walk with a dog, how do I find out what distance the dog walks?	Science Art Geography	Measurement • Time • Distance Geometry • 2D shapes Number place and value • Comparison Algebra • Generalisation • Variables

The common theme running through each of these investigative lessons is that they encourage an interdisciplinary approach and ensure that children have the opportunity to engage with mathematics in a way that uses all elements of what makes good teaching as stated earlier. It may be that children do not refer to any of the subjects we have listed in the second column but have their own sense of how they can answer and address the question posed as the main focus of the lesson – we have merely given some possibilities. Furthermore, this way of working embeds conceptual understanding and develops reasoning, problem-solving and fluency skills which are all aims of the current National Curriculum. The suggestion being made here is that instead of starting with a mathematical concept or process as we traditionally do, to have lessons that are based around tinkering with, unpicking and thinking about fascinating elements of the world that children are naturally interested in understanding. This will achieve a number of key outcomes which will address some of the criticisms that have been discussed in this chapter, and move away from a narrow way of teaching to a more discovery-based approach which is far more sustainable. Also, as you can see from the simple examples, there is still full coverage of the National Curriculum areas when working on these investigations. We would further suggest that the way to approach the investigations is to allow children to initiate the questions that might be considered. This would involve working with children over a period of time to establish a bank of possible investigations and then mapping the National Curriculum to these questions to ensure that there is full coverage and greater engagement.

CHAPTER SUMMARY

In this chapter, we have explored some of the reasons why we find ourselves in the current landscape in relation to mathematics education. We have challenged the narrative that has been engrained in our thinking regarding the teaching and learning of mathematics, and hopefully started a spark in thinking how to develop an alternative approach to balance the need to teach for measurable outcomes with the teaching for more sustained meaning and purpose.

KEY POINTS TO CONSIDER

- Ideas around how and why we teach mathematics in the way that we do.
- The value of not teaching discrete subjects and having a more organic approach to knowledge assimilation.
- The nature of mathematics and why it is so different to what we are currently teaching.
- Some ideas on how to deliver a different approach to the teaching of mathematics without losing sight of the curriculum content and the love for learning.

Further reading

Briggs, M. and Davis, S. (2008) *Creative Teaching: Mathematics in the Early Years and Primary Classroom.* Abindon: Routledge.

Cotton, A. (2016) *Understanding and Teaching in Primary Mathematics.* Abingdon: Routledge.

NRICH: https://nrich.maths.org/

References

Askew, M. (2012) *Transforming Primary Mathematics.* Abingon: Routledge.

Benjamin, A. (2013) *The Magic of Fibonacci Numbers.* TED talk, viewed 24 February 2019. **https://www.ted.com/talks/arthur_benjamin_the_magic_of_fibonacci_numbers**

Boaler, J. (2015) *The Elephant in the Classroom: Helping Children Learn and Love Maths*, 2nd edition. London: Souvenir Press.

Boylan, M., **Maxwell**, B., **Wolstenholme**, C., **Jay**, T. and **Demack**, S. (2018) The mathematics teacher exchange and 'mastery' in England: the evidence for the efficacy of component practices. *Education Sciences*, 8: 202.

Claxton, G. (2008) *What's the Point of School? Rediscovering the Heart of Education.* Oxford: Oneworld.

Davis, P.J. and **Hersh**, R. (1990) *The Mathematical Experience.* London: Penguin.

Dowker, A., **Sarkar**, A. and **Looi**, C.Y. (2016) Mathematics anxiety: what have we learned in 60 years? *Frontiers in Psychology*, 7: 508.

Gibb, N. (2017) *Importance of Core Knowledge See Return of Textbooks.* Transcript of speech delivered by the School Standards Minister at a panel discussion at the Policy Exchange on 30 November 2017 (viewed 26 February 2019), **https://www.gov.uk/government/speeches/nick-gibb-importance-of-core-knowledge-sees-return-of-textbooks**

Harel, G. (2008) What is mathematics? A pedagogical answer to a philosophical question. In B. Gold and R. Simons (eds) *Proof and Other Dilemmas. Mathematics and Philosophy.* Washington, DC: Mathematical Association of America, pp. 265–90.

Maths Anxiety Trust (2019) **http://mathsanxietytrust.com/** (viewed 26 February 2019).

Moustafa, A.A., Tindle, R., Ansari, Z., Doyle, M.J., Hewedi, D.H. and Eissa, A. (2017) Mathematics, anxiety, and the brain. *Reviews in the Neurosciences*, *28*: 417–29.

Organisation for Economic Cooperation and Development (OECD) (2019) *Mathematics Performance* (PISA) (Indicator). Available at: **https://www.oecd-ilibrary.org/education/mathematics-performance-pisa/indicator/english_0471174-en** (accessed on 28 March 2019).

Robinson, K. and Aronica, L. (2009) *Finding Your Element*. London: Penguin.

Shellard, E. and Moyer, P.S. (2002) *What Principals Need to Know About Teaching Math*. Alexandria VA: National Association of Elementary School Principals and Education Research Service.

Skemp, R.R. (1976). Relational understanding and instrumental understanding. *Mathematics Teaching*, *77*: 20–6.

Skemp, R.R. (1987) *The Psychology of Learning Mathematics*. Hillsdale, NJ: Lawrence Erlbaum.

Thurston, W. (2009) William Paul Thurston. In M. Cook and R.C. Gunning (eds) *Mathematicians: An Outer View of the Inner World*. Princeton, NJ: University Press, pp. 76–7.

Toffler, A. (1970) *A Future Shock*. New York: Random House.

12

CONNECTING STEM WITH THE ARTS: BECAUSE IT MAKES SENSE

SUSAN OGIER WITH NICK CORSTON

EVERY GREAT ADVANCE IN SCIENCE HAS ISSUED FROM A NEW
AUDACITY OF IMAGINATION.

(JOHN DEWEY, 1929)

KEYWORDS: STEM; STEAM CO.; CREATIVE; ENQUIRY; PROJECT-BASED LEARNING; INCLUSION; PARENT ENGAGEMENT; COMMUNITY;
ENGAGEMENT; IMAGINATION; INNOVATION.

CHAPTER OBJECTIVES

This chapter:

- contextualises the current focus on STEM subjects and discusses myths and misconceptions about what this means for education
- dispels the notion that there is a gap between science and arts knowledge and skills, and explores how there is a natural symbiosis between the two areas of knowledge and skills
- discusses some of the prevalent stereotypes that potentially limit children's engagement with STEM subjects, and explores how the arts can be used to promote deep learning of concepts in STEM subjects to help motivate and engage pupils in an inclusive way
- illustrates how children can be introduced to linking the arts and STEM through community engagement projects and provides exemplars that show how this can work in practice in the primary classroom, with case studies and personal reflections

─── **LINKS TO THE TEACHERS' STANDARDS** ───

Working through this chapter will enable you to meet all of the Teachers' Standards, but in particular:

TS 1:   Establish high expectations which inspire, motivate and challenge pupils

TS 2:   Promote good progress and outcomes by pupils

TS 5:   Adapt teaching to respond to the strengths and needs of pupils

TS 8:   Fulfil wider professional responsibilities

Introduction

In this chapter, we discuss the current emphasis on Science, Technology, Engineering and Mathematics (STEM) subjects in our schools. While acknowledging that these important subjects are key elements of our young people's education and critical preparation (in economic terms) for the future, we argue that they should not exist on their own as an isolated set of skills and knowledge, especially at primary level. The mental image that is conjured by the word *STEM* has connotations of a strong, sturdy, central structure that supports smaller parts, and from which other areas can grow and develop. Now, however, picture a stem without leaves and without a bloom, and you have an image of a stalk without the bit that brings it to life – this is STEM without its lifeblood: creativity. We shall explore the danger of teaching and learning in STEM subjects in the absence of creativity and we will question the rationale for dividing arts and sciences as separate entities, when both ours and children's lives outside of school are so connected across these disciplines. The chapter concludes with a case study and personal perspective by a parent, engineer and artist, Nick Corston, which will highlight just how those connections can be made in any primary school.

What is STEM?

─── **REFLECTION** ───

Ask yourself this question: What is an inventor?

(a) a scientist; (b) a mathematician; (c) a designer?

The answer is that s/he is all of those things: an inventor, quite simply, cannot not *invent* if they don't have the skills and understanding and conviction that allows them to imagine, to dream and to forecast that the things in our lives can be made better – or at the very least improved upon what is currently accepted as being fit for purpose. How will we ever progress as a society, or as a nation or as a planet, if only the ideas of the past are acceptable? Contrary to what is a common understanding of STEM subjects, where children are encouraged to learn facts and figures (knowledge) relating to Science, Technology, Engineering and Maths, these important aspects of children's experience in schools actually rely on features of creativity, enquiry and skills to make any progress at all. Progression in all of the STEM subjects requires divergent thinking, a creative attitude and an acceptance of risk. These aspects are all learned through studying arts-based subjects and creative pedagogy, where risk-taking and the exploration of new ideas and new concepts are actively encouraged. And it is these attributes and attitudes that are so important to establish in childhood, from where they can grow and develop as the child progresses.

Why the focus on STEM subjects?

The focus on STEM subjects in schools came about in England for a very simple reason: economic necessity (DfE, 2009). There was a desperate shortage of young people coming through the education system wanting to pursue any of the subjects, whether science, technology, engineering or mathematics. In 2011, a great deal of funding and resources were put into promoting STEM subjects in schools, not only by the government, which realised they needed to support businesses that required this kind of knowledge for their future recruitment programmes, but also to provide bursaries for prospective student teachers who would teach these subjects. You can read more about the 2009 STEM Strategy here: **https://www.education-ni.gov.uk/articles/stem-strategy**.

Currently, however, while the need for children to be encouraged into the sciences continues to be a key focus for the future, there appear to be some difficulties in changing fundamental preconceptions that exist, and a parliamentary report in 2018 was critical of the lack of progress in this area. Read the report here: **https://bit.ly/2ByQzkW**.

REFLECTION

What do we do, as teachers of primary-aged children, to either reinforce stereotypes or to negate them?

THEORY FOCUS

The above is an important question, and one that requires us to truly look at our own attitudes and values and to be very honest with ourselves. Halpern *et al.* (2007) state that in order to encourage girls into STEM careers, there are five key evidence-based recommendations for

(Continued)

(Continued)

schools to implement. These, we believe, are relevant for *all* children and not just girls. We have adapted the points to illustrate this:

1. To teach that academic abilities are expandable and improvable, to enhance their confidence in their abilities.

2. To provide feedback that focuses on the process of learning, the strategies used during learning and acknowledging the effort that has been made.

3. To expose children to positive role-models that challenge negative stereotypes and promote positive beliefs about their abilities.

4. To create a classroom environment that sparks curiosity and fosters long-term interest through project-based learning, innovative tasks and technology.

5. To provide opportunities for children to engage in spatial skills training.

There is nothing here about getting children to work harder, faster or pass more tests, which is what has happened in recent years in English schools, by means of increasing pressure to show performance results.

Let's have a look at these recommendations and think how we can facilitate the five key points in our own classroom practice through engaging with creative learning pedagogy – not only to encourage girls, but to aid inclusivity in the primary classroom more generally.

1. Children's academic abilities are expandable and improvable

Lucas and Claxton (2010) suggest that intelligence is not something that can easily be measured and yet we attempt to make judgements about children at a very young age. If, however, this is the accepted case, then it shows us is that *ability* is not finite and that learners change and develop as they progress. This has implications for teaching strategies where primary aged children are set in ability groupings, which is common practice, especially in subjects such as maths.

2. That feedback should focus on the process of learning, the strategies used during learning and acknowledging the effort that has been made

Again, this recommendation is about teaching children to value the process of learning as much as the outcomes, raising their awareness of what works for them as individuals and recognising their efforts. In a publication, *Inside the Black Box* (1998), Black and Wiliam disseminated research findings on their investigation into the complexities of teaching and learning. They discovered that children who learned in a formative way achieved better long-term results than others.

The Assessment Reform Group (2002) produced a guide that displays ten principles for assessing in this way. At the heart of this is a collaborative model which states: *Assessment for Learning is the process of seeking and interpreting evidence for use by learners and their teachers to decide where the learners are in their learning, where they need to go and how best to get there.* It is important to remember that if we subscribe to the idea of expandable intelligence, then perhaps outcome-based assessment should not be how we measure whether a child has 'got there', as this, once again, places a lid on children's learning.

3. Role-models should be introduced to challenge negative stereotypes and promote positive self-beliefs

And there are a lot to choose from! With inclusion in mind here, it is important to show not only role-models who are female, but also those from different ethnic and socio-economic groups, with a range of abilities and disabilities, from different times in history to contemporary figures. These can be introduced to children in a multitude of imaginative ways, including a visit to your local museum or art gallery, such as the National Portrait Gallery in London (or Scottish National Portrait Gallery in Edinburgh), where children can come face to face with a range of key innovators of the past and present, for example the inspirational physician Elizabeth Garret Anderson, who overcame enormous prejudice to qualify as the first female doctor in 1865. There are so many examples of people who have changed our world and our thinking, sometimes *because* of their own personal challenges. An example of this could be someone like Temple Grandin, who was diagnosed with autism as a child and went on to achieve a degree in animal science and then a PhD. She has influenced the humane care of livestock worldwide. You can watch her TED talk here: **https://bit.ly/1KCLbNQ**.

REFLECTION

Some of these examples might help you to be reflective of the potential of children in your own class. Are there some children who you have already decided are 'low ability' or 'low achievers', based on stereotypical perceptions? Is it because you have not given them a chance to show you just what they CAN do, or what they are interested in?

4. Create a classroom environment that sparks curiosity and fosters long-term interest through project-based learning, innovative tasks and technology

What should a classroom environment that 'sparks curiosity' look like? I doubt that it is one that has posters of WOW words and how to do fractions all over it! The classroom that sparks curiosity and is supportive of 'extendable intelligence' is much more likely to be a creative space, a place where enquiry is central: where children are encouraged to explore and experiment physically and intellectually; a creative environment where open-ended questions are more common than correct answers; where appropriate resources are freely available; where there is the emotionally supportive space to think, discuss and debate, without the fear of being wrong or being ridiculed. Learning in and through the arts can provide this space: to facilitate good enquiry-based learning in practical and non-competitive ways that are inclusive for all learners.

5. To provide opportunities to engage in spatial skills training

There is no question that this is important for everyone. Spatial awareness is one of those things that if you don't have it – you ain't goin' nowhere! Hugely underestimated as a key skill, spatial awareness can be learned and is a necessary skill for just living your life. If you did not have this understanding, you would not have passed your driving test (you would not be able to avoid other cars, and you certainly would not be able to park your own car!); you would not even be able to walk down the street without crashing into other people and objects. This skill is commonly taught on foundation courses for art and design with simple activities that you can easily replicate in the primary classroom.

Think like an engineer

We are all very aware of the need to educate children for jobs for the future, and this whole book is about exactly that. STE(A)M careers, such as engineering, are certainly at the forefront of what we shall need in years ahead. The Royal Academy of Engineers commissioned research into the way that engineers work and think, which highlights essential life skills and knowledge for developing what they describe as 'habits of mind', such as questioning, problem-solving and problem-finding. In the report *Thinking Like an Engineer* conducted by the Centre for Real World Learning, Lucas *et al.* (2014) make the case that 'engineering habits of mind' (EHoM) should begin to be formed in very young children, because children are natural engineers at an early age, and this disposition should be maintained and developed through the primary phase. It accuses the current school system, in many instances, of extinguishing opportunities for them to flourish as engineers (p. 3) and gives the example that the key features of engineering, that is *designing, making* and *tinkering*, are what children do instinctively. They cite Piagetian theory – that progress tends to be measured by how children need less practical, less applied ways of thinking and working: this is wholly inappropriate in engineering terms. They state that 'making stuff' is at 'the heart of what engineers do' (p. 32). The practical, hands-on, experimental, creative activities that we offer primary aged children through arts, design technology, forest school activities, etc. are at the heart of EHoM.

Read the report: **https://www.raeng.org.uk/publications/reports/thinking-like-an-engineer-implications-full-report**.

┌─── **REFLECTION** ───┐

Consider Figure 12.1. When and where in your daily work with children do you foster these 'engineering habits of mind'? How could you change things in your practice to make sure you are including opportunities for children to develop dispositions for 'thinking like an engineer'?

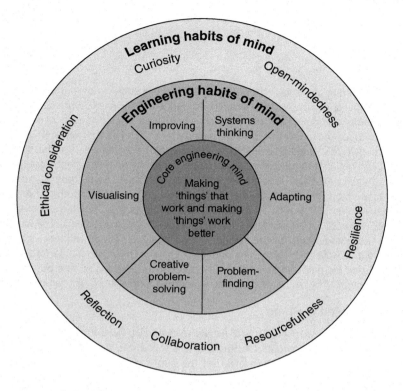

Figure 12.1 Engineering habits of mind. Lucas et.al. Thinking like an Engineer (2014)

CASE STUDY

Nick Corston, with an MA in engineering, founded the national, non-profit community enterprise *STEAM Co.* in 2014. Here he talks about why he is so motivated to do this and what has inspired him:

I think we can see from the examples in this chapter that here is one little problem with the notion of STEM: on its own it is not enough to engage and attract the broadest number of young people, not only for those who need a creative pathway to pursue their talents in their working lives, but also for those who have the potential to acquire the skills they will need to flourish and thrive in life beyond work. It has never been enough for some of the most successful innovators and disruptors we have known, such as leading scientist Professor Robert Winston, Chairman of the Royal College of Music until 2017; Leonardo da Vinci, who was a scientist, mathematician and artist, known equally for his work in these spheres; Sir Joseph Bazelgette, the engineer who built London's sewer systems, and every pumping house had the most beautiful artwork installed, such was his passion for the combination of art and engineering. The list can go on and on.

(Continued)

(Continued)

Just an acronym?

There can be little denial of the fact that a focus on the core subjects of maths and English alone has impacted negatively on arts and the sciences too, which I believe will ultimately be detrimental. Schools become a dry and dull place when the focus is only on academic aspects of the curriculum, and we will not produce the innovators, disruptors and game-changers that we need to solve some of society's – and the world's – biggest challenges. At the same time, many arts and design technology subjects have been reduced to functional skills, with the most important aspect – creativity – almost removed from them, in an effort to make these into subjects that can be taught and tested in the same way as academic subjects, which is a nonsense. This is why I talk about STEAM rather than STEM. STEAM is not just STEM with an A for Art added in: it must be much more meaningful than that. For me, STEAM is about creativity, so that the profile of creative subjects is raised (such as the arts and design technology), with children being able to engage creatively and teachers teaching creatively. These creative ways of teaching and engaging learners might be summarised by approaches such as *project-based learning*, where subjects are taught over a period of time with a major project theme running through. This can be over a week, a month, a term or a whole year in some schools.

What is project-based learning?

Have you seen the movie *Most Likely to Succeed* (directed by Greg Whiteley, 2017)? It features the work of a high-tech high school in America where the whole curriculum is taught using project-based learning. For example, the work that the pupils do is learned, taught and presented through real-life projects and *making*. Although this is based in an American high school, the lessons are the same for you as a primary teacher: how important is it to make learning meaningful and purposeful for the children in your class? For many pupils in the film, their learning is transformative, and this is fundamentally because of the creative pedagogy employed by the teachers. It reflects the way that information is no longer disseminated exclusively through educational institutions. Information is readily available for children at the press of a button or the swipe of a screen, and the role of the teacher, the role of school itself, has been transformed – or needs to be transformed – to become more of a facilitative, coaching and guiding role, and not just for disseminating information.

Most importantly to me, through STEAM and the work we do at STEAM Co., we understand that in many teachers and within many schools there is so much passion, creativity and inspiration which can be tapped into to develop the school community. The benefits of creativity know no bounds: the benefit of inspiring and celebrating creativity across education, work and life. The power of creativity is in technology, in making things and in people who inspire children to want to learn. Jobs for the future are developed through creative industries, which powers the economy and connects people with their communities. And that is why, to me, creativity is so much more important than any acronym can suggest.

Take a risk

The STEAM Co. approach presents a fantastic opportunity to showcase and to champion arts subjects which are under pressure at the moment, as well as promoting creative pedagogy in schools, which is what we should be considering as we move forward in the twenty-first century. One of the most contentious statements made in this area is by Ken Robinson in his very well-known TED talk, in which he says that schools can teach creativity out of children, and that 'creativity is as important as literacy'. Certainly, the things that creativity teaches children are as important as anything else we can teach them, such as risk-taking and that it is OK to make mistakes.

Figure 12.2   Children making wire sculptures on a STEAM Co. Day at St Saviour's C of E Primary, Paddington (Photo. Gabby Ritchie)

Seth Godin's book, *The Icarus Deception* (2013), describes the Greek fable of how Icarus tries to fly with wings fashioned from feathers, sticks and wax. He is told not to fly too close to the sun because the heat of the sun would melt the wax and his wings would fail. What is often overlooked in recounting this famous fable is that Icarus is also warned not to fly too low, for fear of going into the sea. Flying too low in itself is perhaps even more dangerous than flying too high because it is deceptively safe: at least when you are flying high you are cautious because you know it is dangerous. In the event Icarus ignored the warnings, flew too high, his wings got burnt and he plunged to his doom. So, for every child who hears that story, the message is that you should play it safe. Don't take risks. Godin claims this was the perfect propaganda for the industrial economy, because what boss wouldn't want their employees to believe that obedience and conformity are the keys to success?

Today we need to be teaching young children to think creatively, to think around problems – to think where the problems are and to think how to solve those problems in creative ways. Godin discusses how we have moved away from an industrial economy to a *connection economy*.

(Continued)

(Continued)

Godin is the bestselling author of many books on marketing and behavioural change who, like many people, when he had a child in school himself became aware of some of the challenges of the current educational system **https://www.youtube.com/watch?v=sXpbONjV1Jc**.

This work by Godin has influenced lot of my personal work with STEAM Co. and, via a desire to redefine art as broadly as possible and make it as accessible as possible, led indirectly to the *I Love Art* campaign, which we are running as a collaboration with $1m prize-winner and French street artist JR, that you can find out about by following this link: **https://www.steamco.org.uk/iloveart/**.

A launch pad for learning

A heavy academic focus on learning will not engage all learners. When this is the only option in schools, many learners can become disengaged at an early age, leading to behavioural issues and, even worse, exclusion. I will never forget the day that I worked in a school in Liverpool for a half-day *RocketKids* project. This entails a whole-school assembly to start, a creative rocket-making workshop for a class of 30 pupils and a real dynamite rocket launch to finish. One young boy was slow to engage with me and seemed very wary at first, but by the end of the day he had made a super rocket and launched it with great pleasure. Funnily enough, his rocket landed in the roof of the school hall – and remains there for posterity! I was very touched when his head teacher came to me to say that this was the first time that this young man had actively engaged in school and stayed on task. He was confident that they would be able to build on that.

Figure 12.3   A parent helps a young rocket kid launch her creation (Photo. Gabby Ritchie)

The power of creativity to strengthen wider community and school engagement is best illustrated by the time that I spent in a school in Luton, with a head teacher who was struggling to get parents and the local community to be engaged in their children's learning. I repeated the *RocketKids* session over a day: 150 parents came to the workshop to make and fire rockets with their children. The head teacher recently told me how they had recruited members of the parental community as members of staff as teaching assistants on the back of that workshop, as they had been so inspired. The head of a school in Bradford informed me that they now have 14 parents from the Bangladeshi community who had never been into school before, coming in every week to do gardening work and other enrichment activities for the children on a voluntary basis.

How can you do this in the classroom?

Some examples of how you might bring in project-based work to your own classroom or school might include collapsing the timetable for a day, maybe once a term or maybe for a week in the year. During this time children can experiment with project-based and creative learning, and I have worked with a number of schools doing this. STEAM Co. itself was established to provide the inspiration and resources for school communities to run mini creative festivals on STEAM Co. Days. This is where, over the course of the day, children are able to choose from up to 20 creative projects which might include activities such as rocket-making, coding, spin-painting, drama improvisations, ukulele playing, inventing, as well as a range of other activities led by teachers working closely with parents.

Figure 12.4   Ukulele is just one activity available on a Pop-Up STEAM Co. Day.
(Photo. Gabby Ritchie)

(Continued)

(Continued)

Creative practitioners, such as artists and musicians, are encouraged to come in to work with children, from both inside and outside of the school community depending on the school budget. You can draw on the expertise of friends and family of the school community to do this. You might be pleasantly surprised at the talent pool right on your school's doorstep.

Figure 12.5   The Cardboard Challenge activity on a STEAM Co. Day at St Saviour's C of E Primary School which was featured the next day on BBC Breakfast. (Photo. Gabby Ritchie)

We sometimes need reminding of the power and inspirational nature of creativity, not only so that children get the most out of their school years, but to inspire them to develop their own creative pathways and careers of the future. There is no reason to see creativity purely as a means to employment, as children will gain skills that are transferable into other areas of their lives. For example, drama is mentioned as a desirable skill and qualification for very many traditional and academic careers, such as law. Hand–eye coordination and fine motor skills, learned through engaging with visual art processes such as drawing and making, are essential for anyone who is going to grow up to become a surgeon.

Community: the ultimate curriculum

They say it takes a village to raise a child, and the STEAM Co. collaboration model connects communities with schools on many levels. Parental engagement is perhaps key here. Many schools still struggle to engage parents. Sometimes this is because they have busy working lives, or it can be because they did not have a very good experience at school themselves. By involving parents in creative activities such as project days, you can show them that they can enjoy school, and that things are changing for the better for their own children.

At STEAM Co. we say that *everyone is an artist and everyone has the ability to connect*. Sometimes it is just about reconnecting with your creative self and rediscovering the excitement and pleasure associated with this. Many artists are brought into work with us on STEAM Co. days, such as inventor and artist Nick Sayers, who has developed giant drawing machines using bicycles turned on their sides, rather like a giant Spirograph (**http://gallery.bridgesmathart.org/exhibitions/2013-bridges-conference/nicksayers**).

And inventor/designer Dominic Wilcox, whose Little Inventors project has gone global.

When Dominic was growing up in Sunderland, the UK capital of the stained-glass industry, he went to Durham Cathedral and was mesmerised by the stained-glass windows. He eventually studied product design at the Royal College of Art in London. He entered a competition to design a new car of the future and designed a stained-glass driverless sleeper car, revisiting his memory of the visit to the cathedral. Is he an engineer or an artist? See his work and link to Little Inventors here: **http://dominicwilcox.com**.

REFLECTION

Does this help you to think about the memories you are helping store up for the children in your class?

What is your understanding of the links between arts and sciences, having read this chapter?

CHAPTER SUMMARY

In this chapter we have considered that participation in arts subjects facilitates learning in science, technology, engineering and maths, and that developing learning in these subjects together are key to building the skills and dispositions children need for the future. We have seen from research that stereotypical notions of children's abilities, gender, ethnic and socio-economic backgrounds can easily be challenged in our own classrooms, by creating learning environments that support expandable intelligence, and by including activities in which enquiry and 'making' are central for engagement in STEM subjects. The STEAM Co. model, suggested by Nick Corston, demonstrates how you can utilise the school and local community to support you in developing STEAM by bringing project-based learning into your own classroom, and making learning meaningful by connecting children's learning across disciplines.

```
┌─────────────── KEY POINTS TO CONSIDER ───────────────┐
```

- Skills and knowledge in arts subjects can and should be utilised to facilitate good learning in STEM subjects, and these are often interdependent in the real world: school experiences should reflect that.
- We need to truthfully examine potential stereotypical perceptions and ensure we counteract these by developing expandable intelligence strategies and learning environments that are inclusive and supportive.
- To consider the value of project-based learning and of promoting creative making.
- To develop relationships with parents and the wider community to facilitate and validate creative ways of working.
- It is essential to develop attributes such as divergent thinking, a creative attitude and an acceptance of risk in primary aged children so that these dispositions are embedded at an early age.

Further reading

Hickey, I. and Robson, D. (2013) *The Leonardo Effect: Motivating Children to Achieve Through Interdisciplinary Learning.* London: David Fulton.

This book describes an interdisciplinary teaching methodology based upon research with 19 schools, mostly primary. Read inspiring case studies where 'synchronised integration' of arts and sciences led to extraordinary results.

Look at the Wellcome Foundation website, which has a section for primary schools showing videos of children engaged in creative science activities: **https://explorify.wellcome.ac.uk/activities**

Look for STEAM resources on the TES: **https://www.tes.com/teaching-resources/steam**

References

Assessment Reform Group (2002) *Assessment for Learning: 10 Research-based Principles to Guide Classroom Practice.* London: Assessment Reform Group.

Black, P. and Wiliam, D. (1998) *Inside the Black Box: Raising Standards Through Classroom Assessment.* London: School of Education, King's College.

Claxton, G., Lucas, B. and Spencer, E. (2012), *Making It: Studio Teaching and its Impact on Teachers and Learners.* Winchester: Centre for Real World Learning.

Department for Education and Department for Employment and Learning (2009) *Report of the STEM Review.* Available at: **https://www.education-ni.gov.uk/sites/default/files/publications/de/Report%20of%20the%20STEM%20Review%202009_1.PDF**

Godin, S. (2013) *The Icarus Deception: How High Will You Fly?* London: Portfolio Penguin.

Halpern, D., Aronson, J., Reimer, N., Simpkins, S., Star, J. and Wentzel, K. (2007) *Encouraging Girls in Math and Science (NCER 2007–2003).* Washington, DC: National Center for Education Research,

Institute of Education Sciences, US Department of Education. Available at: **https://ies.ed.gov/ ncee/wwc/Docs/PracticeGuide/20072003.pdf**

Lucas, **B. and Claxton**, **G.** (2010) *New Kinds of Smart: How the Science of Learnable Intelligence is Changing Education*. Berkshire: Open University Press.

Lucas, **B.**, **Hanson**, **J. and Claxton**, **G.** (2014) *Thinking Like an Engineer: Implications for the Education System*. London: Royal Academy of Engineering.

Ogier, **S.** (2017) *Teaching Primary Art and Design*. London: Learning Matters.

STEAM Co. website has a wealth of videos of STEAM Co. Days and talks at their events. See: **www. steamco.org.uk**

UNESCO (2017) *Cracking the Code: Girls' and Women's Education in Science, Technology, Engineering and Mathematics (STEM)*. France: UNESCO. Available at: **https://unesdoc.unesco.org/ark:/48223/ pf0000253479**

Whiteley, G. (dir.) (2017) *Most Likely to Succeed*.

13
ASSESSING THE WHOLE CHILD

MARIA VINNEY

NOT EVERYTHING THAT COUNTS CAN BE COUNTED AND NOT
EVERYTHING THAT CAN BE COUNTED COUNTS.

(WILLIAM BRUCE CAMERON, 1963)

KEYWORDS: WHOLE CHILD; ASSESSMENT; STRATEGIES; LISTENING; OBSERVATION; SELF-ASSESSMENT; SOCIAL EMOTIONAL; WELL-BEING; GOOD PRACTICE.

CHAPTER OBJECTIVES

This chapter will help you to:

- understand what assessment is and think about how you can make sure that you assess the things that really matter for your children's learning and development

- consider different strategies which make assessment not just valuable, but manageable for you and enjoyable for your children

- reflect on what you can learn from the way early years practitioners already successfully assess children's capabilities, right across the primary age range

- find out about good assessment practice in UK schools but also further afield by looking at how other countries assess the whole child in all aspects of their learning and development

Introduction

Looking back, my interest in assessing the whole child was prompted when I took on the headship of a large urban primary school in challenging circumstances, which had been at the bottom of the league tables for several years. Challenging behaviour, a tradition of poor standards and a rock-bottom reputation meant staff turnover was high and morale was low, not just among the staff, but among the children, their families and the local community. Physically and mentally exhausted by the challenges surrounding them, and fed-up with being made to feel 'bottom of the heap', most staff recognised that change was necessary, and as a new head teacher, I was excited by the challenge. So, conscious that to bring about a positive shift in attitudes and expectations, as well as standards, the school community would need to work together, we began our journey, one step at a time. We began by creating a huge mind map which we kept on the wall in the staff room, where we explored the question: 'What do *our* children need?'

After two years of hard work, determination and some much needed energy and enthusiasm, we were thrilled to be invited to become part of a 'Vibrant School' research project, in collaboration with Bath Spa University and our local authority. Rather than doing more of the same old, usually focused on more literacy or more numeracy, we had been identified as a school which was prepared to be brave and try something different in order to truly make a difference to the children in our care.

It was this experience more than anything, I think, which ignited my interest and determination to show teachers – and consequently the student teachers I now teach – just how important it is to enable every child to show who they are and what they can do, because children, as we all know, are very good at surprising you.

Human beings are complex and unique; each of us is different and because of this, assessing children is a complicated business. As such, it continues to be the subject of much debate and controversy, both in this country and around the world. Teachers and school staff consciously, and subconsciously, continually assess their children; each time they work alongside a child, observe or listen to a child, either in or out of the classroom, they consider how well that child is doing. This chapter will consider what we mean by assessment and why we assess children. It will explore how we can ensure that we focus our attention on the things that matter for children. How can we give each and every child the opportunity to show, in many different ways, what they can do and what they have learnt?

The ebb and flow of assessment

The way we are asked to assess our children continues to evolve, as does our curriculum; education doesn't stand still. The shifting sands of assessment come and go, tied up in what we choose to value, so when we talk about 'assessing children's progress' we are usually referring to the ability of teachers to consider and make a judgement about what Ofsted and the current government have asked us to measure. Good teachers are interested in so much more than this. They recognise the need to notice not just how well their children are progressing academically but how well their children are developing socially, emotionally and physically, even though it is not always easy to judge due to the complexity of children's lives – often in school we just see the tip of the iceberg.

REFLECTION

How do you view assessment? What is the ethos for assessing pupils in your school?

The methods we use and the way we choose to assess our children in the UK continues to be the source of much discussion and debate, both in the media and among society as a whole. Growing awareness of, and a concern about the need to protect children's positive mental health is a worry for both teachers and parents, especially in relation to what we refer to as *summative* assessment. Known as assessment *of* learning, this is where we test children's understanding at particular points in their education. Statutory Assessment Tests, known as SATs, currently in Years 2 and 6 at primary school, and GCSEs and A levels at secondary school are examples. But actually any kind of assessment which provides a 'snapshot' view of where that child is in their learning – or rather what they are able to show they have retained on that day at that time – is summative.

The Children Act (Her Majesty's Government, 2004) and the White Paper, *The Importance of Teaching* (DfE, 2010), outline that it is a statutory duty of maintained schools to promote children's well-being and also that schools should focus on improving academic attainment. However, despite understanding the need for governments to demonstrate that children in the UK are being well educated and that schools are making good use of public funding, the impact and pressure of the current testing culture in our schools for both children and teachers has been found to result in the narrowing of the curriculum and 'teaching to the test', where core subjects are prioritised because they are being measured in this way, to the detriment of other subjects.

Ofsted have also voiced their concerns about young people spending too much time practising for the tests and not enough studying a range of subjects in depth, which has of course been driven by their focus on data. Funding and training has pretty much been focused on those subjects that provide the data they have wanted to see, but it is not all doom and gloom. There have been many creative and positive examples where primary schools have thought hard about how to minimise the impact of statutory testing on children's self-esteem and well-being, such as the school which referred to the Year 2 SATS as 'Secret Agent Training' and involved the children in what they called a series of challenges rather than tests, resulting in the children being visibly excited at the thought of doing their 'Secret Agent Training'.

Changes ahead

The new Ofsted framework, due for publication in September 2019, will aim to address the narrowing of the curriculum and inspectors will be looking for evidence of children receiving high-quality, rich experiences right across the curriculum, not in just a few subjects, and they will be interested in how the curriculum supports children's health and well-being. They will be *inspecting and reporting on the things that really matter for a good education* (Ofsted, 2017) and this level of renewed scrutiny of the foundation subjects should result in schools spending time and energy looking at their curriculum in order to provide a better balance for children. They will, therefore, be keen to be able to show not just what children are doing, but how well they are doing in all of those subject areas. So how do we make this manageable for staff and enjoyable for children?

Assessment for Learning

Formative assessment strategies, known as *assessment for learning*, are where teachers use their skills to assess children's understanding as they go along. Continually, throughout a lesson, teachers may address any misconceptions or use their questioning, listening and observation skills to adapt their teaching to make it more or less challenging, to support children's learning and move them forward in their thinking and their understanding.

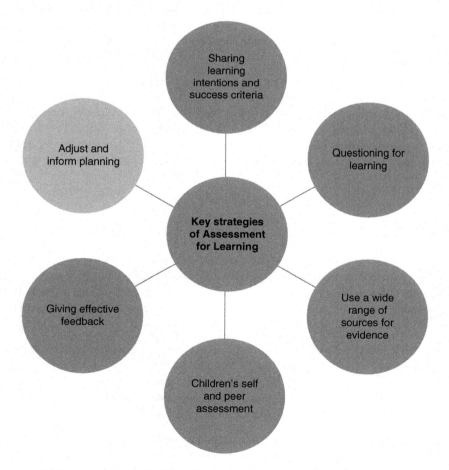

Figure 13.1   A range of strategies are available to the class teacher for making assessments

Let's explore what some of these strategies might these look like in the classroom, for teachers and, critically, for children.

Time to think, time to talk, time to reflect

There are some potentially exciting advancements which could really help to move your assessment practice forward and give you a greater understanding of your children and their learning just by listening to what they have to say and asking questions.

Strategies such as 'pair and share' or the use of 'talk partners', where children share their ideas initially with a partner before then offering their thoughts to the class, are well established in UK classrooms as a way of building children's confidence and giving them time to think through an idea and then verbalise their response. These can of course help you to assess children's learning and, rather than remaining at the front of the class, it also encourages you as the teacher, and any supporting adults, to move around the group in order to 'tune in' to children's conversations so that you can then assess their understanding by skilfully pursuing a line of enquiry. By asking further questions you can encourage children to clarify their thinking and to consider their answer in more depth, as well as address any misconceptions children may have. You are then able to adapt and personalise your teaching accordingly.

Some schools have developed this strategy further and organise for their children to have a 'study buddy' which again supports the idea of children working and learning together and from each other at various times of the day. Vygotsky's social constructivist approach underpins this way of working. It recognises that when children are in what he called the *Zone of Optimal Development* they are learning alongside someone else, be that a more experienced adult or peer. This enhances their own learning and they are then more able to apply that learning independently (Smidt, 2014).

Be flexible

As you know, each child is unique and learns in different ways so it is important that, whenever possible, we give them a variety of opportunities and ways to share what they can do. Sometimes the way they do this may be your choice as the teacher, influenced by factors such as time and resources, but sometimes it should be the child's decision, and sometimes it will depend on what it is that they have been learning that influences this.

In the longer term, many schools build in an opportunity for children to proudly showcase their learning at the end of a block or unit of work. We used to call this our 'Fab Finish', and it always involved inviting families in to see the culmination of whatever it was we had been learning about. Without fail, these were well attended, joyful celebrations where children took great pleasure in surprising their families, and sometimes us, with how much they had achieved.

There are many different strategies which not only help you to assess children and decide where they need to go next on their learning journey, but they are also opportunities for children to self-assess their own learning and progress. Learning something on your own feels good and provides a great deal of satisfaction, but learning something all together and sharing that real sense of achievement feels even more powerful. We need to create lots of opportunities for children to show us who they are because as you know, they continually surprise and delight us when they are given the chance to show what they can do.

REFLECTION

How many different ways can you think of for children to evidence their learning and share what they can do, such as presentations, posters, etc.? Be honest – would you say you usually ask children to present their learning in a particular way, or could you extend these methods? How could you evidence learning for parents, or for Ofsted?

Conferencing

Several schools around the UK have taken these strategies to a whole new level and are inviting their children to regularly share their ideas and thoughts about their learning in a more structured way, by trialling the idea of 'conferencing'. The aim is to support children's independence and ownership of their learning and potentially accelerate progress. Children are given individual time with their teacher and encouraged to find ways to improve their learning by reflecting on what they have already achieved: in effect, self-assessing their progress. Schools have found that their children really enjoy being able to select a piece of work from across the curriculum and are keen to share and discuss their work and to talk through what they need to do to improve. Some schools have linked this in with the work they have been doing around 'learning values' and Guy Claxton's 'Learning Power' skills such as resilience, reflectiveness and resourcefulness.

REFLECTION

How well do you understand where each of your pupils is currently at in their learning and what they need to do in order to progress? How often do you discuss expectations and progress with your pupils?

'Bubble Time'

This idea of teachers making time to talk to their children may not be such a new concept – as a class teacher I remember having what we called 'Bubble Time' with my children at various points in the year, and always when I was about to write their report. In effect this was a 'conference' with each child in my class while the other children got on with their learning independently. This was really much more than an opportunity for the child to tell me what they were most proud of and to flag up anything they wanted specific help with, or for me to suggest some targets and offer support, it was precious time to connect with each child, have a real unrushed conversation and check in on their well-being.

REFLECTION

Think about your class. How can you build in some time, perhaps during one or two afternoons a week, where you could work in this way and find 20 minutes to talk to one individual child in detail?

Some schools have extended this idea of 'conferencing' with their children in small groups in a very powerful way, which proves to have a significant impact on their learning as well as on their enjoyment and independence, as we can see in the following case study.

CASE STUDY

Personal Learning Time

Sally is the head teacher of a rural primary school with four classes which have recently introduced Personal Learning Time (PLT) for their children. Following a good Ofsted inspection but some disappointing Key Stage 2 results, they were forced to take a long hard look at how they worked and, with the support of their Leading Learning Partner from the local authority, realised that in order to move forward they had to make some significant changes. Their current approach was, they realised, resulting in children becoming more, rather than less dependent on the teacher as they moved up through the school. With this in mind, they decided to make a change in the way they planned, taught, marked and assessed because each of these are closely interlinked. It was a brave and bold move which Sally had to work hard to convince staff to try, but with her help and gentle encouragement, plus a 'let's try it and see' approach, they began to realise that children had been waiting to be told what to do and how to do it rather than being empowered to take ownership of their learning and continuing to be the autonomous self-initiated learners they had previously been when they were in the Early Years.

They began by explaining to the children that they would be going on a 'learning journey' together and then they asked them questions such as 'Do you prefer your teacher to write and give you feedback in your book or to talk to you?' Perhaps unsurprisingly, the children were positive about wanting to talk more to their teacher so, encouraged by this, teachers began making some significant changes. They adopted a flexible approach to grouping children so they did far less whole-class teaching and, instead, taught small groups for 20 minutes at a time, sharply focused on what those children needed, so observation became a really key skill for the teachers. Based on what they saw and heard when they worked with the children, they planned their next step. This had an immediate impact on progress, and the need for marking became minimal as feedback was instant.

Time that had been spent marking is now spent redirecting teaching and planning Personal Learning Tasks that the rest of the children can get on with independently.

This menu of tasks is introduced in different ways, according to the age and stage of the children, so Year 1 has the guidance of a teaching assistant to remind them of the tasks on offer that day – usually but not always these are based in their outdoor environment. Year 3 has a series of PLT tasks to complete in a particular week but, critically, the children choose what they want to do and when – they are in control of their learning, they make the decisions that are right for them. Admittedly, to start with some of the PLT tasks were things that children could get on with easily. However, as teachers became more confident about trusting children to work through the challenges and problem-solve, tasks also became much more creative. The rewards are palpable. When asked to explain how PLT works to governors during one of their visits, the children were, as always, very honest, 'We used to waste a lot of time sitting on the carpet waiting for children', 'I just wanted to get on and now I can', 'I like choosing what to do first', 'I like doing a new challenge'. This isn't just working for children as staff are talking more, smiling more. Teachers feel like they have a much clearer understanding of what their children can do and what they need next. This is not just about children's learning, it's about how children learn, so although it is early days, Sally is entirely convinced that her school will not look back, only forward to a bright and happy future.

Steps to success

Of course, there are other ways you can involve your children in showing what they can do, not only that they understand their learning, whatever that might be, but that they understand the journey they need to make to get there, and that there is flexibility in the way they do this. Give them ownership of this process by talking through a task in a clear and accessible way using age-appropriate language, and then give time to think together about what the 'steps to success' or learning objectives need to be along the way. Explain that they may need to take the scenic route, in other words the journey will be different for different children, and there will be some areas where they can whizz along but others where they might need to slow down or try a different way or return to something. Just as in Bruner's spiral curriculum, they may need to revisit and build on what they know: you need to be open and honest with your children about the need to either accelerate or slow learning down to ensure they succeed, but that's OK. Try to create a safe and positive climate which helps children to understand that learning anything new can be difficult to start with, but by encouraging them to keep trying and perhaps changing their approach or way of working, in other words building skills of resilience and problem-solving, they will get there. Show them that you value the journey by displaying and celebrating not just the outcome – the end of their destination – but the steps they took to get there. Help them to be proud of the effort it took to achieve what they did, whatever the subject. Later, we shall look briefly at the Reggio Emilia approach to education which does this very successfully.

Figure 13.2   Shows nursery portraits where the different stages of the children's learning journey are highlighted and valued, the children's own speech bubbles contain what they want to say about their learning in the form of mark making, reinforced by the teacher's annotation.

Supporting children in their ability to reflect on their own and others' learning, giving them the time and the space they need to identify what they need to do to move forward, is crucial. Often classrooms are busy places, where children move from one subject to the next without really having time to stop and think about what their next step should be, or to show that they have actually achieved what it was they were aiming to do. This doesn't have to take long but it is vitally important. So get into the habit of planning ten minutes at the end of your art lesson, for example, where children gather and review their artwork as a group. They can make comments about what they feel has worked well by considering not just their own, but other people's work, and suggest what could happen next.

REFLECTION

How will you make sure when you are working with your children across the curriculum that you have planned time for them to reflect, review and celebrate their learning, whatever that might be? How can you make sure this happens?

What can we learn from the way other countries assess their children?

Having considered the English approach to assessment, let's look at alternative models from other countries and cultures who do this differently. After the Second World War, many countries reviewed their curricula and considered how they wanted to educate their future citizens. Attempts to predict the skills children need growing up in an increasingly complex world, such as good communication, a positive attitude and the ability to get on well with other people, are seen by many to be important and have therefore been incorporated into the primary school curriculum.

Tokubetsu Katsudo (Tokkatsu for short) is practised throughout Japan, for example. Tokkatsu is a series of special activities which focus on educating the whole child and are intertwined and systematically built into the curriculum, alongside academic lessons. Children are expected to obtain the same level of knowledge in these activities as they do in all other subjects, including moral education. In Japanese education Tokkatsu involves children developing their body and mind; primary school is seen as a place to make happy memories. Children take it in turns, for example, to prepare and serve lunch; they are part of a school council where they are encouraged to give their views but also respect the opinions of others; they work together to help organise a cultural event, clean their classroom and generally learn how to live a better life, both collectively and as an individual.

Scandinavian countries have a well-documented interest in promoting life skills with their children and have a reputation for giving children time to be children. They value a unhurried pace to make learning more effective which often involves learning outdoors. In Finland, for example, early childhood education is focused on health and well-being rather than cognitive development (Sahlberg, 2014). The emphasis on educative play until children are age six and seven, combined with very low rates of child poverty at around 4 per cent, means that by age 11 Finnish children perform better than their English counterparts in the areas assessed by the Programme for International Student Assessment (PISA). Despite a fall in their success in 2015 attributed to greater multiculturalism in their schools and an increase in technology and screen time impacting on children's reading skills in particular, the reputation of Finnish schools remains: teachers are held in high esteem and are given autonomy to teach what they feel their children need in a way that is right for those children. The teacher's judgement is trusted to assess children: there is no national assessment for primary aged children and they are not ranked according to educational success so the idea of 'failure' is removed. We can learn much from this.

The Reggio Emilia approach to education is renowned throughout the world and indeed resonates with good early years practice in the UK. After the Second World War, the community in a small town in northern Italy decided to build a school from the bricks of bombed-out buildings and the proceeds from the sale of a tank. People were keen to rebuild their lives and wanted their children to have a better future so together they created a new kind of school where children were treated as citizens, encouraged to ask questions, collaborate and work together. The school became a symbol of hope for the future under the guidance of Loris Malaguzzi, a primary school teacher who, having been inspired by what was happening at the school, dedicated his life to sharing the approach. Today, the guiding values and principles of Reggio inform high-quality early years practice but we can potentially apply this way of working, not just in the early years but across the primary school.

CHAPTER SUMMARY

Do what comes naturally

We have established that teachers are naturally interested in people – we are curious about why we do what we do, as humans. More than anything we want our children to enjoy learning and to help them move forward in their development – it is a fundamental skill of being a teacher! We know that teachers are skilled observers of children; we continually collect a variety of data about each child's learning and development and we continually assess children's understanding and reflect on the impact of our teaching. As we have heard, we know that by learning alongside children, observing them carefully, listening, documenting observations and conversations and asking questions, we can find out who they are and more about what they can do and are capable of.

We have considered some of the successful strategies good schools are using both in the UK and abroad, so together with your colleagues, create that supportive climate, work together and when you can, take time to stand back and make the most of those valuable opportunities when you are able to watch your class while someone else teaches. Team teaching, collaboration and discussion with your support staff who are also actively involved in evidencing what children can do and where they need to go next will really help. Use your own knowledge and understanding about how children learn – this is, after all, at the heart of good assessment. But above all talk and listen, celebrate the uniqueness of each and every child you teach and enjoy sharing the many different aspects of their achievement. They are growing up in a complex society where we can only predict what knowledge and skills they will need, so it is vital that they (and we) recognise and value that we are all different and have different strengths, and should feel proud about who we are and what we can achieve.

KEY POINTS TO CONSIDER

- Assessment in the UK is currently out of step with what children need in relation to teaching holistically. We asked how this could be improved to evidence that we value the whole child, not just their academic progress in a few select subjects.
- Focus attention on and assess things that really matter for children's learning and development by considering innovative strategies, to make assessment not just valuable but manageable for staff and enjoyable for children.

- Consider some of the many ways that good schools can and do assess all aspects of their children's learning and development, and compare this approach with what happens in other countries.
- Think about some of the ways schools can evidence that they know who their children are, what they can do and how they can share and celebrate success, individually and collectively.

Further reading

Barnes, J. (2015) How can we assess cross curricular learning? *Cross Curricular Learning 3–14*. London: Sage, p. 245.

See also: **www.p.u-tokyo.ac.jp/~tsunelab/tokkatsu.**

References

Barnes, J. (2015) *Cross Curricular learning 3–14*. London: Sage.

Cameron, B. (1963) *Informal Sociology: A Casual Introduction to Sociological Thinking*. New York: Random House.

Department for Education (DfE) (2010) *The Importance of Teaching. The Schools White Paper 2010*, available at: **www.gov.uk/government/uploads/system/uploads/attachment_data/file/175429/CM-7980.pdf** (accessed 24 October 2018).

Her Majesty's Government (2004) *Children Act 2004*. Available at: **http://www.legislation.gov.uk/ukpga/2004/31/pdfs/ukpga_20040031_en.pdf** (accessed 29 October 2018).

Ofsted (2017) **https://www.gov.uk/government/speeches/amanda-spielmans-speech-at-the-festival-of-education** (accessed 11 January 2019).

Sahlberg, P. (2014) *Finnish Lessons 2.0: What can the World Learn from Educational Change in Finland*, 2nd edn. New York and London: Teachers College Press.

Smidt, S. (2014) in T. Cremin and J. Arthur, *Learning to Teach in the Primary School*, Routledge: London.

Teaching Schools Council (2016) *Effective Primary Teaching Practice*. TCS. Available at: **https://www.tscouncil.org.uk/wp-content/uploads/2016/12/Effective-primary-teaching-practice-2016-report-web.pdf**

UNICEF (2011) *Children's Wellbeing the UK, Sweden and Spain: The Role of Inequality and Materialism*. London: UNICEF.

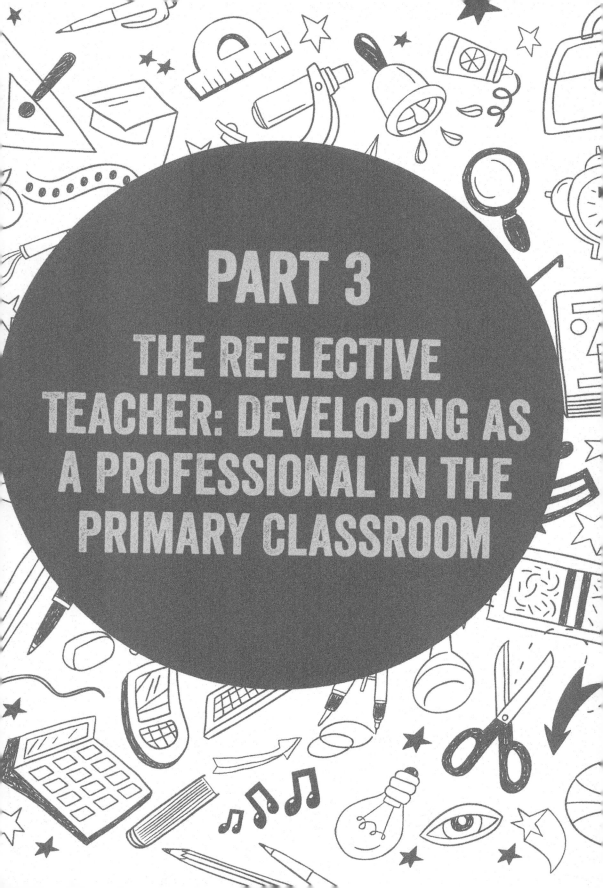

PART 3

THE REFLECTIVE TEACHER: DEVELOPING AS A PROFESSIONAL IN THE PRIMARY CLASSROOM

14

THE TEACHER'S PALETTE: CREATIVE AND HOLISTIC LEARNING SPACES

GENEA ALEXANDER AND JULIE SUTTON

THE ARTIST IS A RECEPTACLE FOR EMOTIONS THAT COME FROM ALL OVER THE PLACE: FROM THE SKY, FROM THE EARTH, FROM A SCRAP OF PAPER, FROM A PASSING SHAPE, FROM A SPIDER'S WEB.

PICASSO, IN BARR (1946)

KEYWORDS: HOLISTIC; CREATIVE; LEARNING SPACES; ENVIRONMENT; PHILOSOPHY; REFLECTION; INNOVATION; STANDARDS; EXCELLENCE; IMPACT.

——— CHAPTER OBJECTIVES ———

This chapter helps you to:

- explore the key components of creative and holistic learning spaces and their impact on learning
- synthesise current research and theory in relation to creative and holistic practice
- examine curriculum design in relation to creative and holistic practice, as part of a broad and balanced curriculum
- identify the tools required in order to maximise impact

LINKS TO THE TEACHERS' STANDARDS

Working through this chapter will enable you to meet all of the Teachers' Standards, in particular:

TS 1:   Promote good progress and outcomes by pupils

TS 2:   Set high expectations which inspire, motivate and challenge pupils

TS 8:   Fulfil wider professional responsibilities

Part 2:   Personal and professional conduct

Introduction

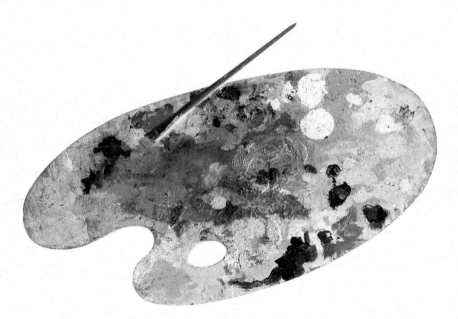

Figure 14.1 The Artist's Palette

When you think of 'an artist', what images come to mind? Is it perhaps a famed painter, such as Picasso or Matisse, or do you picture an eager child with a brand new set of paints and a crisp, white sheet of plain paper? As a teacher, do your picture yourself as an artist?

The artist's palette in Figure 14.1 is seemingly paradoxical – it is messy and disorganised, yet unique as an amalgamation of carefully considered colour mixes. It portrays the passion and hard work that are essential components in the creation of an artist's labour of love. The artist, we propose, comes in many guises and it is this idea – a broad-brush stroke, if you will – that underpins our approach to the design of creative and holistic learning spaces. In this chapter, we consider the role of teacher-as-artist: co-creators of learning spaces. We refer to 'space' as it implies by its very nature that it is free to be created – a blank canvas. We embrace the intrinsic relationship between environment and space and as such refer to both of these elements throughout this chapter.

As Csikszentmihalyi suggests, the most fundamental question in creativity is *where is creativity?* and not *what is creativity?* (1988, in de Souza Fleith, 2000: 148) Cronin and Hiett suggest that *teachers who teach creatively are more likely to provide the environment which allows creativity to flourish in their learners* (Denby, 2015: 232), and Cremin and Barnes discuss *creating environments of possibility* (Cremin and Arthur, 2014: 475). We seek to support teachers in achieving this goal in order to impact positively on learners, and as Kinsella and Fautley observe, . . . *this begins with us and the environments we create for our own creativity and our own learners* (2017: 1).

Developing a philosophy

Creative and holistic learning spaces start with your own ideas – and involve much more than just carefully considered placement of furniture. Ashbridge and Josephidou involve that *classroom organisation reflects your educational philosophy* (in Cooper and Elton – Chalcraft, 2018: 129). A classroom, an outdoor environment or any other space in which learning takes place says a great deal about you as a teacher. It captures your vision, your values and how you nurture and inspire those learning within (and beyond) it. Defining your philosophy of education is a good starting point in beginning to understand how you view learning spaces, which in turn, will assist in their creation.

REFLECTION

What is your philosophy of education and how could this impact on the learning and teaching environment?

The National Advisory Committee on Creative and Cultural Education (1999: 6) states:

> *Creativity is possible in all areas of human activity, including the arts, sciences, at work, at play and in all other areas of daily life. All people have creative abilities and we all have them differently. When individuals find their creative strengths, it can have an enormous impact on self-esteem and on overall achievement.*

Available at: **http://sirkenrobinson.com/pdf/allourfutures.pdf** (accessed 17 December 2018)

Learning spaces have capacity to foster creativity in addition to being creative in their design and, as such, have capacity to impact on the individuals who engage with them. Miller (2000) proposes that holistic education *nurtures a sense of wonder* and as Alexander and Sutton in Carden (2018: 340) identify, learning environments have the potential to be a *wonderland* for children. As a teacher, we suggest that the development of creative and holistic learning spaces is a significant part of your craft. This goes beyond the creation of effective learning environments, but teachers actively seeking to maximise the impact of the creative and holistic development of children through the medium of learning spaces – wherever they happen to be.

Preparing Your palette

Here we examine what we define as the four crucial components in the design of an effective learning space through the key principles of 'The RISE Approach' (Alexander and Sutton, in Carden, 2018: 346):

1. *Reflection*: Critically reflect on theory and practice in order to impact on your own professional practice.

2. *Innovation*: Creative spaces, happy faces! Design stimulating learning environments, alongside your pupils, to allow them to thrive.

3. *Standards*: Maintain high expectations.

4. *Excellence*: Display a commitment to professional development and improved experiences and outcomes for your pupils.

We shall look at these in more detail, as each section will guide you through a range of practical considerations, underpinned by theory, in order to support you on your journey to becoming 'the artist'.

1. Reflection: the tools

REFLECTION

Critically reflect on literature with which you have engaged in relation to creative and holistic learning spaces. Ask yourself: 'So what?' and consider the impact of this on your own practice.

Kinsella and Fautley on creative classroom behaviours state that *all learners can be creative if given the opportunity* (2017: 64). They propose that *creative teaching involves creativity in pedagogy, and teaching for creativity is the focus on the development of creativity in the learner*. Yet as Davies, Newton and Newton (2018: 888) found in their exploratory study of provision and reality in relation to creativity as a twenty-first-century competence: *even at schools which claimed to have 'creativity at the heart of their*

Figure 14.2   The tools

curriculum', teachers' responses suggested a lack of understanding as to how creativity could be fostered in different domains and confusion between teaching creatively and teaching for creativity. We would agree that all learners have the capacity to be creative if afforded the opportunity, but an understanding of ways in which this can be achieved is an essential component of a teacher's toolkit, in addition to an openness and desire to foster creativity – not only in children but as a whole school ethos. In order for this to be successful, it is important that all stakeholders within the school including teachers, leadership and management and governors are given time and space to consider this crucial aspect of their role.

It could be argued that one of the most important 'tools' within any creative activity is that of *relationships* and the ability to work together towards a common aim. Jeffrey and Woods introduce the concept of *ownership of knowledge* (2009: 45), believing that this occurs *when young participants learn for themselves, not just for the teacher, examiner or society.* They describe *collaborative projects* where children work together towards an end product and believe that *collective ownership* will emerge as each child contributes. From this collaboration, children can become involved in evaluating their successes, natural leaders may emerge and self-esteem will be raised. Working collaboratively and taking ownership instils a sense of responsibility where children learn how to manage themselves in different situations, especially when given the autonomy to do so (Wilson, 2009).

However, it is not just the relationships between pupils that are important. The teacher–pupil relationship also plays a crucial role in supporting creative practice. Knowing and understanding your pupils so that your response is personalised is an important part of teacher presence (Paige *et al.*, 2017) and as Alexander and Sutton in Carden concur, *in such an environment, the teacher's role [becomes] that of facilitator, interacting with children to support, challenge, question and so provide opportunities to further deepen knowledge and understanding* (2018: 339).

Cronin and Hiett propose that *a safe environment where risk taking and thinking out-loud are encouraged is an important nurturing space for creative activity* (2015: 233). The promotion of 'thinking' as part of creative teaching and learning is a topic that has been explored by many (Cremin and Barnes in Cremin and Arthur, 2014; Kinsella and Faultley, 2017; Desailly, 2015) and we would argue is of significance when designing holistic and creative learning spaces. Discussing the work of Guilford (1967, in Grigg and Lewis, 2019), it is stated that, in particular, divergent thinking *generates alternative answers and options without the limits of preconceived ideas* (2019: 18). We return to the idea of risk-taking within a safe environment in which divergent thinking is fostered and valued by all.

Giving children the tools to immerse themselves in creative activity is closely aligned with the concept of *growth mindset* (Dweck, 2012). As Carden and Bower remind us *the promotion of a growth mindset . . . will support learners with embracing challenge, taking risks, learning from mistakes and developing tenacity – the perfect mindset to flourish* (2018: 19).

Robinson (2015) reminds us that *there are two other concepts to keep in mind: imagination and innovation*, proposing that *imagination is the root of creativity. It is the ability to bring to mind things that aren't present to our senses*. This proposal underpins one of the core aims of the Cambridge Primary Review Trust, whose mission was to *advance the cause of high quality primary education for all children* (Alexander, 2010). *Exciting the imagination* and, more specifically, *the intrinsic value of exciting children's imagination* was a child-focused aim which has the potential to develop children more holistically. Imagination and the opportunity to both spark and channel this is a concept that has been widely considered as central to creativity, although it is important to remember that creativity differs from innovation (Driscoll *et al.*, 2015). Robinson makes a clear distinction between imagination and innovation, stating that: *Creativity is putting your imagination to work. It is applied imagination. Innovation is putting new ideas into practice* (2015). Both, we would argue, have a place in the creative and holistic learning environment.

THEORY FOCUS

See: **http://sirkenrobinson.com/**

Explore the works of Sir Ken Robinson, an influential voice on the subject of creativity. Recent works include: Robinson and Aronica (2015). *Creative Schools: The Grassroots Revolution That's Transforming Education*. New York: Viking.

---

2. Innovation: a vignette to showcase creative and holistic practice

When thinking about developing creative teaching and learning in its holistic sense, it is not unusual for the discerning teacher to research into what could be described as 'creative approaches' used to ensure effective teaching and learning takes place. Indeed, when designing this chapter, we, by default, considered including reference to some of these. However, innovation, by its very definition, implies the creation of something new – so, to make reference to teaching approaches already well-known, is a contradiction of terms. To this extent, this section is focused on a vignette and how the term 'learning environment' is encapsulated through its innovative curriculum design.

A local primary school has deservedly been given an 'outstanding' award by Ofsted (2009) in its last two inspections, being described as a *school [where] excellent teaching and an inspirational curriculum all contribute to [pupils'] thorough enjoyment of learning* http://www.wyche.worcs.sch.uk .

The school has formed its own curriculum, namely 'The Wyche Curriculum' (Rutherford, 2012), where the ethos of the school, together with its core values, are at the heart of its development. Understanding the moral purpose behind what the school is trying to achieve is instrumental to its success. Sinek (in Rutherford, 2019: 13) proposes that in any institution undergoing a form of organisational change, it is important to start with *why* we are doing something rather than simply 'how' we might achieve it or 'what' it will look like. In the context of creativity, the notion of *why* develop a creative curriculum should therefore be at the core of what one is trying to do rather than a focus on how it might be achieved and in what way. This, therefore, takes us back to our initial thoughts on why we teach creatively, and the importance of the holistic learning environment within this.

REFLECTION

Why is creative teaching and learning important to you as a teacher?

The aims of 'The Wyche Curriculum (Rutherford, 2012)' reflect this 'why', with key features such as 'Happy Memories', 'Enjoyment and Fun', 'Love of Learning', Friendship and Community', 'Relationships', 'Self-Esteem and Confidence', among many others. The moral purpose behind the curriculum is clear. The ethos of a creative curriculum should be to provide building blocks for every child to succeed in life and in learning. Developing a sense of curiosity about the world around them, questioning, exploring, teamwork, problem-solving, taking risks, being resourceful are all essential skills children should be developing and these lie at the heart of 'The Wyche Curriculum'.

As well as promoting the concept of a 'growth mindset' described earlier, these aims are closely linked with the ideology behind 'Building Learning Power' devised by Guy Claxton (2002). He argues that giving individuals confidence to face the future through introducing them to essential life skills develops their capacity to learn. It is of no consequence that some of the words which feature prominently in Claxton's writings mirror those already described above as aims of 'The Wyche Curriculum'.

Learning should be considered as a process where time is given for reflection, discussion and revision in order to reach a specified goal. It should not be about jumping through hoops in order to reach an end goal. One could argue that in such an environment as this, no real learning takes place at all. The final product might be achieved, but the means of realising it can soon be lost as the next goal comes around the corner. We can all reach an end destination by travelling at speed up a motorway, but the journey becomes far more memorable if we choose to take the minor roads, stop off in a lay-by, pause and reflect on the surroundings.

'The Wyche Curriculum' is delivered through the concept of a 'curricular vehicle' described by Rutherford as *not a 'topic' in the traditional sense because it is designed to deliver much more than the national curriculum subjects . . . [it] should provide opportunities for children to learn about the management of themselves, relationships and situations . . .* (2012: 21). This philosophy links with our earlier discussion about relationships and the importance of ownership and collaboration.

So, what about the learning environment?

The learning environment should be everything about the school, not just those things that are visible but should include behaviours, attitudes and relationships. *It doesn't matter where you go with [the children], whether it is to a lesson or after school club or the lunch hall you will find the same ethos and the same culture operating between teacher and child, teacher and teacher and child with their peers* (Rutherford, 2019: 34). The environment in which children learn builds on the ethos of the school and will run through the school like letters through a stick of rock, wherever you break it you will see the same moral purpose within.

In a curriculum where developing relationships, with both oneself and others, are at the core of everything one does, the idea of the learning environment being anything but 'holistic' is unquestionable. From the moment the child enters school to the point where they leave at the end of the day, they are part of a holistic learning environment.

> IT IS IMPORTANT FOR THE TEACHER TO RECOGNISE THAT A CONDUCIVE LEARNING ENVIRONMENT EXTENDS FAR BEYOND WHAT YOU CAN SEE. IT IS NOT JUST ABOUT THE IMMEDIATE ENVIRONMENT; HOW THE FURNITURE IS ARRANGED IN A CLASSROOM, THE DISPLAYS ON THE WALL OR HOW THE RESOURCES ARE ORGANISED – IT IS SO MUCH MORE. A VIBRANT LEARNING ENVIRONMENT ENCOMPASSES THE PHYSICAL ENVIRONMENT OF THE WHOLE SCHOOL, TOGETHER WITH ITS ETHOS AND VALUES.
>
> (Alexander and Sutton, 2018: 340)

Although very much a child-centred curriculum, the role of the teacher is instrumental, being described as *the inspiration behind the work* with *their own personal enthusiasm often driving the vehicle.* This facilitating role again links our earlier discussion (see *1. Reflection*). In practice, the delivery of the curriculum is very fluid and is not restricted to rigid timetables or prescriptive subject content. Instead, it is a fun, engaging and fully immersive curriculum in a rich, fully encompassing learning environment.

3. Standards: high expectations

Alexander and Sutton argue that although the word 'environment' is only mentioned once in the Teachers' Standards [TS1] in establishing *a safe and stimulating environment for pupils, rooted in mutual respect* (DfE, 2013), establishing such an environment pervades all of the standards in different ways, providing *opportunities for teachers to maximise the potential for [the learning environment] to be used effectively in its widest, most holistic sense* (Alexander and Sutton, 2018: 339).

─── **REFLECTION** ───

How can you maintain high expectations within a broad and balanced curriculum when embracing creative approaches?

To answer this question, we need to return to the concept of teacher presence, more specifically 'being present' as described by Paige in Paige *et al.* (2017), alongside an understanding of the importance of relationships within this. A teacher who spends time building positive relationships with the children in their class, getting to know them not just academically but socially and emotionally as well, will be rewarded with children who are respectful and, in turn, demonstrate a willingness to learn.

A classroom which reflects the children's interests and is personalised, engaging, inspirational and fun will be a place where children will want to be. They will feel safe, nurtured and valued for being themselves. But, as discussed in section 2 (*Innovation*) above, it is important to remember that the learning environment is not just the classroom space but a part of the whole school experience. This school ethos is pivotal in ensuring positive relationships are developed.

Building a firm foundation for learning, therefore, is essential to developing high expectations. This firm foundation is centred upon the moral purpose of the school and from this the curriculum will grow and develop.

Let us pause for a moment and think what the term 'firm foundation' means. Why is it so important? When constructing anything of significance, its foundation is key to its success. Before building the walls of a house, for example, considerable time must be spent laying the foundation. Not only is it a concrete base but within it is the infrastructure needed to ensure that the building, once erected, functions well. The roots of any plant lie deep in the ground, anchoring the plant securely and providing the mechanism for the essential nutrients to travel to the surface so that it can develop and grow.

The same principles are true when considering the foundation of a school. Its philosophy for learning, shared core values, culture and ethos – factors that are often not tangible – underpin the whole curriculum. Rutherford (2019) describes this using the analogy of an iceberg as shown in Figure 14.3. Although 90 per cent of the foundation appears invisible, it is an essential solid base on which to build the curriculum. Without it the curriculum may at first, appear solid, but cracks will soon appear and therefore high expectations will be lost.

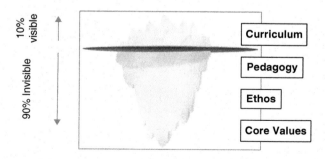

Figure 14.3   An adaptation of Rutherford's Iceberg (2019: 26)

So . . . to return to the classroom. Once the foundation is secure, the relationships that have been built can transcend into curriculum planning and design. Teachers and children can work collaboratively and creatively, moulding the learning based on needs and interests. Careful questioning and challenge from both the teacher and peers will encourage the learner to do the same and so deepen their understanding. In a holistic learning environment, the learner will feel confident to take risks, make mistakes, reflect and refine. Constructing the learning in this way empowers the children to take control of their learning and move on to the next stage. In such a learning environment, expectations remain consistently high.

It is easy to see how the Teachers' Standards (DfE, 2013) are reflected in a creative pedagogy. If, as has been argued throughout, a holistic learning environment is an integral part of the whole school experience, then establishing the correct environment for learning from the outset is an essential part of our toolkit.

THEORY FOCUS

Research and discover ways in which philosophies underpinning education (relationships, teacher presence, foundations for learning, etc.) can be exemplified within the Teachers' Standards. You may find Carroll and Alexander (2016) supportive. Carroll, J. and Alexander, G. N. (2016) *The Teachers' Standards in Primary Schools: Understanding and Evidencing Effective Practice*. London: Sage.

4. Excellence: The Teacher's Palette

Figure 14.4   The Teacher's Palette

As a teacher, you have the opportunity to become an artist. Your classroom could be described as a blank canvas and much like the artist's palette and brushes, you require certain tools in order to ensure that you have provided maximum opportunity for the learning environment to be inspiring and impact on learners who, in an environment which supports a collaborative ethos, can become contributing artists.

(Alexander and Sutton, in Carden, 2018: 343)

Thus far, we have explored a range of key principles pertaining to creative and holistic learning spaces and it is now that we wish to present a practical tool, based on a theory-into-practice approach. We hope this will support you to enable learners to develop holistically as creative individuals, within and beyond carefully designed learning spaces.

The primary colours

To begin, you will require three colours in your palette: red, yellow and blue. Each colour represents an important component in the design process

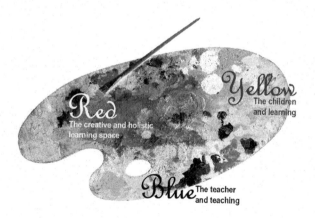

Figure 14.5   Palette of primary components

The power of three

Each element within the palette of primary components should be considered as part of your design in order to maximise the potential for impact on learners. Each component can be broken down into practical, impact-focused considerations when designing creative and holistic learning spaces (Figure 14.5). Provision of opportunity for each aspect should be planned for or, if it arises, the opportunity should be seized by both teachers and learners and in this way an ethos to facilitate this should be established.

The children and learning

Figure 14.6   Yellow: the children and learning

- Find their own identity
- Collaborate and interact
- Are engaged
- Question
- Demonstrate a growth mindset
- Feel comfortable and safe to take risks
- Have a sense of true shared ownership
- Are afforded time, space and freedom to reflect and for creative thinking and exploration

The teacher and teaching

Figure 14.7   Blue: the teacher and teaching

- Values contribute to an embedded philosophy that is omnipresent in teaching and learning spaces
- Environments of possibility are created
- Presence has a positive impact
- Risk-taking is modelled and supported
- Critical and divergent thinking are valued, encouraged and praised
- Innovative practice is demonstrated
- Interaction and exploration are encouraged
- Mistakes are accepted
- Questioning is modelled and promoted

The creative and holistic learning space

Figure 14.8   Red: the creative and holistic learning space

- Is learner-centred
- Nurtures a sense of wonder
- Excites the imagination
- Is *safe*: form relationships, acquire life skills, develop their self-efficacy and learn new knowledge and skills. They feel comfortable to interact and teachers know their pupils
- Is *enabling*: the inclusive environment allows children to learn and encourages them to want to learn. Children demonstrate a sense of ownership and autonomy. Successes are celebrated
- Is *engaging*: inspiring and stimulating, rich opportunities, personalised
- Is *flexible*: dynamic and responsive to the needs of all children
- Is *collaborative*: constructed by all within it

(Based on Alexander and Sutton, in Carden, 2018: 343)

REFLECTION

Critically reflect on the impact-focused element within each component. In what way do you plan for each in your professional practice, and how does this relate to learning theory and pedagogical approaches?

The Art of Colour Mixing

The art of designing creative and holistic learning spaces is knowing how to create secondary and tertiary colours from the colours in your palette. This is achieved through combining components in order to achieve your masterpiece and each component may vary in its quantity at different times. This could also be viewed as identifying the interconnectedness of the components in order to find the best 'mix' to support holistic learning, e.g. combining the components of 'create environments of possibility' (Cremin and Barnes in Cremin and Arthur, 2014: 475) with 'nurtures a sense of wonder' (Miller, 2000).

CHAPTER SUMMARY

A rainbow of possibility

In this chapter, we have explored the idea of teacher-as-artist in the development of the holistic and creative learning space and, at the heart of this, we have highlighted the significance of the impact on learners and the learning process.

The Teacher's Palette creates possibilities for teachers and learners. It is a tool from which teachers can extract and combine components in order to enhance learning spaces and impact positively on learners and the learning experience. We are keen to emphasise the significance of the relationship between learner and teacher (Muijis and Reynolds, 2018) and the interchanges between the individual and environment (de Souza Fleith, 2000). By carefully combining these components, we would argue that the creation of an enhancing, harmonious and meaningful environment can contribute to the development of creative potential (de Souza Fleith, 2000) and the holistic development of the child. However, before mixing the colours, it is important to consider the base for your creation. Is it constructed from paper where the more you mix, the thinner it becomes until tiny holes start to appear, or is it more resilient, wood or canvas perhaps, which remains durable throughout each creation, never failing to support the trial and error involved in creating the perfect masterpiece?

In conclusion, we return to 'the power of three': the *children and learning*; the *teacher and teaching* and the *creative and holistic learning space*, relating these components to Cremin and Barnes in Cremin and Arthur (2014: 475) and their 'environments of possibility'. In the context of teacher-as-artist, we invite you to critically reflect on your practice in order to ensure that the environments of possibility you design – wherever they happen to be – are truly holistic and creative and *impact* positively on learners.

KEY POINTS TO CONSIDER

- Understand the concept of teacher-as-artist: using a metaphorical palette of primary colours from which to construct a holistic space for children to thrive in their learning.
- Understand the significance of relationships that exist and can be developed between learner and teacher, and between the individual and environment to promote high standards for learning.
- Reflect on how to implement the 'Rise Approach' and the four crucial components, *Reflection, Innovation, Standards* and *Excellence*, for developing creative, nurturing and purposeful learning spaces in the primary school.

Further reading

Claxton, G. (2002) *Building Learning Power*. Bristol: TLO.

Further develop your understanding of building learning power and reflect on how this aligns with your philosophy of education.

Kinsella, V. and Fautley, M. (2017) *Creativity: Getting It Right in a Week*. St Albans: Critical Publishing.

This accessible book contains practical examples of creative teaching and learning for the busy teacher and offers supportive links to theory.

References

Alexander, G. and Sutton, J., (2018) in Carden, C. (ed.) *Primary Teaching: An Exploration of Learning and Teaching in Primary Schools Today*. London: Learning Matters, 337–54.

Alexander, R. J. (ed.) (2010) *Children, Their World, Their Education: Final Report and Recommendations of the Cambridge Primary Review*. London: Routledge, pp. 197–9. Available at: **https://cprtrust.org.uk/about_cprt/aims/**

Ashbridge, J. and Josephidou, J. (2018), in H. Cooper and S. Elton-Chalcraft, *Professional Studies in Primary Education*. London: Sage, 57–72.

Barr Jr, A.H. (1946) *Picasso: Fifty Years of his Art* New York. Museum of Modern Art, available at: **www.oxfordreference.com/view/10.1093/acref/9780191826719.001.0001/q-oro-ed4-00008311** (accessed 17 December 2018).

Carden, C. and Bower, V. (2018) in C. Carden (ed.) *Primary Teaching: An Exploration of Learning and Teaching in Primary Schools Today*. London: Learning Matters, 3–22.

Carroll, J. and Alexander, G.N. (2016) *The Teachers' Standards in Primary Schools. Understanding and Evidencing Effective Practice*. London: Sage.

Claxton, G. (2002) *Building Learning Power*. Bristol: TLO.

Cooper, H. and Elton-Chalcraft, S. (2018) *Professional Studies in Primary Education*. London: Sage.

Cremin, T. and Barnes, J. (2014) in T. Cremin and J. Arthur, (2014) *Learning to Teach in the Primary School*. Oxon: Routledge, 357–73.

Cronin, S. and Hiett, S. (2015) in N. Denby, *Training to Teach: A Guide for Students*. London: Sage.

Davies, L.M., Newton, L.D. and Newton, D.P. (2018) Creativity as a twenty-first century competence: an exploratory study of provision and reality. *Education 3-13: International Journal of Primary, Elementary and Early Years Education, 46*: 7. Available at: **doi.org/10.1080/03004279.2017.1385641**.

De Souza Fleith, D. (2000) Teacher and student perceptions of creativity in the classroom environment. *Roeper Review, 22* (3): 148–53: doi.org/10.1080/02783190009554022

Desailly, J. (2015) *Creativity in the Primary Classroom*. London. Sage.

DfE (2013) *Teachers' Standards*. London: Crown.

Driscoll, P., Lambrith, A. and Roden, J. (2015) *The Primary Curriculum: A Creative Approach*. London: Sage.

Dweck, C. (2012) *Mindset: How You Can Fulfil Your Potential*. London: Robinson.

Grigg, R. and Lewis, H. (2019) *Teaching Creative and Critical Thinking in Schools*. London: Sage.

Jeffrey, B. and Woods, P. (2009) *Creative Learning in the Primary School*. Oxon: Routledge.

Kinsella, V. and Fautley, M. (2017) *Creativity: Getting It Right in a Week*. St Albans: Critical Publishing.

Miller, R. (2000) A brief introduction to holistic education. *The Encyclopaedia of Informal Education*. Available at: **http://infed.org/mobi/a-brief-introduction-to-holistic-education/**

Muijis, D. and Reynolds, D. (2018) *Effective Teaching Evidence and Practice*. London: Sage.

National Advisory Committee on Creative and Cultural Education (1999) *All Our Futures: Creativity, Culture and Education*. London: DfEE. Available at: **http://sirkenrobinson.com/pdf/allourfutures.pdf** (accessed 17 December 2018).

Ofsted (2009) Available at: **https://files.api.ofsted.gov.uk/v1/file/927477**

Paige in Paige, R., Lambert, S. and Geeson, R. (2017) *Building Skills for Effective Primary Teaching*. London: Learning Matters.

Robinson, K. (2015) *Creativity is in Everything, Especially Teaching*. Available at: **https://www.kqed.org/mindshift/40217/sir-ken-robinson-creativity-is-in-everything-especially-teaching**

Robinson, K. and Aronica, L. (2015) *Creative Schools: The Grassroots Revolution That's Transforming Education*. New York: Viking.

Rutherford, G. (2012) *The Wyche Curriculum: Designing a Curriculum for the 21st Century*. Gloucester: Little Inky Fingers.

Sinek, S. (2019) in G. Rutherford, *Wyche Way to Lead* (n.p.).

Wilson, A. (2009) *Creativity in Primary Education* (2nd edition). Exeter: Learning Matters.

15

THE PERSONAL IN THE PROFESSIONAL

TERESA CREMIN

KEYWORDS: PERSONAL, PROFESSIONAL; IDENTITIES; TEACHERS' AND CHILDREN'S OUT-OF-SCHOOL LIVES AND INTERESTS.

CHAPTER OBJECTIVES

This chapter:

- Explores teachers' personal and professional identities
- Considers the importance of teachers' and children's interests and lives beyond the classroom
- Enables an understanding of ways in which you can connect to your own and children's interests and out-of-school lives in the classroom
- Examines research and practice examples that reveal the value of teachers' authentic personal engagement in school

---

LINKS TO THE TEACHERS' STANDARDS

Working through this chapter will enable you to meet all of the Teachers' Standards, in particular:

TS 2:   Set high expectation which inspire, motivate and challenge pupils

TS 4:   Plan and teach well-structured lessons

Part 2: Personal and professional conduct

At the heart of this [education] is a deep sense of the personal, of interaction and confianza. Of 'becoming somebody', somebody who has a growing sense of their own strengths and resources and is enabled to use them.

(Cremin *et al.*, 2015: 187)

Introduction

This book is designed to support the profession in educating 'the whole child', but what about the 'whole teacher'? What about you? We enter classrooms as people, humans with interests, value and morals, and lives outside school, and while our focus as teachers is of course on the children, who we are and what we bring inevitably influences our teaching and thus impacts on every child we teach. Why did you choose teaching, I wonder? What in your personality or your past might have drawn you to this challenging profession?

Your personal take on education and what you might uniquely offer will depend in part on your conception of *teaching*. Do you see it as an 'objective' science like Hattie (2012) and Coe and Waring (2017), for example? Perhaps you see it as a craft, as Marland (1975) does – a set of techniques you can learn to use regardless of circumstance? Certainly policy-makers tend to favour these two pur-portedly simple conceptions. Others see teaching as an art (Eisner, 1979; Bennett, 2012), a *complex creative enterprise concerned with the promotion of human learning and involving imagination, sensitivity and personal response* (Richards, 2018: 8). I too view teaching as a complex artistic and professional enterprise, albeit with science and craft elements, and one in which relationships matter: indeed, the relationship between teacher and child is at the heart of the practice of education. So *who* each teacher is counts, as well as *who* each child is. How can we remove the humans from the enterprise, the children from the learning, the teacher from the teaching, the personal from the professional? We simply cannot.

In this chapter, we consider these issues, explore our interests and values, our personal and pro-fessional identities, and develop strategies to help us learn about young people as unique learners. We discuss ways to bridge from this knowledge and understanding into the classroom in order to create culturally responsive child-centred curricula and communities of learners. We also examine two projects in which teachers were invited to engage personally as well as professionally by look-ing at case studies of three teachers: Carol found out more about a boy's pleasure in hunting with his father and found ways to link to this; Sophie opened up as a learner in class and taught more authentically; and Claire, after reflecting on herself and the children as readers, began to teach dif-ferently from her previous practice. Over time their altered practices impacted positively on the young people's learning and helped build stronger learning communities. Teachers' (and children's) life experiences and teachers' personal and professional identities matter, and you can draw on these to support young learners in your class.

REFLECTION

What do you personally bring to the education profession?

You come to the profession as a person, a family member, an individual with particular interests and a life history. What do you like to do in your 'own time'? Read, write, make art (pottery, painting, dance, drama, music), play a sport, keep fit, engage in cultural activities (visiting museums, theatre, concerts, gardens), engage with friends on social media, travel? My hobbies include reading and baking – what are yours? Perhaps you have had a previous career? Across nearly 20 years in initial teacher education, I taught student teachers who had worked as linguists, farmers, nannies, chefs, soldiers, in the ambulance/police/financial services, the theatre, the circus and in real estate, to mention but a few! Each brought different knowledge, skills and aptitudes as well as related interests and individual values which they could use to support children's education. Many had worked with children in different capacities, in voluntary work for example, as youth leaders in choirs, clubs and holiday camps, and most, as teenagers, had been involved in looking after siblings, cousins or the children of family friends.

Recognising your skills and interests, however small they may seem to you, is a first step in acknowledging that you bring something unique to the profession. Considering your values and beliefs is important too. I am sure you have experienced the difference that someone's principles, knowledge and enthusiasm make, and can remember teachers whose love of a subject or intriguing lives altered your engagement and openness to learning. You do not have to leave your values or sense of self at the school gate; you can and should be genuinely engaged, both personally and professionally, in the classroom.

THEORY FOCUS

Studies of highly creative teachers show that regardless of the subject or age of the students, they draw on their own lives to personalise their teaching and make imaginative connections that support learning (Grainger et al., 2004; Henriksen and Mishra, 2015). For example, one practitioner I observed shared her great grandfather's war medals and read an extract from his diary in order to introduce Tom Palmer's (2018) novel *Armistice Runner*. Her authentic engagement prompted the class to listen intently, ask pertinent questions, and make connections. Such creative teachers are likely to have a wide range of personal interests and often share their curiosity about the wider world, encouraging children to develop their own (Cremin, 2015). They are also seen to be risk-takers, disposed to trialling new ideas and approaches to teaching and learning due to their personal and professional engagement in various communities of practice beyond the classroom (Henriksen and Mishra, 2015). You too will benefit from joining such communities: action research teams, Open University/UK Literacy Association (UKLA) Teachers' Reading Groups and Chartered College of Teaching networks, for instance. In such communities you can 'forge positive professional relationships' in line with the Teacher Standards (DfE, 2011), and sustain yourself as a learner and a teacher.

Does becoming a professional mean ignoring who you are?

By becoming a teacher, you will be becoming a professional and embarking upon a life-long learning journey. In describing the development of teachers' professional identities, Hargreaves and Fullen

(2012) recognise that teachers' personal resources, such as being friendly, open, caring and resilient, and their talents of various kinds, are critical. They call this 'human capital'. As you develop as a professional you'll use these resources to help you build 'social capital', that is reciprocal trusting relationships with others in the education community which, Hargreaves and Fullen argue, will enable you to experience the *collaborative power of the group* (2012: 37). Their vision of professional identity also includes a third strand called 'decisional capital': this relates to your ability to make wise and informed decisions about the young learners that enable you to support them effectively. If you recognise your own resources and talents you will be in a stronger position to build respectful relationships with children and parents, as well as other teachers and teaching assistants. It is worth reflecting on what you have already learnt from working with others, whether within or beyond school, and considering some specific situations of challenge and the extent to which you feel you have made wise decisions in them.

Over the years you are likely to encounter personal/professional tensions, school circumstances when you feel your own personal values and beliefs are being compromised. For example, student teacher Jo felt unsure when working in a placement school, as the children were expected to complete science worksheets and follow prescribed experiments. Yet Jo's childhood and previous placement experience had taught him that problem-finding and solving was key to developing enquiring minds, and he wanted to make science, at least occasionally, child-led and enquiry-based. The 'at least occasionally' hints at how he, through discussion of his values and experience, negotiated a way forward with the class teacher. Drawing on your personal and professional resources, you too will find appropriate ways forward as you become socialised into the education community.

Challengingly, however, Ball (2003) argues that teachers' identities are being redefined by the culture of performativity, in which teachers and schools are subjected to accountability measures such as children's performance in standardised tests and inspection evidence. He even suggests that many teachers experience a *kind of values schizophrenia* and that as a consequence their *commitment, judgement and authenticity within practice* may be surrendered (p. 221). So it is essential you retain a strong sense of your own values and beliefs and exercise your professional judgement thoughtfully. The teacher you become will be shaped by your unique journey and how you handle the conflicts and tensions you experience. Your professional identity will also be influenced by the relationships you build with children and your openness to learning from them.

How might you develop knowledge of the children and build bridges to support their learning?

Children develop their conceptual understanding, in part, by making connections to their prior knowledge and understanding. They do this more easily when they are motivated by a curriculum which has relevance to them. So in order to teach effectively you need to know about the children's home lives and practices, including their use of digital technologies, interest in and experience of popular culture, sport, hobbies and home languages. Their life experiences from a very early age give them knowledge, understanding and capabilities that they can draw upon in later learning. These *funds of knowledge* (Moll *et al.*, 1992) represent rich resources for education, although too often they are unknown, unacknowledged and unused in schools, particularly when the curriculum is prescribed (Thomson and Hall, 2008; Cremin *et al.*, 2015).

Figure 15.1   Children work creatively to make their personal identity box

Figure 15.2   Girl aged 7 decorates her identity box to reflect her personality

There are many ways to learn about children as rounded and unique individuals. You could invite them to create *Identity Boxes* with a number of items inside which reflect a sense of who they are. Sharing your own decorated shoebox of personal items acts as a useful model, and helps them to get to know you too. Alternatively, you and the class could create *Interest Trees* with leaves about your personal passions, or *Timelines of Life* with notations of significant memories across the years (doing this for homework helps trigger family memories). Alternatively, you might invite children to take photographs on the theme of *My Life beyond School* and display these ready for discussion. Listening to the children talk about their objects, memories or photos is key; such small-group conversations will help you learn a great deal about individual children and their friends and families outside school.

CASE STUDY

Carole and Sophie build on children's knowledge and share their own learning

The new knowledge about the children's lives and communities that you develop needs to be built upon within the curriculum. For example, at a very basic level if you find out that several children enjoy particular sports outside school you will want to ensure there are appropriate magazines or books available that they can connect to and will find motivating. You could also offer writing opportunities connected to their life experiences, as one teacher Carol did when she found out that Cole, a five year old who struggled with literacy, regularly went hunting, fishing and ferreting with his father. Initially, she invited him to bring in his fishing rod and net and talk to the class; later he had the chance to write about his interests. Over time Carol noted *[Cole] has completely changed his attitude towards writing, from very negative 'I can't do it' to a much more positive view. This only began after encouraging him to write about his out-of-school experiences and showing him it was okay to do so* (Cremin et al., 2015: 79). In discussing one of Cole's stories in which a hunter shot a rabbit, Carol asked what happened next. He explained it was skinned, gutted and cooked for supper. On being encouraged to write exactly that, he replied with surprise *Can I?* Carol wondered whether she might have responded differently and expressed shock or displeasure at the rabbit's demise if she hadn't known about Cole's interests. She realised that, without meaning to do so, she often implied what was deemed to be acceptable in school and in effect prevented children from drawing on their personal resources and funds of knowledge from home. So, in order to support children's learning, Carol began to offer opportunities for children to use the *texts of their lives* (Fecho, 2011) as resources to retell, re-present and remake in multiple ways and you can do so too.

Working with 10–11 year olds, Sophie decided to position herself as a learner more overtly alongside the children and shared her challenges in setting up a Facebook account with her class. She also chose her own project on the class theme of 'Exploration' and when stuck for ideas in her creative writing planning she turned to the children to help her. Whatever our skills and passions, there are always areas where we are less assured, and being open about this helps children appreciate that we are all learners and need to find practical ways forward. As evidenced through interviews and observations in Sophie's class, her openness, honesty and authenticity had consequences for the children's engagement and a stronger sense of a learning community was built (Cremin *et al.*, 2015). In finding out more about the children as learners and sharing more of your own learning challenges as appropriate, you can build closer relationships, reduce hierarchies and support children's education, while still observing proper professional boundaries.

THEORY FOCUS

Both Carol and Sophie were teacher-researchers in the project *Building Communities: Researching Literacy Lives*. In this study, teachers from ten schools were supported to develop new knowledge about children's out-of-school literacy practices in order to build bridges to learning in the classroom (Cremin *et al.*, 2015). The Learner Visits they undertook to children's homes often challenged their beliefs and implicit assumptions about the children and their parents. The teachers visited not as authority figures taking information to tell the parents, but as learners and researchers seeking to understand more about the children's everyday literacy lives. They chatted with parents and family members, observed the children informally in their homes, and brought back new insights that enabled them to make connections and personalise the curriculum. During these Learner Visits it was clear that when the teachers shared something of themselves as adults/parents/daughters or sons/learners, and responded intuitively and authentically in their conversations, new connections were created between teachers and the families. Over time, stronger, more personal and mutually respectful adult and child relationships were built.

Analysis

The practitioners in the project began with very limited knowledge about the children's lives and interests – they knew about their literacy abilities (as measured by the National Curriculum) but little else. They realised that the existing home–school contact books, parents' evenings and homework diaries all centred on school expectations and indicated almost nothing about children as learners at home. The Learner Visits proved revealing; the teachers were surprised by the breadth and depth of children's funds of knowledge which included specific cultural and religious practices as well as other social practices. Collectively they also found that children who were not keen literacy learners in school behaved rather differently at home; there they seized self-chosen opportunities for learning. At home these children: read, wrote, talked and learnt about issues that interested them; employed a wide range of digital texts for their own purposes; learnt in social and collaborative contexts; demonstrated considerable independence and agency as learners, and took the time/space they needed, frequently concentrating for long periods when reading, drawing, playing with digital texts and playing sport. The teachers sought to develop *pedagogies of re-connection* (Comber and Kamler, 2004) to build on children's personal passions, interests and practices in the home. For example, many offered more choice and responsibility in school since they realised at home the children were agentic learners who developed their knowledge and skills for real and personally relevant purposes.

CASE STUDY

Claire drawing on her love of reading and the consequences for the children

On her initial teacher education course Claire was invited to review her knowledge of children's literature and found to her consternation that, like the teachers in the study *Teachers as Readers*, she was reliant upon childhood favourites and celebrity writers (Cremin *et al.*, 2008). So through taking up tutors' and friends' recommendations and setting herself personal reading goals (including, for example, reading the UKLA Children's Book Award winners), Claire widened her repertoire and rejuvenated her childhood pleasure in reading.

Perhaps more significantly though, once in school Claire also drew on the notion of being a Reading Teacher - a teacher who reads and a reader who teaches (Commeyras *et al.*, 2003) - and reflected on her personal reading preferences and practices. Metaphorically she held up a mirror to herself as a reader and considered the possible pedagogic consequences of her experience of reading. For example, she found that she liked to read in bed or on the sofa curled up with a drink and that she often, although not always, chatted to friends or family members about what she was reading. In recognising the environmental conditions of comfort and conversation that supported her as a reader, she wondered if it would help her class to relax and sit in more informal spaces near their friends during reading time (rather than sitting on hard chairs at their assigned tables). She tried this and found that even after the novelty wore off, the children valued the comfort and affinity of their friends and concentrated on their books. Booktalk arose naturally, sometimes during or at the end of this time and children eagerly shared their views, as indeed Claire shared hers. When the class annotated pictures of Claire with things they considered were important to her, two-thirds of them mentioned her love of reading. As she observed, *this revealed a far deeper understanding of my reading life than I expected*; their knowledge included her favourite books and authors, her habit of encircling publication dates, her collection of signed books and much more (see Figure 15.3). Claire noticed, however, that no one mentioned poetry or non-fiction, which she also enjoys, so she sought to make clearer the variety of texts that she tackles as a Reading Teacher.

In addition to a new appreciation of reading and relaxation, the role of interaction in motivating readers and sharing herself as a reader, Claire developed her knowledge of the children as readers and invited them to create *reading rivers* (collages which document out-of-school reading practices). This enabled her to make tailored book recommendations to individual children drawing on her developed knowledge of texts and of children as readers. These opportunities impacted strongly on her class. They became more motivated and engaged as readers and read more frequently and enthusiastically at home and at school. A community of readers emerged, of which Claire was a full member. Over time and through reflection, Claire developed an enhanced personal and professional awareness of what it means to be a reader and shaped her pedagogic practice in responsive ways. As research has shown (Cremin *et al.*, 2014), and her case study demonstrates, this has positive consequences for children's pleasure in reading and helps develop reciprocal and interactive reading communities.

She gets lots of her books signed.

Book queen

10000,0000,000 of Books

She reads at home and we know that because she tells us.

She is a Book worm

I think she likes to buy books so she can share them with us so we can see if we like them too.

She loves HARRY POTTER because she got a Huge version of it for her Birthday

She always orders new books to read and share to us.

We know miss william loves Mini Grey because

She invented mini Hay festival so we can relax with a book outside.

She has a dress that has a lot of books on.

She always loves to put the new books in her calendar.

She recommends books to us.

She screams whenever she reads a new book!

Mini Grey

Figure 15.3   One child's view of Claire as a reader (Cremin et al., 2018: 9)

Conclusion

As a teacher you do not need to seek permission to bring your values, skills, interests and expertise into the classroom in order to support children's learning. By drawing on your life experience, passions and practices as a learner you will be more authentically and personally engaged in the classroom and open to developing new knowledge about the children as unique individuals too. You will also be professionally engaged, thoughtfully considering the most appropriate ways forward to build on the children's own strengths and resources to enrich their learning. While tensions between your personal and professional identities will arise, treat these challenges as opportunities for reflection on the kind of teacher you want to be and shape your journey accordingly. As a reflective professional you can draw on your personal attributes and values, this will make a difference both to your teaching and to the children's learning. You can, and I trust you will, always work at becoming a better teacher, developing a sense of your own strengths and resources, personally and professionally, and using these to benefit the children.

CHAPTER SUMMARY

In this chapter we have:

- examined our own identities as adults and the nature of our emerging professional identities;
- explored research which highlights the value of teachers' capitalising upon their own lives and values to support young learners;
- considered the importance of teachers' developing rich knowledge of the children they teach to create responsive pedagogies of connection;
- asserted the potential for authenticity, humanity and the personal in the professional.

Further reading

Cremin, T., Mottram, M., Powell, S., Collins, R. and Drury, R. (2015) *Researching Literacy Lives: Building Home School Communities*. London and New York: Routledge.

This book won the UKLA Academic Book Award in 2016. It explores how re-positioning teachers as researchers enabled new understandings about children and their families to develop, and how this new knowledge shaped the curriculum and helped build stronger relationships and home–school communities.

Twiselton, S. and Goepel, J. (2018) Becoming a professional in the current context. In T. Cremin and C. Burnett (eds), *Learning to Teach in the Primary School* (4th edition). London: Routledge, pp. 17–31.

This chapter looks in detail at the Teaching Standards highlighting that the professionalism that you develop will extend well beyond these government standards and will be informed by your personal resources, social capital and wise decision-making.

https://researchrichpedagogies.org/research/reading-for-pleasure

This research-informed reading for pleasure website offers support materials for teachers to use. It has sections on Reading Teachers and Developing Knowledge of Children as Readers, videos featuring Claire and Teresa, and examples of teachers' research-informed practice to inspire you to develop motivated and able readers.

References

Ball, S.J. (2003) The teacher's soul and the terrors of performativity. *Journal of Education Policy, 18*: 215–28.

Bennett, T. (2012) *Teacher: Mastering the Art and Craft of Teaching*. London: Continuum.

Coe, R. and Waring, M. (2017) *Research Methods and Methodologies in Education.* London: Sage.

Comber, B. and Kamler, B. (2004) Getting out of deficit: pedagogies of re-connection. *Teaching Education, 15* (3): 293–310.

Commeyras, M., Bisplinhoff, B.S. and Olson, J. (2003) *Teachers as Readers: Perspectives on the Importance of Reading in Teachers' Classrooms and Lives.* Newark, DE: International Reading Association.

Cremin, T. (2015) Creative teaching and creative teachers. In A. Wilson (ed.), *Creativity in Primary Education* (3rd edition). London: Sage, pp. 33–44.

Cremin, T., Mottram, M., Bearne, E. and Goodwin, P. (2008) Exploring teachers' knowledge of children's literature. *Cambridge Journal of Education, 38* (4): 449–64.

Cremin, T., Thomson, B., Williams, C. and Davies, S. (2018) Reading teachers. *English 4–11, 62* (Spring).

Cremin, T., Mottram, M., Powell, S., Collins, R. and Drury, R. (2015) *Researching Literacy Lives: Building Home School Communities.* London and New York: Routledge.

Cremin, T., Mottram, M., Powell, S., Collins, R. and Safford, K. (2014) *Building Communities of Engaged Readers: Reading for Pleasure.* London and New York: Routledge.

Department for Education (2011) *Teachers Standards.* Retrieved from **https://www.gov.uk/ government/publications/teachers-standards** (accessed 19 December 2018).

Eisner, E. (1979) *The Educational Imagination.* New York: Collier-Macmillan.

Fecho, B. (2011) *Writing in the Dialogical Classroom. Students and Teachers Responding to the Texts of Their Lives.* Urbana, IL: National Council of Teachers of English.

Grainger, T., Barnes, J. and Scoffham, S. (2004) A creative cocktail: creative teaching in initial teacher education. *Journal of Education and Teaching, 38* (3): 243–53.

Hargreaves, A. and Fullan, M. (2013) The power of professional capital. *Journal of Staff Development, 34* (3): 36–9.

Hattie, J. (2012) *Visible Learning for Teachers: Maximising Impact on Learning.* London: Routledge.

Henriksen, D. and Mishra, P. (2015) We teach who we are: creativity in the lives and practices of accomplished teachers. *Teachers College Record, 117* (7): 1–46.

Marland, M. (1975) *The Craft of the Classroom.* London: Heinemann.

Moll, L., Amanti, C., Neff, D. and Gonzalez, N. (1992) Funds of knowledge for teaching: using a qualitative approach to connect homes and classrooms. *Theory into Practice, 31* (2): 132–41.

Palmer, T. (2018) *Armistice Runner.* Edinburgh: Barrington Stoke.

Richards, C. (2018) Primary teaching: a personal perspective. In T. Cremin and C. Burnett (eds), *Learning to Teach in the Primary School* (4th edition). London: Routledge, pp. 5–16.

Thomson, P. and Hall, C. (2008) Opportunities missed and/or thwarted? Funds of knowledge meet the English curriculum. *Curriculum Journal, 19* (2): 87–103.

16

DIFFERING VIEWS OF PROFESSIONALISM: IMPLICATIONS FOR PRIMARY TEACHERS

TONY EAUDE

TEACHERS' SENSE OF WELLBEING IS DEEPLY CONNECTED WITH HOW THEY DEFINE THEMSELVES AS PROFESSIONALS, AND HOW THEY SEE THEIR PROFESSIONALISM BEING DEFINED BY OTHERS.

(DAY ET AL., 2007: 244)

KEYWORDS: PROFESSIONALISM; PRIMARY TEACHERS; IDENTITY; EXTENDED PROFESSIONALITY; JUDGEMENT; AUTONOMY.

CHAPTER OBJECTIVES

This chapter helps you to:

- explore what it means to act and think as a professional, drawing on lessons from research in different professions
- consider different views of what teacher professionalism involves
- realise that what acting as a professional entails may vary over time and according to context and is linked to one's well-being

---

- recognise that professional identity is partly defined by the teacher him or herself but strongly influenced by how the role is perceived by other people
- compare 'restricted' and 'extended' professionality and the implications for primary teachers throughout their careers, especially in the early career phase

LINKS TO THE TEACHERS' STANDARDS

Working through this chapter will enable you to meet all of the Teachers' Standards, in particular:

TS 1: Establish high expectations which inspire, motivate and challenge pupils

TS 5: Adapt teaching to respond to the strengths and needs of all pupils

TS 8: Fulfil wider professional responsibilities

Part 2: Personal and professional conduct

Introduction

Most people see teaching as a profession, without necessarily thinking exactly what this entails. About fifty years ago, Etzioni (1969) described teaching, like nursing and social work, as a semi-profession, without the prestige attached to medicine or law. Many would argue that teachers have been expected in recent years to act more like executive technicians than to exercise professional judgement. Let us start by thinking how professionals should, and should not, act.

What does being a professional mean in practice?

CASE STUDY

Consider the following incident and note any points where you think that Anita acted in a professional or an unprofessional way.

Anita is a teacher towards the end of her first year of teaching. She is asked to take a group of children whom she does not know well on a day trip. She is worried about doing this on her own and sends an email to her head teacher refusing to do so unless a more senior person is present and tweeting to her friends that this is what she had done. Eventually, another, more experienced person is asked to accompany the group and Anita leads the trip, but complains in the staffroom that her arm was twisted.

Most people, including me, would see Anita criticising other colleagues on social media as unprofessional. Indeed, teachers should be exceptionally careful how they use social media and never involve children – and remember that what they post online from their personal life as a bit of fun may not be seen that way by their head teacher or by someone interviewing them for a job in a few years' time. While all teachers may want at times to complain about the head teacher or another colleague, it is not appropriate to do so in the staffroom or on social media.

While the children's safety must be a priority and is an essential part of acting as a professional, she could have gone about ensuring this in a more appropriate way. It would have been more professional to talk to her head teacher (or another senior leader) to express her concerns and ask for their advice.

This is a relatively simple example. To explore further what acting as a professional means, complete the following activity, on your own and perhaps with a group of other teachers.

REFLECTION

How would you describe what acting as a professional teacher involves? *(It may help to think of a teacher you know and admire.)*

You may have written words such as smart, compliant or well-organised; knowledgeable, caring or hard-working; or self-motivated, independent or idealistic. Or many others, as no list captures the complexity of acting as a professional.

Acting as a professional involves much more than:

- looking smart – though teachers do need to dress appropriately;

- doing what they are told – though teachers cannot do what they want and then expect to be treated as a professional;

- being well-prepared and organised – though these are essential.

Being knowledgeable, caring and hard-working are all necessary, but many people with these qualities would not really be regarded as professionals. While being self-motivated, independent or idealistic may be appropriate, some people may place more emphasis on fitting into a team or abiding by the school's and government policies.

Part 2 of the Teachers' Standards refers to personal and professional conduct and highlights that teachers must maintain high standards of ethics and behaviour, within and outside school, for instance safeguarding pupil's well-being and not undermining fundamental British values, though exactly what these entail is debatable (see Chapter 3). Do note that how teachers behave out of school is seen as part of how they should act as professionals, so you need to be careful about what you do in your own time and how this is presented by you, or others, especially since one's indiscretions can soon become public through social media.

How is, and has been, acting as a professional been understood in different professions?

THEORY FOCUS

Shulman (2004: 530) proposes that all professions are characterised by:

- service to others;
- understanding of a scholarly or theoretical kind;
- skilled performance or practice;
- the exercise of judgement under conditions of considerable uncertainty;
- learning from experience as theory and practice interact;
- a professional community to monitor quality and aggregate knowledge.

John (2008: 12) highlights as characteristics common to all professions:

- mastery of a knowledge base requiring a long period of training;
- tasks that are inherently valuable to society;
- a desire to prioritise the client's welfare;
- a high level of autonomy;
- a code of ethics to guide practice.

Much of Shulman's work was with doctors and lawyers as well as teachers. From this, and John's summary, it is worth noting the emphasis on whose welfare is prioritised, the emphasis on knowledge and skilled performance and how these are learned, who makes decisions (given the emphasis on judgement and autonomy) and membership of a professional community. Stop for a minute and think how well this fits in with your view of what professionalism entails.

We will explore the implications for primary school teachers, but let us first look at some different models of how being a professional has been described theoretically (see Eaude, 2018, Chapter 8 for a more detailed discussion).

'The exercise of judgement under conditions of considerable uncertainty' calls for teachers to be trusted to make such judgements, rather than just doing what someone outside the classroom says. This, and John's emphasis on prioritising the client's welfare and a high level of autonomy, reflect what is called a *covenantal* view. A covenant is based on trust rather than someone constantly checking whether the teacher is acting as they should. In a covenantal model, teachers as professionals are trusted to make good judgements in the best interests of the children in their care. The danger is that some teachers may not make good judgements.

In contrast, in the last thirty years, teachers, along with many other professionals, have increasingly been expected to adopt a *contractual* view of professionalism. A contract is based on exact expectations, which can be monitored and checked to see whether the person involved is doing what is expected. A contractual model of professionalism involves delivery and compliance – doing what one is told – with people regularly checking whether you are doing so and achieving externally set expectations. The danger is that what is expected may not be in children's best interests.

Being professional or being a professional?

Another view is that of Hargreaves and Fullan (2012: 80) who distinguish between being professional – how teachers act – and being a professional – related more to status and how other people regard teachers. This may seem a small difference but think about a farmer, an estate agent or a sports coach. Any of these may act in a professional way, in the sense that they are knowledgeable, efficient and trustworthy. However, people in such occupations would not normally be regarded as having the status associated with a profession such as medicine or teaching.

This highlights the importance of the knowledge required, and of the years necessary to acquire this level of teacher identity, who teachers are and who they are seen to be. This depends both on how teachers feel and see themselves and on other people's perceptions. Teachers are often respected as individuals, but not, as a group, as much as previously. Many politicians and parents believe that primary teachers do not require the same depth of knowledge or training as teachers of older students. You may still come across the view that teaching in primary schools is easier than secondary schools and that people become primary teachers because they are not academic enough to teach in a secondary school. If you do, make sure that people recognise the breadth of knowledge and skills necessary!

> *Teachers are not deliverers but developers of learning. Those who focus only on teaching techniques and curriculum standards . . . promote a diminished view of teaching and teacher professionalism that has no place in a sophisticated knowledge society.*
>
> (Hargreaves, 2003: 161)

REFLECTION

Do you agree with Hargreaves' view?

What are the implications of being a developer rather than a deliverer of learning?

Professional identity as a teacher matters for several reasons, which are associated with how children learn and the teacher's own role. For instance:

- The example which teachers set has a direct influence on children, especially in terms of passion and enthusiasm.

- A robust but flexible sense of identity and an extended sense of professionality – discussed below – helps teachers to avoid acting just as technicians, making them unlikely to exercise, and develop, a high level of expertise and judgement.

- Developing an identity as a teacher helps to secure teachers' commitment to their work and adherence to professional norms of practice.

- How teachers see themselves, and how they are seen, affects their confidence, morale and resilience and whether they enjoy teaching and wish to continue as teachers.

- A lack of status and confidence, individually and collectively, means that teachers' identity may not be sufficiently stable, and robust, to resist the imposition of inappropriate methods of teaching.

Therefore, how professionalism is understood affects to what extent the profession, collectively, can try and ensure that how children are taught is not left to those with little understanding of how they learn.

We will pick up these themes in relation to primary teachers, but first let us consider a third way of understanding what being a professional entails.

Restricted or extended professionality?

Drawing on Hoyle's work, Hargreaves and Goodson (1996) distinguish between *restricted* and *extended professionality*, as summarised in Table 16.1. This helps in identifying features of what being a professional entails and how the necessary skills and attitudes are developed.

Table 16.1

Restricted professionality	Extended professionality
Skills derived from experience	Skills derived from a mediation between experience and theory
A perspective limited to the here-and-now and classroom events being perceived in isolation	Having a perspective beyond the classroom embracing the broader social context
Introspection about methodology	Developing one's teaching methodology by comparing it to others
Individual autonomy	Collective autonomy
Limited involvement in professional activities outside teaching, reading professional literature and attending training other than practical courses	Placing a high value on professional activities and literature and training which combines theoretical and practical elements
Teaching being seen as largely intuitive	Seeing teaching as a rational rather than an intuitive activity

Adapted from Hargreaves and Goodson (1996): 14.

Table 16.1 emphasises features such as skills, the perspective adopted, ways of teaching, autonomy and professional development. I disagree with teaching being seen as rational rather than intuitive as teachers with a high level of expertise rely strongly on intuition (see Eaude, 2018: 160–4). However, this model emphasises that acting as a professional is mainly about how you teach and how you learn to do so with greater expertise – rather about how you dress or how neat your desk is. As Evans (2008: 29) observes, *a meaningful conception of professionalism must reflect the reality of daily practices.*

Table 16.1 mentions skills, but not knowledge as such. Teachers need to know how to teach and be able to do so – procedural knowledge – rather than just what to do – propositional knowledge. This difference is like that between knowing what riding a horse entails in theory and actually being able to do so. This is why methodology and learning from other teachers are important aspects of extended professionality.

Look back at Table 16.1 and consider:

- to what extent your own teaching reflects a restricted or an extended professionality, remembering that when anyone is starting to learn something as complicated as teaching their abilities will be limited at first;

- how much autonomy you have – and how confident you feel in exercising judgement;

- what *really* helps you in learning how to teach a class of young children.

What does extended professionality imply for primary teachers?

Teaching a class of young children is demanding; and learning to do so with extended professionality takes a long time. To see why, let us consider the challenges of teaching young children, especially a whole class.

REFLECTION

What makes teaching a class of young children so difficult?

You may find it hard to articulate why teaching a class of young children, which looks easy when done by a very good teacher, is so hard when one tries to do it oneself.

Most obviously, the teacher is dealing with young children who tend to be more volatile and usually more enthusiastic than older children. This makes the task enjoyable at times, exasperating at others. Classrooms are places of considerable uncertainty, where teachers often have little time to think what to do but have to act in the moment, intuitively. This is linked to a natural fear of loss of control, which often leads to a lack of confidence in oneself and an understandable tendency to over-control what happens – and so restrict opportunities for children to act independently and imaginatively.

Primary teachers have to ensure that children have a balanced and broadly based curriculum and must deal with the needs of the whole child, both pastoral and academic, and liaise with the family and other professionals. What really matters as a primary teacher is how well children learn across the whole curriculum and beyond and how teachers enable that. Primary teachers do not have such an obvious base of subject knowledge as secondary subject teachers, but they require a breadth of knowledge, especially of how young children learn, and repertoire of teaching methods. In Eaude (2018), I argue that pedagogical content knowledge (PCK) – the ways of formulating the subject that make it comprehensible to other people (see Shulman, 2004: 203) – is more important than subject knowledge as such. In addition, being able to act accordingly, especially when one is uncertain, depends heavily on case knowledge – 'I've been in a similar position before and know roughly what to do' – to guide one's judgement. Case knowledge is built up partly by experience, but also by thinking and seeing how general lessons can be applied to one's own teaching.

How do primary teachers develop as extended professionals?

Teaching young children is hard, especially at first. There is usually a lot of pressure and too little time, so that teachers are often too busy to reflect deeply and tend to focus more on their mistakes than their successes. A short course of training, however good, will not enable one to learn all the expertise associated with outstanding teaching, which is learned mostly in the years soon after qualification. Let us consider the following.

REFLECTION

What must primary teachers do to develop as extended professionals?

The obvious answer to how one develops as a teacher is continuing professional development (CPD). You probably think of CPD as going on courses, but the research on CPD (see TDT, 2015) which really changes how teachers teach suggests a much more nuanced view. Usually, short courses, however worthwhile and interesting, out of context, make little impact on how teachers actually teach in the long term. What really makes a difference is:

- practice, so that good habits gradually become embedded; and

- beliefs about learning, teaching and children.

As Hargreaves and Fullan (2012: 54) point out, *expert teachers are always consolidating what they know to be effective, testing it and continually adding to it.* However, one needs to practise the right things – for instance pre-empting or responding to disruptive behaviour, asking open questions and listening more and talking less – repeatedly and in a real classroom with real children.

Observing other teachers is useful, but expertise is often tacit, so how and why teachers make decisions has to be articulated and then practised. Feedback from others who are more experienced is helpful, though skilled teachers gradually become better at observing themselves. This involves reflection on what has gone well and on what they could do differently. However, Schön (1987) makes the distinction between reflection-on-action, after the event, and reflection-in-action, which happens in the moment. It is important to reflect on what has gone well and what one might do differently, but usually teachers do not have much time to reflect. Reflection-in-action involves what Sawyer (2004: 13) calls *disciplined improvisation* which requires confidence in one's own judgement, which many teachers lack, especially when they are new to the profession and/or when under stress.

How one actually teaches depends heavily on one's beliefs about learning, teaching and children. Primary teachers who are extended professionals draw on theory about how young children learn and do not always follow what is prescribed, so that, for instance, they give a wide range of opportunities to all children, as discussed elsewhere in this volume, rather than a narrow curriculum which disengages many children, especially those from disadvantaged backgrounds.

Can one develop extended professionality on one's own?

It is very difficult to develop extended professionality on one's own, especially for those new to the profession. The best context for doing so is in professional learning communities.

> *Learning communities become arenas for professional learning because the people imbue activities with shared meanings, develop a sense of belonging, and create new identities based, in part, on their relationships with one another.*
>
> (Lieberman, 2007: 199)

Schools are not automatically places where professional learning takes place, especially if teachers are isolated or under too much pressure. Lieberman highlights the importance of relationships and how these help to create a sense of belonging and, gradually, greater understanding of what being a teacher involves and the ability to act accordingly.

While acting as a professional requires teachers to exercise judgement and some autonomy, in professional learning communities, autonomy is collective rather than individual. This helps to set some parameters on what teachers can and cannot do and so protects children and teachers, especially those who are unsure. One important aspect is that mistakes are normalised – a collective recognition that all teachers make mistakes and can learn from them. Otherwise, teachers easily become discouraged and unlikely to try out new ideas.

Primary schools often have good and supportive social relationships, but professional learning sometimes involves being challenged in constructive ways. Therefore, teachers need opportunities to learn from each other by watching and being watched in a non-threatening way, rather than being constantly monitored. Other teachers and support staff can be very helpful and willing to help, but one usually needs to ask for their advice. Mentoring is valuable, as long as it is developmental, and the benefit is ideally reciprocal, where both the teacher and mentor learn from each other.

CHAPTER SUMMARY

There are different ways of understanding what acting as a professional entails, but how teachers do so, and how they act as a result is important both for their own well-being and that of the children. Fulfilling a role as complex as teaching a class of young children must be just a matter of following a pre-prepared plan exactly, but requires professional judgement to make appropriate decisions very quickly, drawing on case knowledge. Learning to act in this way with confidence takes a long time, with the years after qualification crucial, and is done best in supportive professional learning communities.

KEY POINTS TO CONSIDER

- Teaching, especially in primary schools, has always struggled to be seen as a profession as prestigious as medicine or law.
- Two contrasting views of what acting as a professional entails are a covenantal one where teachers have considerable autonomy and are trusted, and a contractual one where teachers are expected to do largely as they are told.
- Primary classroom teachers need to exercise judgement especially when there is no easy or obvious answer as to what to do.
- Developing 'extended professionality' involves much more than going on courses and happens best within professional learning communities, with the years soon after qualification being especially important

Further reading

Eaude, T. (2018) *Developing the Expertise of Primary and Elementary Classroom Teachers: Professional Learning for a Changing World.* London: Bloomsbury.

Chapters 8 and 9 discuss professional identity and how this can be developed throughout a primary teacher's career, but especially in the years soon after qualification.

Nias, J. (1989) *Primary Teachers Talking: A Study of Teaching as Work.* London: Routledge.

A classic text, though a little dated, but one which helps to explain how primary teachers think and act.

Pollard, A. (ed.) (2010) *Professionalism and Pedagogy: A Contemporary Opportunity. A Commentary by TLRP and GTCE.* London: TLRP. Available at **https://dera.ioe.ac.uk/11320/**

A very helpful discussion of many different aspects of pedagogy and the implications for professionalism.

References

Day, **C.**, **Sammons**, **P.**, **Stobart**, **G.**, **Kington**, **A. and Gu**, **Q.** (2007) *Teachers Matter: Connecting Lives, Work and Effectiveness*. Maidenhead: Open University Press

Etzioni, **A.** (ed.) (1969) *The Semi-professions and Their Organization: Teachers, Nurses, Social Workers*. New York: Free Press.

Evans, **L.** (2008) Professionalism, professionality and the development of education professionals. *British Journal of Educational Studies*, *56* (1): 20–38.

Hargreaves, **A.** (2003) *Teaching in the Knowledge Society – Education in the Age of Insecurity*. Maidenhead: Open University Press.

Hargreaves, **A. and Fullan**, **M.** (2012) *Professional Capital – Transforming Teaching in Every School*. New York: Teachers College Press.

Hargreaves, **A. and Goodson**, **I.F.** (1996) Teachers' professional lives: aspirations and actualities. In I.F. Goodson and A. Hargreaves (eds), *Teachers Professional Lives*. London: Farmer Press, pp. 1–27.

John, **P.** (2008) The predicament of the teaching profession and the revival of professional authority: a Parsonian perspective. In D. Johnson and R. Maclean (eds), *Teaching: Professionalization, Development and Leadership*, 11–24. **Springer.com**

Lieberman, **A.** (2007) Professional learning communities: a reflection. In L. Stoll and K. S. Louis (eds), *Professional Learning Communities: Divergence, Depth and Dilemmas*. Maidenhead: Open University Press, pp. 199–203.

Sawyer, **R.K.** (2004) Creative teaching: collaborative discussion as disciplined improvisation. *Educational Researcher*, *33* (2): 12–20.

Schön, **D.** (1987) *Educating the Reflective Practitioner: Toward a New Design for Teaching and Learning the Profession*. San Francisco: Jossey-Bass

Shulman, **L.S.** (2004) *The Wisdom of Practice – Essays on Teaching, Learning and Learning to Teach*. San Francisco: Jossey-Bass

TDT (Teacher Development Trust) (2015) *Developing Great Teaching – Lessons from the International Reviews into Effective Professional Development*. Available at **http://tdtrust.org/about/dgt**

17

THE CREATIVE TEACHER: AGENCY AND EMPOWERMENT

KATE THORPE

> TEACHERS SHOULD WORK TOWARDS A PEDAGOGY OF REPERTOIRE RATHER THAN A RECIPE.
>
> (ALEXANDER, 2010)

KEYWORDS: AGENCY; EMPOWERMENT; PROFESSIONAL; ASSESSMENT; DOCUMENTATION; REAL-LIFE/EXPERIENTIAL LEARNING; REFLECTIVE PRACTITIONER; LEARNING OUTSIDE THE CLASSROOM (LOTC); CONTEXT-BASED CURRICULA; PLANNING; CREATIVE PRACTICE.

CHAPTER OBJECTIVES

This chapter:

- empowers class teachers to value creative teaching and the subsequently enriched responses from the children
- explores how agency, motivation and creative thinking are intrinsically bound and will enhance a child's education and life journey
- informs and empowers teachers to recognise the validity of multiple pedagogies, that are adaptable equally to each teacher and each class, and to recognise that this is a reciprocal union and thus a mutually respectful journey
- offers practical and adaptable ideas for use in the classroom
- examines holistic benefits of Learning Outside the Classroom (LOtC)

```
┌─────────── LINKS TO THE TEACHERS' STANDARDS ───────────┐
│                                                         │
│  Working through this chapter will enable you to meet all of the Teachers' Standards, in particular:│
│                                                         │
│  TS 1:   Set high expectations which inspire, motivate and challenge pupils│
│                                                         │
│  TS 4:   Plan and teach well-structured lessons         │
│                                                         │
│  TS 5:   Adapt teaching to respond to the strengths and needs of all pupils│
│                                                         │
│  TS 6:   Make accurate and productive use of assessment │
│                                                         │
│  TS 8:   Fulfil wider professional responsibilities     │
│                                                         │
│  Part 2: Personal and professional conduct              │
│                                                         │
└─────────────────────────────────────────────────────────┘
```

Introduction

In this chapter we shall explore how agency and empowerment are part of the creative teacher's repertoire, how reflective practice is integral to the practitioner maintaining agency, as well as being a resourcing and nourishing element of practice. We'll consider current Ofsted recommendations and NC requirements and contextualise this with theoretical and practice evidence. Our three sections are:

- *Agency and empowerment: a reciprocal union* explores the impact of creative teaching, experiential learning and off-the-script teaching.

- *A forum for creativity: assessment and documentation as agency and empowerment* analyses how different mediums of assessment and documentation become a tool for agency and empowerment and can create links with the community.

- *The creative teacher: pedagogy that supports/stimulates teaching and learning* empowers teachers to believe in their own agency and creativity, and explores how to become a reflexive practitioner.

This chapter looks beyond just the agency of the teacher and child and seeks to evoke an emerging understanding of the many complexities and influences at play in classroom relationships through a series of case studies from the classroom.

Agency and empowerment: a reciprocal union

Let us consider how we might define *agency*. Each of us – child or teacher – have a latent potential capacity to act. When we recognise that we have choice and can do something positive about it, we are acting with agency: our actions are actualised. It is through agency that we are empowered to act in ways that are in the best interests for the children in our charge; through deciding to use this power to act our self-confidence and self-belief increases and intensifies, and we are empowered. This is a reciprocal union: in using our actions, we feel empowered, and each occasion we act our empowerment is confirmed, thereby completing a cycle.

We should therefore find that if our professional decisions are challenged, we can feel that it is possible to maintain our position, our sense of what is best for our own class and our responsibility to consider their education and well-being as of the utmost importance. In this chapter we explore how an imaginative and curious teacher will utilise the National Curriculum as a means to support teaching and learning, not as a constraint, but as a point from which to expand. The professional will enrich the curriculum at every opportunity, and remain flexible and adaptable towards the interests and needs of their class.

Teacher agency is at the very heart of professionalism. As we have seen throughout this book, in creating meaningful, holistic learning experiences for every child, the teacher is acting with agency, and this is pivotal to meaningful teaching and learning.

Teaching for creativity is a powerful means to give agency to both teacher and pupil. We will see what this could look like, how experiential learning and off-the-script teaching demonstrates agency and empowerment for teacher and child, indicating the reciprocity between the two and how this will enhance a child's education and life journey.

Increasing agency: taking learning outside

One of the environments we can explore further, that immediately stimulates curiosity and creativity, is that of *learning outside of the classroom* (LOtC). This could be, for example, within the school grounds or in museums, galleries and educational centres, etc. Taking learning outside of the classroom fundamentally involves the teacher being able to work in a different way with children, and this immediately invokes excitement and curiosity. It will often show the children in a different light (as illustrated by the case studies in this chapter), drawing out their skills and confidence in a way that learning in a more formal setting so rarely can (EOtC, 2005).

REFLECTION

Recall when you went on a school trip.

Why can you still recall these learning experiences?

How can you bring such excitement and deep learning to your class?

You can probably remember your own school trips because they were immersive experiences, where the learning is made meaningful. *Meaningful learning* can be contextualised through the way that the experience is introduced, so that the children have a clear understanding of either what they are to do or see. For example, if they are to search for mini-bugs, how will you plan to keep them focused and excited? Are they to hypothesise in which habitat the insects will be present and which not? How will they record their findings – on pre-designed sheets, or was this jointly negotiated and created between teacher and class? The latter example demonstrates how easily agency, motivation and creative thinking can be built in to this activity. This is also an example of how teachers can develop *context-based curricula* (Reiss, 2018), which will enrich and deepen learning while also contributing to children's *physical, personal and social education* (EOtC, 2005), thereby fostering teaching and learning of high quality that *enriches the curriculum and can improve educational attainment* (EOtC, 2005). LOtC can become a fantastic cross-curriculum vehicle for learning where the child may pose their own problems and find their own solutions.

Imagine visiting, for example, a natural beauty spot with the class. Suddenly their interest in rocks, rivers, etc. has purpose: their learning is experiential. The fieldwork fosters child agency and critical thinking as the learning opportunities represented by such visits open up new ideas and ways of thinking (EOtC, 2005) which can be explored back in the classroom.

Powerful pedagogy

LOtC is a means through which a teacher may plan real-life experiences that will *provide each learner with an education that enables them to acquire the knowledge, the skills and the understandings that prove powerful for them* (Reiss, 2018). This will foster the individuals' capacity to flourish, influencing their attitude towards learning, motivating the child to make sense of the world and to draw links between feelings and learning. Such powerful and memorable learning experiences promote not just the acquisition of skills but the transfer of skills, thus metacognitive learning is embedded. This demonstrates the reciprocity between LOtC, critical thinking and learning in the classroom, thereby developing agency and empowering both practitioner and pupil. Research also evidences that experiential and LOtC pedagogy raises academic achievement (LOtC, 2006; EOtC, 2005; NASUWT, 2017).

Such a pedagogy would develop *attributes such as risk-taking, independent judgement, commitment, resilience, intrinsic motivation and curiosity* (NACCCE, 1999), all of which are key elements in creative thinking. The practitioner who plans for learning sequences that build these attributes in their class is not merely giving children agency, but significantly is sensitively providing a platform for creativity, through motivating them *to believe in their creative potential, to engage their sense of possibility and to give them the confidence to try* (NACCCE, 1999).

CASE STUDY

School garden

Year 1 teacher, Yasmin, planned a sequence of creative science lessons through a cross-curricular approach, maximising their experience by using the school grounds as a direct stimulus. She planned to engage the children with this familiar environment in specific ways: close observation, classification of plants, understanding of the life cycle of a plant, etc. through immersive, sensory, hands-on experience. She provided opportunities for the children to extend and consolidate their knowledge base, and to collaborate, hypothesise and pose questions. They also worked with the school gardener who was present and ready to assist during their sessions outside, and who provided an expert source of knowledge.

This 'real-life' experiential approach was combined with a narrative element, whereby the children were introduced to fictional characters of the same age as them (created by their teacher), Lucy and Leon, with whom the children could relate. The teacher remarked: *The characters posed the problems and the children looked forward to answering them.*

The teacher knew a narrative approach would stimulate and foster curiosity and engagement from her children. She was acting with agency.

Figure 17.1   The fictional characters of Lucy and Leon

REFLECTION

Does the above seem strange and yet exciting?

Have we begun as practitioners, as schools, to deliver an education that seeks *to enable all children to develop their creativity and unlock their creative potential* (NACCCE, 1999)?

If we are to deliver an education which promotes creativity, motivation and agency, how can we effectively implement and dynamically change our current education system? The above case study provides a platform from which we can critically consider our planning and learning to include opportunities for creative thinking.

The NACCCE report recommended a longitudinal shift in the curriculum and pedagogy to fulfil the goal of inspiring the future generation to be innovative and creative thinkers. The above case study illustrates how to *develop lively, inquiring minds, the ability to question . . . and to apply themselves to tasks* (NACCCE, 1999), all of which foster creativity. Experiential learning, through partnerships with schools, museums and other centres for education can provide immersive, interactive and informative learning experiences. A cross-curriculum approach, one where the arts are utilised as a vehicle to stimulate and cross-fertilise a range of subjects, fulfils the needs of the child, to resource their spirit and promote motivation and academic engagement:

> *It is through the arts in all their forms that young people experiment with and try to articulate their deepest feelings and their own sense of cultural identity and belonging. A balanced arts education has essential roles in the creative and cultural development of young people.*

> (NACCCE, 1999)

THEORY FOCUS

NASUWT (2017), Report: Creativity and the arts in the curriculum

The NASUWT 2017 report into Creativity and the Arts in the Curriculum evidences that when a child receives an education that provides cultural learning significant gain is made by all children, holistically, academically and cognitively. Such children will flourish and become responsible members of society, for example continuing to higher education, voting and volunteering. Cultural learning has a particularly significant positive effect on children from low-income families, evidencing how creative and cultural learning addresses inequalities in our society.

Surely this is a potent argument to ensure that our curriculum includes cultural and arts education as a fundamental part of the child's education? Is this not the approach we wish to take as practitioners, that educates the whole child for their future journey in life and not just for school performativity tests? This is an *approach [which] is failing young people*, according to Amanda Spielman, the head of Ofsted (Spielman, 2018).

The proposed 'quality of education' framework represents Ofsted's commitment to a change in the curriculum, seemingly taking note of the longitudinal shift defined by NACCCE, their understanding of the necessity for a broad and balanced curriculum, and the redirecting of agency and empowerment to school leaders, teachers and the child. As Spielman states:

> *By shifting our focus away from performance measures in isolation, we will empower schools to put the child first.*

> (Spielman, 2018)

The current punitive assessment systems in the UK do not motivate creative teaching and learning and therefore decrease teacher agency and empowerment. The NASUWT (2017) report recommends that all strata of the education community should be involved in curricula explicitly considering creative teaching and learning, alongside frameworks to value these transposable skills. Comparing the NC of England with its counterparts in Wales and Scotland, it is clear that English version has a poverty in its description of creativity (Wyse and Ferrari, 2015). However, considering Spielman's recent changes to OfSTED's foci, creative teaching and learning are now being considered to be of significance once again in education.

A forum for creativity

Assessment and documentation as agency and empowerment

Let us now consider what might a forum for creativity look like? How can *assessment* and *documentation* become a tool for agency and empowerment? These will be the guiding elements of this section and should also be kept in mind as we progress through the chapter. We shall explore what this can look like in the classroom and how the reflective questions can support our pedagogy as practitioners.

As teachers we need to be mindful to seek to educate children beyond bureaucratic and performativity demands, to foster a creative education and curriculum, to tailor our teaching – to act with agency. The approach we take to assessment and the influence this has on children, be that positive or negative, is significant. A child's attitude towards assessment *will play a major role in shaping their identity as learners* (Hayward and Hayward, 2016). If we as teachers involve children in the processes and dialogue about assessment and learning, we can foster 'optimistic learners' (ibid., 2016) who will have agency and a sense of empowerment as a result. This will promote a positive attitude, a greater depth of understanding and engagement with the learning. Agency and empowerment is reciprocated through the teacher holding an inclusive, dialogic approach to assessment.

REFLECTION

What methods do you currently use to document children's progress in learning? How effective are these in capturing the process of learning?

How can current records be used in collaboration with children to stimulate further learning?

How effectively do your records communicate children's experiences and learning processes to parents?

Do both children and parents contribute to the documentation process?

How can/do methods of assessment empower teachers?

These questions could be a motivator to rethink assessment and documentation approaches and suitability for you and your class.

How does the teacher demonstrate an inclusive, dialogic approach to assessment in the case study below?

Figure 17.2   Poster demonstrating use of direct speech

The creative teacher

Pedagogy that supports/stimulates teaching and learning

The creative teacher who maintains agency is well versed in the subjects they will teach. They have rigorously researched their themes and explored cross-curricula links (Barnes, 2015), which they can highlight explicitly so that children are aware of these connections, or so that they are well-prepared in case a child's thinking spontaneously diverts the interest and focus of the class. The creative teacher is not challenged by an off-the-script diversion. They are excited by the learning opportunity and enriched engagement, questioning, thinking, reasoning or expertise that the pupil ignites in the class. The creative teacher is ready to adapt, to move with the interest of the class, to follow their motivation and exploit an instance of deep learning: they are acting with agency.

CASE STUDY

An off-the-script instance/planning dilemma

A Year 3 class were studying their locality which, being near to Westminster, was close to the River Thames and the many bridges which cross this waterway. The class teacher, Josie, had a two-week plan for studying bridges and other local geographical features through time. But several days into the topic, a pupil unexpectedly brought to the class's notice some 'green and yellow stuff' growing on the bridges. What could it be? Did anyone know?

Josie was unexpectedly faced with a decision: should she follow the class's interest which diverted from the topic, or stick to her planning?

Their interest was piqued. They were curious, wanted to know and understand more. If she was to go off script, adapt her teaching to follow their interest, how would she cover the areas planned and within the NC? Time pressures meant a balance would be tricky at best. But they were deeply motivated, and an unexpected meaningful learning opportunity had presented itself.

Josie decided to adapt the topic to encompass this intriguing new learning. Yes, it resulted in a bit more planning, but both the teacher and the children were highly motivated, and the new direction of the topic meant that other areas of the NC, of skills and knowledge, could be included. The resulting learning was of a high calibre. All the children felt included as they had directed the focus of the learning. The teacher carefully scaffolded the how and what of the learning, so that the expected skills and knowledge were explored and acquired.

REFLECTION

How could you maximise the learning impetus from an off-the-script diversion?

How can listening and following the child's interests be valued?

Pivotal to this is the teacher's ability to create a forum in which the children will discuss and listen. If the teacher creates an environment (see Chapter 1) where the child feels encouraged to take risks and make mistakes, then their participation, reasoning, thinking and ability to share will develop immensely. The teacher who develops an adaptable approach to teaching will be ready to enjoy those off-the-script diversions. This may well result in a higher level of cognition as the children are self-motivated, and through their critical thinking and discussions will reach deeper understandings (Crichton and McDaid, 2015; Clarke, 1998; Craft, 2000; Fisher, 2006).

Reflective teacher – reflective child

A natural extension of listening and reasoning skills would be fostering children to become self-evaluative (Clarke, 1998; Black and Wiliam, 1998; ARG, 2006): the child who is engaging in listening and reasoning is also capable of learning to self-evaluate. Plenaries, whether mid-way through or at the end of an activity, are an ideal time to develop this skill with the class. Clarke recommends that in the early stages of the acquisition the teacher will give a range of question types and a range of answers (Clarke, 1998). Introducing children to think critically and evaluatively while modelling explicitly will increase their understanding of expectations and their motivation and opportunity for success.

Here are some sample questions from Clarke:

What did you find easy?

What did you find difficult/where did you get stuck? What helped you get out of the difficulty? (Was it something a friend said or did, something the teacher did, something to do with equipment, something you did yourself?)

(Clarke, 1998)

This verbalising of the evaluative process could be combined with the children creating a display or poster (Clarke, 1998). It could be made from them photographing or sketching stages of the process or their end product – a form of self-evaluation in which all phases of primary could engage. This could develop into a written formulation of their self-evaluation, depending upon the learning stage of the child. These skills will empower the child to *understand the main purposes of their learning and thereby grasp what they need to do to achieve* (Black and Wiliam, 1998). Thus both teacher and child are acting with agency.

REFLECTION

Take a look at Figure 17.3 and reflect upon instances of your own practice when you pose these questions:

- Have you had the opportunity to reflect in this way with a colleague or a group of colleagues, so that cross-fertilisation of ideas and expertise takes place?
- How might this work for you in your weekly/daily practice?
- Are those informal 'chats' during break time, those 'I don't know how to . . .' moments in the staff room, actually more reflective than you had consciously considered?

The reflective practitioner will take time to reflect and note their thinking. I would suggest at times a mental note is sufficient while at others it is clearer to put it in writing and adapt the planning accordingly. Such a *pedagogical practice promotes children's learning and creativity* (Blandford and Knowles, 2012).

Professional identity and the 'everyday'

A significant ingredient to include in our reflections on practice is to consider what *we* bring to this – what might *our* biases be? What has influenced *them*? If we engage with Figure 17.4, we are challenging our assumptions, freshening our outlook, and through collaborative sharing with colleagues, parents, carers and children, we can create an inclusive, welcoming and meaningful environment.

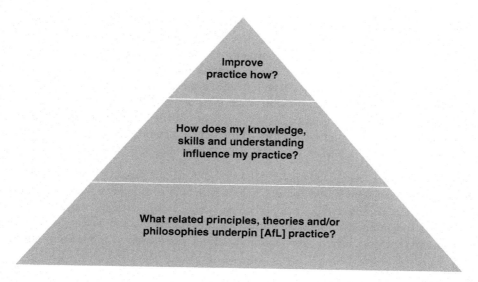

Figure 17.3   Enhancing practice (adapted from Blandford and Knowles, 2012)

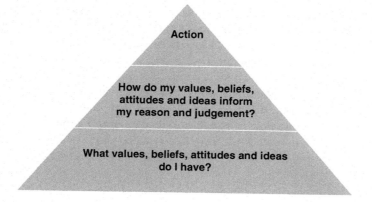

Figure 17.4   Improving pedagogical practice (adapted from Blandford and Knowles, 2012)

Another ingredient is the potential gender differences in subject knowledge and skills and how to remain objective and impartial to support a sense of teacher-agency. Being aware of gender-biased systems means we can re-balance this, through recognising and valuing other *values, beliefs, attitudes and ideas* (Blandford and Knowles, 2012), such as subjective and intuitive knowledge, *tentativeness and uncertainty* (Craft, 1996).

Integral to this awareness of our influences, to facilitate the planning of curricula and learning experiences, is considering the child and the influences outside of school which will frame the child's experience and knowledge, their everyday knowledge. Consider Figure 17.4 with the parent or carer rather than the practitioner as the focus, to give us insights into *what counts as 'everyday'* (Reiss, 2018) knowledge for the child, and how this will be influenced directly by their home experience and the values, beliefs, attitudes and expectations with which they are familiar. These too will be influenced by more complex nuances than a parent's enjoyment or knowledge of a particular subject, their beliefs, culture and their expectations for their child, which may be gender specific. Therefore, we need to be sensitively aware that *what is everyday to one student may be exotic to another* (Reiss, 2018).

The creative teacher will maximise all opportunities to motivate and promote learning and this could result in project or home–school linked work being individual or collaborative. We can promote pupil agency through collaborative project work or home–school linked projects between peers and/or involving the local community. Approaches involving the community will develop rapport between school and locality, and are a means to communicate children's experiences and learning effectively.

Organising for optimal agency

Back in the classroom, grouping children and deciding the type of setting is additionally influenced by the aim of the learning, especially when promoting creative thinking and agency. It is important for the teacher to provide opportunities for children to work and choose to do so, in a range of settings, such as individual, pair, small/large group to whole class (Hayward and Hayward, 2016). This provides different types of evidence of learning for formative assessment, which will inform planning and will confirm whether the teacher should, for example, intervene or stand back, or allocate more or less time (Craft and Chappell, 2016; Cremin *et al.*, 2006). The teacher scaffolds the learning through maintaining a 'speculative stance' which invites the children to pose questions to peers and to the teacher (Cremin *et al.*, 2006). Significantly to foster possibility or creative thinking, the responses the teacher gives need to be of the type that open up possibilities, that promote the child to challenge their thinking, consider new solutions, pose new problems, thereby ensuring the child's *sense of agency and influence over their work* (Cremin *et al.*, 2006). The child could be said to be intrinsically motivated, and therefore *will perform more creatively if they are motivated by interest in the activity itself* (Amabile, 1988).

CASE STUDY

Empowering children

Ayesha had planned a sequence of cross-curriculum creative teaching and learning for a Year 1 class. The initial stimulus was an image. The children were working in carefully selected groups (e.g. those who would work well together and mixed ability), with specified aims for each segment of the lesson sensitively scaffolded. The children were responsive not only to this pedagogical approach, but their sense of agency was activated through this; they were confident in the knowledge that they understood the what and the how of the learning. When the teacher directed a child from each group to tiptoe around and garner ideas from other groups, the children were excited and proud to be given this important role.

In this example the children could be said to be working at times independently and at times in a group. The teacher provided scaffolding through minimal intervention and maintained a speculative stance, which evidently enthused the children with confidence and agency.

CHAPTER SUMMARY

In this chapter we have explored the reciprocity between agency and empowerment and how this could look in the classroom. The plethora of research that we have examined demonstrates the demand from practitioners for guidance and continuing professional development to enhance their practice to teach in a confident and informed way. I hope this chapter has gone some way to advancing this guidance.

We have developed a firm understanding of how the forum for creativity can be utilised as a vehicle not only to inform teaching, but also to support our pedagogical approach, making the NC work for us. Each teacher is personally responsible for making assessment for learning their own: to make it work for you and your children, according to your pattern of teaching (Black and Wiliam, 1998), the uniqueness of each child and the dynamics of your particular class. Therefore you will demonstrate fluency and adaptability - a repertoire of pedagogies (Alexander, 2010) which are integral to creative professional practice. We, as trained professionals, possess the skills and expertise to create meaningful, experiential learning, both inside and beyond the classroom, and should feel empowered to maximise this agency.

KEY POINTS TO CONSIDER

- Experiential learning, creative/possibility thinking, LOtC, are within the agency of both teacher and child, and empower each to value experiences, skills and knowledge beyond the bounds of the school.
- We have established the place of the arts as an essential component to a holistic education that, embedded into education, will provide social mobility and thus is a motivator for inclusivity and change.
- A creative curriculum provides opportunities for memorable, deep learning experiences, involving the community beyond the school, where sharing child achievement and a different perspective become tangible and meaningful.
- It is through a creative, enquiry-based education that we can provide children with opportunities for self-reflection, develop an understanding of bias and influences, and motivate the development of informed perspectives (NACCCE, 1999), which will enrich their sense of identity and their place within an increasingly global culture.

Further reading

Marshall, T. (2014) New teachers need access to powerful educational knowledge. *British Journal of Educational Studies*, 62 (3): 265–79.

Priestley, M., Biesta, G.J.J., Philippou, S. and Robinson, S. (2015) The teacher and the curriculum: exploring teacher agency. In D. Wyse, L. Hayward and J. Pandya (eds), *The Sage Handbook of Curriculum, Pedagogy and Assessment*. London: Sage. Available at: https://pdfs.semanticscholar.org/4573/7ce723a8788ad268928fcbfa57fe4e6bb5ffc.pdf

References

Alexander, R. (ed.) (2010) Conclusions and recommendations. In *Children, Their World, Their Education: Final Report and Recommendations of the Cambridge Primary Review*. Abingdon: Routledge.

Amabile, T.M. (1988) A model of creativity and innovation in organizations. In B. M. Staw and L. L. Cummings (eds), *Research in Organizational Behaviour, 10*: 123–67.

ARG (2006) *The Role of Teachers in the Assessment of Learning*. Report. Nuffield Foundation, Assessment Reform Group, UK.

Barnes, J. (2015) An introduction to cross-curricular learning. In P. Driscoll, A. Lambirth and J. Roden (eds), *The Primary Curriculum: A Creative Approach* (2nd edition). London: Sage, pp. 260–83.

Black, P. and Wiliam, D. (1998) Inside the black box: raising standards through classroom assessment. *Phi Delta Kappan, 80* (2): 139–48.

Blandford, S. and Knowles, C. (2012) Assessment for learning: a model for the development of a child's self-competence in the early years of education. *Education 3–13: International Journal of Primary, Elementary and Early Years Education, 40* (5): 487–99.

CLA (2017) *ImagineNation: The Value of Cultural Learning*. Cultural Learning Alliance.

Clarke, S. (1998) *Targeting Assessment in the Primary Classroom: Strategies for Planning, Assessment, Pupil Feedback and Target Setting*. London: Hodder & Stoughton.

Craft, A. (1996) Nourishing educator creativity: an holistic approach to continuing professional development. *Journal of In-Service Education, 22* (3): 309–23.

Craft, A. (2000) *Creativity Across the Primary Curriculum: Framing and Developing Practice*. London: Routledge.

Craft, A. (2001) *An Analysis of Research and Literature on Creativity in Education*. Report prepared for the Qualifications and Curriculum Authority, UK.

Craft, A. and Chappell, K. (2016) Possibility thinking and social change in primary schools. *Education 3–13: International Journal of Primary, Elementary and Early Years Education, 44* (4): 407–25.

Cremin, T., Burnard, P. and Craft, A. (2006) Pedagogy and possibility thinking in the Early Years. *Thinking Skills and Creativity, 1* (2): 108–19.

Crichton, H. and McDaid, A. (2015) Learning intentions and success criteria: learners' and teachers' views. *Curriculum Journal, 27* (2): 190–203.

Dewey, J. (1910) *How We Think*. Boston: D. C. Heath.

Early Education (2012) *Development Matters in the EYFS*. DfE.

EOtC (2005) *Education Outside the Classroom*. House of Commons Education and Skills Committee, Second Report of Session 2004–05, HC 120. London: The Stationery Office.

Fisher, R. (2006) *Thinking to Learn: Helping pupils take greater responsibility for their own learning.* Scottland: The Highland Council. Available at: **https:www.steveslearning.com/Teacher%20 Training%20resources/Fisher,%20R.%20Tools%20for%20Thinking.pdf**

Hayward, L. and Hayward, S. (2016) Assessment and learning. In D. Wyse and S. Rogers (eds), *A Guide to Early Years and Primary Teaching.* London: Sage, pp. 165–83.

LOtC (2006) *Learning Outside the Classroom: Manifesto.* DfES Publications, Nottingham.

NACCCE (1999) *All Our Futures: Creativity, Culture and Education,* Chaired by K. Robinson, National Advisobry Committee on Creative and Cultural Education (NACCCE). Sudbury: DfEE.

NASUWT (2017) *Creativity and the Arts in the Curriculum: A Report of Policies and Practices in England, Northern Ireland, Scotland and Wales.* NASUWT, The Teachers' Union, April.

Reiss, M.J. (2018) The curriculum arguments of Michael Young and John White. In D. Guile, D. Lambert and M. J. Reiss (eds), *Sociology, Curriculum Studies and Professional Knowledge: New Perspectives on the Work of Michael Young.* Abingdon: Routledge, pp. 121–31.

Rogers, S. and Wyse, D. (2015) Agency, pedagogy and the curriculum. In D. Wyse, R. Davis, P. Jones and S. Rogers (eds), *Exploring Education and Childhood: From Current Certainties to New Visions.* London: Routledge, pp. 56–70.

Spielman, A. (2018) Her Majesty's Chief Inspector, Ofsted, Letter dated 30 October. **https://assets. publishing.service.gov.uk/government/uploads/system/uploads/attachment_data/ file/752721/HMCI_PAC_letter_311018.pdf**

Valentine, M. (2006) *The Reggio Emilia Approach to Early Years Education* (2nd edition). Learning and Teaching Scotland, Glasgow.

Wyse, D. and Ferrari, A. (2015) Creativity and education: comparing the national curricula of the states of the European Union and the United Kingdom. *British Educational Research Journal, 41* (1): 30–47.

18
MYTH BUSTING IN THE CONTEMPORARY PRIMARY CLASSROOM

ROBERT MORGAN

FREEDOM IS NOT A GIFT WHICH IS GIVEN OR TAKEN, BUT A POWER WHICH GROWS OR FAILS TO GROW AND IT IS A POWER OF SPECIAL VALUE TO CHILDREN AT SCHOOL. SCHOOL IS A PLACE TO WHICH CHILDREN GO TO LEARN; AND CHILDREN LEARN BEST WHEN THEY EXERCISE, NOT ONLY THEIR IMAGINATION, THEIR INTELLIGENCE AND THEIR MEMORY, BUT ALSO THEIR GROWING POWER TO CHOOSE.

(SCHILLER, 1979: 49)

KEYWORDS: BEHAVIOURISM; HIERARCHY; AUTONOMY; HABITUS; POWER; CONTROL; PEDAGOGY; SANCTION; REWARD.

CHAPTER OBJECTIVES

This chapter:

- explores the common features of an English primary classroom in relation to organisation/behaviour management/inclusion
- asks why teachers do the things they do
- explodes myths of what teachers perceive as 'what works'
- requires readers to engage in a re-examination of classroom pedagogy

Introduction

Myth 1: Behaviourism is no longer a key pedagogy in primary schools in the UK today.

Behaviourism lives in many primary schools that I have visited in the last five years. It is a myth that the idea of social constructivism, as favoured by many initial teacher training institutions, is the favoured pedagogy used by teachers in the classroom. I shall argue that behaviourism is bound in the idea that power, as a form of discipline and sanction, is the dominant form of the teacher/child relationship within primary schools today. This chapter will seek to explore how the current primary school structure employs a system of control that not only reduces the child to a passive role within a hierarchical model, but also the teacher. My argument is that the teacher, in employing various examples of controlling pedagogy, can be viewed as complicit and possibly, at the same time, unaware of doing so.

By *behaviourism* I mean a form of teaching and learning in which there is *a high degree of adult control in the process* (Pollard, 2014). Behaviourism is the pedagogical theory that learning is *acquired from a stimulus-response relationship* (Grigg, 2010) which translates into the teachers being the transmitters of learning. It is characterised by learners sitting in rows facing the teacher because the learner is *cast in a passive role* (Pollard et al., 2019). This didactic role gives power to the teacher who is able to control the teaching and assessing of learning (Pollard et al., 2019). The difficulty is in assessing the learners' progress, but its strength lies in the efficiency of transmission of knowledge and subject expertise. Such a theory of teaching is known as *traditional teaching methods* (Pollard et al., 2019). Prominent behaviourist theorists, notably Skinner, believed that scholarship involves learning by association. Curtis and Pettigrew (2010) wrote that such learning does not motivate learners, inhibits curiosity and favours an approach that prioritises the transmission of knowledge. This has the effect of learners being conditioned by qualities namely passivity and studying for external rewards rather than for the sake of learning.

Social constructivism, as the term implies, uses the interaction of others, whether that be a teacher or a child. It is this theory that has *influenced the development of the curriculum* (Grigg, 2010) and its most influential theorist was Lev Vygotsky. Vygotsky (1978) described how 'adult guidance' would further children's development and although he did not specify any adult other than the teacher. He did write how learning would happen when a learning environment takes language development and problem-solving into account:

> Using imitation [internalised learning], children are capable of doing much more in collective activity or under the guidance of adults.
>
> (Vygotsky, 1978: 88)

It is social constructivism which requires a teacher to design and develop a *learning-oriented class-room climate* (Pollard *et al.*, 2019). Therefore, it calls on teachers to draw more widely on pedagogical knowledge and repertoire and, in order to be successful in teaching, requires a good level of skill and judgement.

A hierarchical system?

The modern English primary school is a hierarchical entity bounded within a larger educational system of top-down control. The Department of Education rests at the top of this model; its policies and curricula flow down and are absorbed by the thousands of schools which, in turn, are publicly accountable through nationally administered tests. If a visitor were to visit a primary school they may, more than likely, be greeted by a display board in which the employees of that school are listed in a descending manner, beginning, perhaps invariably, with the head teacher, the leadership team, the staff, the teaching assistants, the mid-day meal supervisors and the peripheral staff, such as the crossing patrol team. This may also be true on drop-down boxes titled 'staff' or 'who's who' on school websites.

The school is a hierarchy and a system of regulated control, existing today as a product of its ancestral conception based in the economic slump of the 1870s and the organisation of society at that time. The Education Act of 1870 paved the way for the beginning of a move toward educating most of the population, not that all were unable to read or write, but to service the empire and the economy. Therefore legislation enabled schooling that was designed for a specific purpose. The idea of 'school' was formed from a Victorian perspective of conformity, and its basic operation and organisation has largely been unchanged to this day.

REFLECTION

Do you recognise this hierarchy in your own school setting?

What do you think the purpose of education should be?

A sense of power

Foucault (1991) wrote how the penal system began to infiltrate the machinations of other societal institutions and how their infrastructure was influenced by it. The penal system's reform was based on requiring docile bodies that had constant observation as a method of enforcing such docility, in that prisoners learnt to conform to the institution's expectations. Such observation was the 'gaze' – a technique that authority uses to monitor behaviour (Danaher *et al.*, 2000). The school, I argue, is no different. Power is brought about by constant observation and the requirement to fit into 'behaviour policies' which is imposed on children. There is a subsequent 'fit in' and be rewarded or 'opt out' and be sanctioned, usually with public displays in the classroom of colourful charts. Power is enforced from above, but that society acquiesces to the demands of the school. Parents send children to schools – and will decide which schools to send their children to – but, importantly, at that point they then subscribe to the organising of the school in terms of curriculum and teaching routines. Children themselves quickly realise that the school classroom has hierarchical divisions. One example is the naming of ability groups according to measurable attainment; there are high ability groups and low ability groups, usually for English and mathematics but sometimes based as the formation for differentiating ability for other subjects too. Children recognise this easily, as we have seen as examples in other chapters of this book, and some choose or are encouraged to conform to this by aiming to get into the 'highest' group possible.

An honest approach?

This chapter is based on my own observations and research in primary schools. One of my roles is as a university moderating tutor, which entails visiting trainee primary teachers during a school experience-based placement to assess their state of training. This usually comprises a lesson observation and then a feedback in which pertinent aspects of the lesson are discussed – you will probably recognise this from your own training. It is, however, during the post-observation discussion when pedagogical decisions can be revealed as superficial, in the sense that they are carried through without having been thought about enough. I argue that behaviourism comes naturally to a trainee teacher, even though she/he may think that the children are being taught and are learning through more constructivist or social constructivist pedagogies and organised environments. Therefore, behaviourism, in the sense of increasing adult control, permeates the primary classroom and should be brought into focus and discussed honestly. There is nothing wrong in behaviourism as a pedagogy: it is efficient and cost effective. It relies on transmission and reward and easy to administer assessment systems. That said, however, it should not be used unwittingly, and care needs to be implemented through a reflective take on primary practice.

REFLECTION

What is your teaching philosophy and style? When do you use behaviourist pedagogy in your teaching? Do you agree that behaviourist strategies are the ones that come most naturally to the beginning teacher?

THEORY FOCUS

Cultural conditioning

It was Bourdieu writing in his book *Distinction* (1984) who introduced his version of sociology and an explanation for the organisation of human institutions, notably education and the media. For

(Continued)

(Continued)

Bourdieu, social institutions or organisations are based on divisions within relationships. People within these structures are engaged in a struggle to exert their positions according to the 'accumulation of being' that they manage to achieve. Society is not equal; the workplace is not equal; and people have perceptions of who and where they are in the world and attempt to navigate their pathways by using strategies that best fit their own purpose. His definition of the 'habitus' works on an unconscious level; an individual is conditioned by a habitus. It is a culturally and socially acquired way of thinking or acting based on an individual's accumulation of knowledge, views, skills, tastes. This accumulation reflects an individual's background or maintains an individual in a social class, which can reflect a social history. There is a sense that too much adult control in the primary classroom today is about subjugation and monitoring of behaviour so that this can be rewarded or sanctioned. Power, by which I mean a force that allows change to be implemented, is denied to the child and is wrapped in the wider school environment. The habitus, or social environment, in a school is fixed and the classroom teacher or trainee teacher who enters it is subconsciously absorbed by it and conforms to the dominant ethos of control.

Models of control

From my visits to primary schools I shall provide four examples of how I perceive trainee primary teachers engaging in behaviourist examples of classroom-based pedagogy. I am not arguing that behaviourism, in itself, is less worthy of any other favoured models; rather I am selecting examples which may indicate how behaviourism dominates classroom practice without being critiqued or reflected on as being the type of pedagogy that is relevant. Within the concept of teaching and learning, the primary classroom is governed by these three examples of control: language, organisation, permission to engage and talk-partners.

Myth 2: Some words in the English language are better than others.

Language

The English language is constantly evolving, having words added to it and recognised by dictionaries on a yearly basis, as well as editing words deemed as out of fashion and falling into obscurity. The fascinating element in the use of the English language in the primary classroom is that increasingly its entry point is being determined by teachers. For example, some English lessons, or literacy lessons as they are titled, despite the National Curriculum labelling it otherwise, have a technique called 'up-levelling'. This is where a child produces a piece of writing and is invited to share it openly with the rest of the class. The child's work is subject to scrutiny at once: from the child's peers through the invitation to share how it can be made better under the 'two stars and a wish' strategy, as well as by the formative assessment of the teacher. Here the teacher begins to exercise the role of language gatekeeper. If the work of the child needs remedying in terms of correcting syntax, grammar, punctuation or spelling, that could be seen as an acceptable form of assessment for improvement, although the debate could be that Standard English, as the dominant dialect in England, could have room for other dialects to be expressed and used within writing. The obvious example is the local dialect of the school's community. If, however, the teacher's assessment moves onto word choice, that is a different issue. This is where the child offers a piece of writing but then is required to substitute a perfectly acceptable word for another because it 'is a better word'. The meaning of the writing or its sentiment will not change but the former word is no longer acceptable. For example, 'I was scared' becomes 'I was petrified'. The obvious question is not why is 'petrified' any better than 'scared' – and this possibly opens up former etymological divisions within modern English – for example a preference for Norman French – but this also shows why the power is residing in a teacher's ability to allow 'up-levelled' words. Lambirth (2011) described how language is 'invested in power', and the question of power here lies with teachers as a way of controlling the words permitted to be used in the classroom.

Children are naturally curious and inquisitive members of a school (as so should you be, by reading this!). It is not that their English vocabulary should be stunted. On the contrary, it should be encouraged and developed. This is not a direct contradiction with the earlier points about up-levelling. I merely wish to point out that no one word within a language is 'better' than another, or that children cannot and should not write in their own dialect. Why is the dialect that is 'Standard English', as expressed in Teachers' Standard 3, the chosen dialect? Originally it was a southern English dialect – could teachers perhaps consider why this has been imposed centrally, and why there is a need for doing so? Do teachers see themselves as advocates of all the richness of the English language used throughout the country, or are they favouring a pyramidal approach to certain words in one dialect, whether consciously or subconsciously?

> **Myth 3:** Carpet time is a good way for me to control a class.

Organisation

Carpet time must be, for me, the most frequent example of mass organisation within any primary school I visit. In many primary schools there is the phenomenon of carpet time. This entails the class teacher requiring as many as 30 children to sit on the carpet: while he or she sits on an adult-sized chair, children sit on a woollen covered hard floor. Then learning and teaching can begin. Why does this happen? How well can children learn in this discomfort? Or is it simply for a closer behaviour management strategy? After around twenty minutes the children are able to leave the carpet to sit at their tables and chairs for activity work. Then they come back to the carpet for what is known as a *plenary* session. It would be interesting to know why teachers model good behaviour, manners, correct use of English, to name but a few, that they should then allow children to sit where most people allow their pets. It is more usual than not to find the teacher sat on a chair, a comfortable one, and certainly in a raised position.

This has a link to a subsequent form of organisation, what I call 'carpet population and evacuation'. This is where the class is called to come to and leave the carpet by being announced according to ability group. 'Will red group come to the carpet, now yellow group and now, blue group.' The question is why are children being systematically manoeuvred according to their existing attainment measurements? Or, why are children not able to come to the carpet in a fashion and time element of their choosing? I do not think this happens at playtime where children are seemingly free to navigate the space afforded to them by their own volition – until, that is, when playtime finishes and children are called into lines ready to re-enter the classroom.

Not only are children curious and inquisitive they are bounded with energy and a desire to move and explore. This may suggest they are more suited to constructivist-based pedagogies, but is the discipline of sitting on a hard, uncomfortable carpet for up to fifteen or more minutes more productive? Arguably the point of carpet time is to have all children in one fixed point where they can all be seen (a case of vigilance) so that the teacher can manage the behaviour in order to 'deliver' the input, 'deliver' the message, 'deliver' the modelling. Could teachers somehow consider the child who has no need to listen? By this I mean the child who has already been assessed as being able to continue with learning without having to engage with a new teacher's input? Or is it that the previous assessment records would surely indicate that not all children require an input? For example, could a child hear just as well by being seated at their own table, or even just get up from the carpet when he feels he has heard enough? This may be a spontaneous act or an act of assertion in the child that he has achieved the learning goal and can dispense with the need to sit and listen. It could be practical for the children to self-select where sitting-on-the-carpet-time is only an option and they have the power to choose whether they need the input of a teacher in the first place.

> **Myth 4:** Children must not call out.

Permissions to engage

By this I mean the various processes and strategies teachers use to allow children to engage during aspects of teaching and learning. These are identified as requiring not only permission but are controlled by time, as demonstrated in the forthcoming examples. I shall begin with the behaviourist elements of teacher's pedagogy of 'hands up' and its subsequent associated forms of control that are common practice in the primary classroom. The notion of raising one's hand demotes that entry into the discussion or assessment or learning is a barrier to be negotiated. How does a child gain entry? One solution is to be seen to be sitting up straight as if somehow adopting an agreeable posture is an indicator of having learnt something. Another is to 'beg' the teacher by showing in great earnest, usually by flapping the hand and making plaintive subtle noises, that the child is in possession of a good answer that should be heard. How do teachers select children to answer? Do they hope the 'high-ability' pupils will do so, especially when an observation is in process, or do they actually have a sampling strategy based on differentiation and democratic principles of learning? This is similar to the practice of selection by lollipop stick. This is where each child is assigned a stick with their name written on it, which is placed in a jar or cup then, when the teacher requires an answer, a child's stick is drawn out. Have you ever wondered whether there is a real strategy behind this?

> **Myth 5:** Children do engage in talk as a feature of social constructivist learning.

Talk partners

This is one example of a teacher usually selecting one particular child as a partner for another. Here the issue is one of time: 'You have thirty seconds to talk to your talk partner' is a frequently heard instruction, in my experience, to pupils who are sitting on the carpet. The teacher is directing the length of dialogue. If this were applied to call centres, for example, or other aspects of lives where talking is required, how could what we think and say be limited to a such a small amount of time? 'You have two minutes to tell me why you wish to change your television satellite subscription company!' If a teacher does enable children to engage in the notion of using talk partners, then could it be that it should not be so severely curtailed by short time frames?

Perhaps children could be choosers of educational pedagogy. Do they need to be chosen by a teacher to have their voice heard or can they express this in another way? It is interesting to discover how much 'talk time' gets devoted to children on a carpet session. Talking for under a minute or two is not long enough, and not all children can express an opinion in that particular lesson in that way. Rather than the teacher choosing responders, perhaps the children can require the teacher to listen to them, or choose a different method of communication. There has long been a call from educationalists to allow more child-centred freedom within education. The Finnish example of creative learning environments is lauded widely as how autonomy and creativity can allow children to flourish. By allowing children the small freedom to talk when they decide can be a small step in re-evaluating other creative pedagogies and revolutionary classroom arrangements that are based on equity (Sahlberg, 2011).

Read more about the Finnish innovation of desk-free learning environments here:

https://innovationhouse.org.ua/en/statti/obrazovanye-v-fynlyandyy-shkoly-bez-sten-ucheba-bez-otsenok/

REFLECTION

Do you recognise these modes of control within your own practice or experience?

Have you considered the reasons why these methods are so commonplace in the classroom?

What kind of mindset might be established in pupils by using these behaviourist strategies?

Drivers of success

I have attempted to take four arguably familiar examples of primary practice that, while some may not view them as obvious examples, they are nonetheless important to discuss within the power relationships that exists between teacher and child.

Where do pedagogical practices such as carpet time or up-levelling originate? They are not new and are likely to be of the same age as the former National Numeracy and Literacy Strategies from the late 1990s. This was also not too long after the call for a basic curriculum was realised with the introduction of the first National Curriculum of 1988, and the subsequent mass introduction of other adults into the classroom, who later became termed teaching assistants. An important example of intervention and accountability followed, notably with the creation of Ofsted and the publication of league tables as a public record of SATs attainment. It was a time of rapidly advancing political interest in and control over what had been a relatively autonomous profession up until this point. It can be assumed that such intervention has resulted in a drive toward behaviourism as a main underpinning in teaching practice because there can be little room for deviation or creative teaching and learning. Allowing children to be more autonomous and decisive is inefficient and time-costly. Teachers may be afraid that they might lose control if children are all making individual decisions without a teacher to influence them and pull them together as one group. Or they might see the attainment of Standards as the key driver towards success, which is generally how the school operates in its philosophy. Perhaps such a dominant habitus of accountability and centralised government directives and control is difficult for a school to do much about. Some schools could advocate more freedom in their teaching and learning and redefine their habitus as an embodiment of their mission statement and, in reality, there is nothing to stop this happening.

Why do teachers do the things they do?

How can teachers take a moment to reflect upon and rediscover their philosophy for *good practice*? How can they question existing paradigms and feel empowered to do something positive about it? Teachers should look at whether their practice merely replicates existing practice with a critical eye. If they cannot do this, then the habitus will not change, and teachers are in fact compliant within the system. But the system can change from a bottom-up perspective by putting the learning preferences of the child first and giving pedagogical consideration to the needs of the child as a learner foremost.

REFLECTION

Do you feel pressurised to replicate teaching strategies that you have observed, or are you encouraged to innovate in your classroom practice? When do you put the learners' preferences first? What difference does it make to the outcomes of their learning?

How can you challenge the myths?

Here we can apply elements of Bourdieu's theory of the habitus to explain how schools are continuing ecosystems of behaviourist control which may exist in the current primary classroom. First, I do not pretend that outright reform of pedagogy and practice and the school's way of doing things is necessary and even achievable. It is a case of small steps and the underpinning thought of 'what is best for the children' in their learning. Reform is welcome – providing it is justifiable. This may be explored with the following three points.

(a) How children are affected – should children be docile bodies in a behaviourist-centred classroom?

Perhaps they should be given more autonomy within a revised understanding of how their learning behaviour can grow. To empower children is to make them responsible and to allow them to receive a greater stake in the classroom. It could be possible that trainee teachers consider how their confidence would grow if they allowed children greater and freer participation within daily learning. Can children access resources by walking around the classroom? Can children orient themselves to produce learning where they feel comfortable? It may be that a teacher encourages the children to feel more central to their learning if the children's own dialect was celebrated and modelled in English story writing. The issue to consider here is whether increased engagement and a different learning behaviour would reduce 'misconduct' and therefore drastically reduce teachers' fears of losing control.

(b) How teachers are (arguably) unwittingly coerced into this

Bourdieu would argue that the habitus of a school (how things are run) is kept that way by those who run it and those who therefore have the power and influence. How can trainee teachers or NQTs even make a contribution to the ethos? The answer here is to justify the adaptation in pedagogy – of course one obvious justification would be the improvement in results and associated data measures. The pressure to conform and being perceived as successful may come at the expense of professional autonomy. This is a call to government education ministers, teaching unions, parents and interest groups. A teacher should be critical of education and the teaching profession, and be prepared to have their abilities, suggestions and desire for innovation for change be recognised and acted upon. In the same way, it should be the responsibility of mentors, head teachers and governing bodies to welcome new innovations and ideas from newer entrants, and not be constrained by their perception of the habitus of the school or the habitus of the demands of accountability. Habitus can be changed – it can be 'undone'.

(c) To question whether teachers are merely replicating existing pedagogy

One potential side to the above paragraph is that if matters do not change then trainees will copy existing practice and the danger of that is a lack of in-depth reflection. A profession would require innovation and open critique to allow for an honest discussion. Initial Teacher Training institutions should give consideration to ensuring they are educating trainee teachers to be critical of policy, pedagogy and the teaching profession. This is a reminder to those involved in teacher training within universities that operate in the increasing QTS market that involves, among others, organisations such as SCITTS, School Direct and Teach First, etc., to consider their uniqueness as institutions that promote thought and criticality. Teachers also need to reflect on their role in a school experience and, as someone expected to manage deployment of another adult, to consider how they would be affected by it.

CHAPTER SUMMARY

This chapter has helped us to reconsider behaviours by classroom teachers that are perpetuated, often without question. It has offered examples to enable us to think about our own values and principles and to consider how we might begin to change the habitus of school culture for the future. If the habitus within the teaching profession is only an arbitrary expression of values and principles, then trainee teachers can effect change. Such change can radiate and influence those who are stakeholders in education: teachers, governors and, importantly, parents. That change is, therefore, the restoring of teaching decisions and the freedom to exercise professional judgement. For the teachers this would allow the habitus to welcome experimentation, freedom (to make mistakes) but to contribute innovation and reform. Teachers can find out for themselves which myths are perpetuated and then they can do something about it. As Christian Schiller wrote at the top of the chapter, if a child should be free in 'their growing power to choose' could not a teacher assist in this?

KEY POINTS TO CONSIDER

This chapter has:

- considered the habitus of school culture from historical perspectives;
- explored common behaviourist strategies for control in an English primary classroom;
- questioned why teachers conform so readily and are compliant in perpetuating these approaches;
- encouraged a more mindful and reflective position to enable teachers to engage in a re-examination of classroom pedagogy.

Further reading

Martin, K. and Harper, A. (2014) *Managing Behaviour in the Primary Classroom: A Research Brief for Primary Practitioners*. Slough and Oxford: NFER and Oxford University Press.

Payne, R. (2015) Using rewards and sanctions in the classroom: pupils' perceptions of their own responses to current behaviour management strategies. *Educational Review, 67* (4): 483–504.

Read more about reflective practice with this online guide: **Cambridge International Education**, *Getting Started with Reflective Practice*. Available at: **https://www.cambridge-community.org. uk/professional-development/gswrp/index.html**

References

Bourdieu, P. (1984) *Distinction*. London: Routledge & Kegan Paul.

Curtis, W. and Pettigrew, A. (2010) *Education Studies Reflective Reader*. London: Learning Matters.

Danaher, G., Schirato, T. and Webb, J. (2000) *Understanding Bourdieu*. London: Sage.

Foucault, M. (1991) *Discipline and Punish*. London: Penguin.

Grigg, R. (2010) *Becoming an Outstanding Primary School Teacher*. Harlow: Pearson.

Lambirth, A. (2011) *Literacy on the Left*. London: Continuum.

Pollard, A. (2014) *Reflective Teaching in Schools*. London: Bloomsbury.

Pollard, A., Black-Hawkins, G., Dudley, P., Hodges, G.C.P., Higgins, S.M., Linklater, H., Swaffield, S., Swann, M., Winterbottom, M. and Wolpert, M. (2019) *Reflective Teaching in Schools* (5th edition). London: Bloomsbury.

Sahlberg, P. (2011) *Finnish Lessons*. New York: Teachers College Press.

Schiller, C. (1979) *Christian Schiller in His Own Words*. London: NAPE/A. & C. Black.

Trudgill, P. (1975) *Accent, Dialect and the School*. London: Edward Arnold.

Vygotsky, L. (1978) *Mind in Society*. London: Harvard University Press.

END PIECE
LOOKING BACK AND LOOKING AHEAD

SUSAN OGIER AND TONY EAUDE

THE FEAR OF FAILURE IS THE ONE THING THAT SCHOOLS SHOULD BE ABLE TO HELP CHILDREN OVERCOME, THOUGH SO OFTEN THEY DO THE OPPOSITE.

(DONALDSON, 1992: 254)

This book has covered a wide and diverse range of themes and topics related to the education of the whole child in primary education. It has presented resoundingly similar messages from leading educationalists who advocate a broad and balanced curriculum to benefit all children, through inclusive, creative, enquiry-based pedagogy. These messages emphasise that it is essential for teachers to really get to know the children as the unique individuals they are. Teachers should not pre-judge or make decisions based on stereotypical, prescriptive ideas of what and where children should be in terms of their learning and development at any one moment. We believe that teachers must help all children to succeed, building on their many talents rather than leaving them with a sense of failure and making them afraid of trying new things, as a narrow, test-driven curriculum does for so many children.

We hope that you recognise, by reading this book, that offering a 'broad and balanced curriculum' is much less about making sure you are ticking boxes to show you are covering foundation subjects at some point and to some extent. It is much more about enabling every child's potential to be made possible, made visible and acknowledged, through demonstrating that learning is an ongoing process and 'success' is to be understood differently for individuals – and involving much more than test scores. This should help you to consider the following question in a reflective way and remind you why you wanted to become a primary teacher in the first place and why teaching young children can be such a wonderful, though demanding, profession.

Why is a broad and balanced curriculum so important?

The essential principle underlying primary education is that learning should be age appropriate and build on each child's strengths. All children should be introduced to a range of opportunities to enable them to develop in many ways – cognitively, socially, emotionally, physically, creatively, spiritually – so that they become well-rounded and responsible citizens of the future. If each of these elements are present within the curriculum, you will almost certainly contribute significantly to the education of the whole child – and towards children's well-being and good mental health and, ultimately, to a more thoughtful and compassionate society of the future.

The current National Curriculum emphasises 'academic' subjects as all important. Here is a little story about the difficulties this can present for real lives.

CASE STUDY

Louisa

Louisa works as a literary agent. Her job is to read and provide feedback to authors on their play scripts, books and articles which have been submitted for publication or performance. When she was at primary school, Louisa was placed in the 'bottom' group for her learning, where she remained throughout her school years. Latterly she was diagnosed as severely dyslexic combined with ADHD. In Louisa's experience, the core subjects of English and maths - subjects at which she did not excel - defined her sense of self and for many years this self-perception prevented her from achieving her potential. Louisa is now a 30-year-old professional who has become successful in her career - not because of her school experience but in spite of it.

Today, Louisa's teachers might be surprised to learn that she has found success in her career as a literary agent! We must reflect on how we should begin to recognise potential in our young people – and how easy it is to pre-judge what we think of each child's potential, often based on inaccurate suppositions. Keeble *et al.*, in the Teaching Schools Council report *Effective Primary School Practice* (2016), argue that, of course, literacy and mathematical understanding is fundamental, but this is not enough. The sorts of opportunities and experiences described in this book are essential. Moreover, Keeble *et al.* remind us *that primary education is valuable for its own sake as much as for future success; joyful learning is something worth celebrating* (2016: 8).

'Joyful learning' is not only worth celebrating, but is a motivating factor for primary aged children which allows them to recognise and feel success in their education and their lives. One important reason for providing a broad and rich range of experiences to your class is that this is likely to engage children, to make them enthused to learn and to feel excited about what the future holds for them. It makes it more likely that talents and interests which children have will be discovered and developed. Maintaining this attitude to learning will help children throughout their lives. If you can encourage and enable this, as their teacher, you will not only have helped to make the children life-long learners but will experience the tremendous fulfilment which teaching a class of primary age children can bring.

There is now a groundswell of interest by educators who wish to regain control of the primary curriculum in order to provide the breadth and balance that young children need. We are not alone in arguing for a curriculum that is broader and better balanced. Her Majesty's Chief Inspector, Amanda Spielman, recently highlighted that Ofsted is very concerned about the lack of balance in the primary curriculum, and that inspectors are actively looking at the breadth of curriculum on offer in primary schools before making a judgment. In this speech she warned:

> If you are putting more resources into providing exam scribes than in teaching your strugglers to read and write or scrapping most of your curriculum through Year 6 to focus just on English and maths. If you are doing any of those things, then you are probably doing most of your students a disservice. This all reflects a tendency to mistake badges and stickers for learning itself. And it is putting the interests of schools ahead of the interests of the children in them. We should be ashamed that we have let such behaviour persist for so long.

Hall (2016) indicates that to achieve an 'Outstanding' grade, schools must now show that:

> The broad and balanced curriculum inspires pupils to learn. The range of subjects and courses helps pupils acquire knowledge, understanding and skills in all aspects of their education, including the humanities and linguistic, mathematical, scientific, technical, social, physical and artistic learning.
>
> (2016: 6)

Providing a wide and varied range of experiences is not just a question of meeting Ofsted requirements. There are other, much better and more principled reasons related to young children's needs in a complicated and changing world and how they learn best. John Dunford, previously a head teacher, reported from a range of education conferences taking place in 2018 on a change in the mindset of educators who are actively questioning the current push on test results and rigid accountability systems. He states that:

> The narrow, knowledge-based curriculum promoted by the government since 2010 was firmly rejected by a range of speakers who, from their different perspectives, argued for the breadth and balance in the curriculum that remains in English law the statutory obligation of schools.
>
> (TES, 18 March 2018)

Speakers such as astronaut Tim Peake, CBI chairman Paul Drechsler and a range of professionals from diverse backgrounds spoke clearly of the challenges ahead for young children being educated in a system that has such a narrow focus. These voices are becoming ever louder, as the curriculum becomes less child-centred and more age-inappropriate. Many people are now arguing that we all need to join together as professionals to ensure that the next generation benefits from the broad and balanced education they need for the future. Some of those voices are in this book and we hope that you will reflect deeply on their arguments.

Are there existing models of excellence?

There are many models of excellence that we can use as starting points for developing personal philosophies for teaching primary children. The *Flourish Movement* supports cognitive, emotional, physical and social growth, that works with nature itself, where well-being is the fundamental factor for good learning and personal growth. The model suggests seven 'Foundations for Well-being':

- growth

- contribution

- fulfilment

- engagement

- independence

- emotional fulfilment

- security.

It is a collaborative and holistic view that values every part of humanity as children develop, highlighting the need for children to feel connected to, and work with, other people. The social and emotional aspects of learning are essential, and it is through offering children a varied diet of subjects, experiences and opportunities and by nurturing their individual talents and interests that we can inspire children to live as thoughtful, compassionate and fulfilled global citizens. Read more about the Flourish Movement here: **https://www.savechildhood.net**.

The 'Too Much Too Soon' campaign by the Save Childhood charity highlights similar concerns and offers another alternative model. This is underpinned by research from around the world arguing that children need time, space and a variety of experiences and should not be put under undue pressure at too young an age, as happens all too frequently.

In his book, *How Children Succeed* (2013), Paul Tough explains his own moment of epiphany when observing a class of four year olds who were fully immersed in their learning, occupied, socialised and working in an atmosphere of purposeful calmness. Their curriculum was based upon the 'Tools of the Mind' approach, based on the view that children learn to self-regulate by being emotionally, physically and socially engaged. When children take responsibility for their own learning, they are able to work independently without distraction, and without the anxiety of whether they are doing the right thing or not. Excellent Early Years practice facilitates this kind of independent learning, giving children skills and a resourcefulness that they can draw upon in their future lives to take charge of their own learning. Tough advocates that it is precisely these skills, dispositions and emotional resilience that stand children in good stead for future success, much more than the current policy to grade children according to narrowly focused academic criteria alone. We would be wise to look to these kinds of models of Early Years practice in deciding what an excellent primary curriculum should be like.

Figure EP.1 The Whole Child © Copyright Wendy Ellyatt, 2017, Flourish Project www.flourishproject.net

The Effective Pre-school, Primary and Secondary Education Project (EPPSE 3–16+) came to similar conclusions (Simms, 2011), emphasising the importance of high-quality early years provision and what they call 'sustained shared thinking'. You can read more about the EPPSE project to develop your understanding of how children learn at **https://bit.ly/2tD1FkS**.

Many examples of excellent practice exist in schools all around the country, and we hope that you will continue to be inspired by these – and indeed some of you reading this book will be the next group of innovators who move thinking and practice further forward. As long as there are teachers who care and are passionate about children's real lives and about their future, our youngest generation will be in safe hands by providing the broad and balanced curriculum that they need and they deserve.

References

Donaldson, **M.** (1992) *Human Minds – An Exploration.* London: Allen Lane

Hall, **J.** (2016) *A Broad and Balanced Curriculum: Key Findings from OFSTED.* Available at: **www.inside government.co.uk/uploads/2016/09/joannahall-1.pdf**.

Keeble, **R.** *et al.* (2016) *Effective Primary School Practice.* Teaching Schools Council. Available at: **https://www.tscouncil.org.uk/wp-content/uploads/2016/12/Effective-primary-teaching-practice-2016-report-web.pdf**

Simms, **M.** (2011) Early childhood matters: evidence from the Effective Pre-school and Primary Education Project. *Early Years, 31* (2): 205–6.

Tough, **P.** (2013) *How Children Succeed.* London: Random House.

INDEX

musicality of writing *see* prosody
Muslims 56

N
National Advisory Committee on
    Creative and Cultural
    Education (NACCCE) 18, 51, 205
National Curriculum 3, 61, 67, 107, 135
    art and design 121
    creativity 17–18
    geography 155–6
    learning with nature 149
national identity 34, 41–2
nature 135–6, 146–59
    learning through harmony 148–9
    as our teacher 153–6
    reconnecting with 149–52
    we are what we eat 152–3
NHS 64
NSPCC 64
Nussbaum, M. 106, 109
Nye, R. 49

O
off-the-script diversion 248–9
Ofsted 209, 246–7
    accountability agenda 264
    assessment and 189–91
    inspections 84
    review of curriculum 149
    SMSC development 48
Olson, D.R. 114
online safety 122
Opalski, M. 36
organisation 261–2
outdoor learning 148–9
ownership of knowledge 207

P
Pagden, Alan 154
'pair and share' 192
Palmer, Samuel 123, 127
Peake, Tim 270
Peaston, H. 90, 91, 94
pedagogical content knowledge (PCK) 237
penal system 258–9
performance, writer friendly environment 142
performativity, culture of 19, 21, 222
permissions to engage 262–3
personal identity 33, 37–40
Personal Learning Time (case study) 194–5
Pettigrew, A. 257
philosophers, stereotype 75–6
philosophical inquiry model 80–4
    overcoming challenges 83–4
    suggested models 81–2

before you start 80–1
Philosophy for Children 120
Philosophy for Children (P4C) 113
philosophy/philosophical inquiry 74–86
    in the classroom 80–4
    developmental stages and readiness 78–9
    importance of 76–8
    meaning 75–6
    subject knowledge barrier 79
photographs 38
    identity cards/passports 42
physical appearance and identity 40–1
physical environment of classroom 24–30
    class ethos 25–7
    immersive learning environments 28–9
Piaget, J. 78
Picasso, Pablo 121
picture books
    case study 84
    images in school 121
PISA tables 163
play 3, 4
Pollack, D. 35
positive identities 35
'possibility thinking' 23, 25, 28
power 258–9
    language and 261
Prevent Strategy 55, 56
professional identity 221–2, 234–5, 250–2
professionalism 230–40
    contractual view of 233–4
    covenantal view of 233
    Hargreaves and Fullan view of 234–5
    meaning in practice 231–2
    restricted or extended professionality 235–9
    understanding in different professions 233–4
Programme for International Student
    Assessment (PISA) 197
project-based learning 180–4
prosody 139–40
publication, writing friendly environment 142

Q
questions/questioning
    case study 25
    critical apparatus in writing 143–4
    immersive learning environment 28
    philosophical enquiry 82
    teaching humanities 113–14
    trigger questions 137–8

R
radicalisation 55
rapport 21–3
Read, Herbert 119, 121, 130
reading rivers 226